THE EIGHTEENTH CENTURY NOVEL

In gratitude to
Sehra
My ever helpful mother

THE EIGHTEENTH CENTURY NOVEL

The Idea of the Gentleman

HOMAI J. SHROFF

ARNOLD-HEINEMANN

© Homai J. Shroff
First Published 1978

Published by Gulab Vazirani for Arnold-Heinemann Publishers (India) Pvt. Ltd. AB/9, Safdarjang Enclave, New Delhi-110016 and Sunil Composing Co. at S.P. Printers. 1067, Ajay Palace, Naraina, New Delhi-110028.

Preface

This book is a study of the attitude of the leading novelists of the eighteenth century to the contemporary class system and to current trends in philosophy and education. The ideas of divergent philosophers and writers like Locke, Shaftesbury, Mandeville, Pope, Johnson, Chesterfield, Rousseau are analysed in order to show how often they are reflected in the plot, characterization and satirical themes of the novels of the century.

The novelists' views on sexual ethics and characteristic eighteenth century controversies about good-breeding, honesty, greatness, happiness are examined in order to understand how they give shape to a new concept of the 'gentleman' quite distinct from the Renaissance concept of the gentleman as the perfect courtier.

A vivid picture of the social and political life of the century emerges as the new concept is described. Surprisingly, in spite of the fact that so many of the novelists concentrate on satirizing the degenerate and tyrannical behaviour of the upper classes not one of them questions the validity of the stratified class structure.

Nevertheless eighteenth century writers are the first to realize that the exploitation and degradation of the ordinary man by social, political and legal institutions, and by the agents of money and power, are themes with which literature must concern itself.

I am very happy that I have this opportunity of recording my keen sense of gratitude to the following persons without whose valuable help the work of writing this book would have been far more difficult and far less pleasant than it has been.

My thanks are primarily due to Professor G.C. Bannerjee, former Head of the Department of English, University of Bombay. From a person of his lively scholarship and extensive knowledge and experience, ever since I came to know him in

1951, I have learnt some of the most worthwhile things that I know about literature, education and life.

I am deeply grateful to Mrs. Shirin Kudchedkar, Reader in English, S.N.D.T. University, Maharashtra, for the continued and ungrudging help she has given me in looking through the preliminary draft of all the chapters. I am also extremely grateful to my colleague Miss Soonu Kapadia for reading the final typescript with meticulous care and for many useful suggestions.

I would also like to express sincere gratitude to Professor D.N. Marshall, Professor of Library Science, University of Bombay, for his exceptionally courteous and friendly assistance.

Elphinstone College,   HOMAI J. SHROFF
Bombay

Contents

Preface	v
1. The Novelist and the Gentleman	9
2. The Importance of Being a Gentleman	17
3. Fashioning the Gentleman	55
4. The Woman's Gentleman, or the Anatomy of the Rake — *Samuel Richardson*	96
5. Greatness, Goodness, Happiness, — A 'Great, useful and Uncommon Doctrine' — *Henry Fielding*	123
6. Angry Young Gentleman and 'A Most Risible Misanthrope' — *Tobias Smollett*	161
7. 'The Heart Rather than the Head' — *Oliver Goldsmith, Henry Mackenzie, Laurence Sterne*	192
8. 'A Young Lady's Entrance into the World' of the Gentleman — *Fanny Burney*	236
9. Who Was then the Gentleman?	254
Notes	281
Key to the Notes	290
Select Bibliography	291
Index	295

1 The Novelist and the Gentleman

... that most to be taken Care of is the Gentleman's Calling. For if those of that Rank ... are once set right, they will quickly bring the rest into Order.
—John Locke.[1]

Samuel Johnson's dictum, 'He that thinks reasonably must think morally', is forcefully expressive of the conviction of his age that it is man's obligation to think both reasonably and morally. On those in particular who chose to think within the framework of the novel, a special duty was imposed. 'That great CHAM of literature', as Smollett called Johnson,[2] pronounced his edict on this 'new species of composition' in the fourth number of *The Rambler* (31 March 1750). Johnson's argument was that since novels are 'written chiefly to the young, the ignorant, and the idle, to whom they serve as lectures of conduct and introductions into life', they must convey the rules of morality even more directly and clearly than other forms of literature.

Like Richardson earlier, and numerous novelists and critics throughout the fifty years that followed the *Rambler* essay, Johnson went so far as to insist that a realistic portrayal of life and character was not by any means required of the novelist. He could not see 'what use it can be to read the account' if the world is 'promiscuously described' in a literary work : 'In narratives where historical veracity has no place, I cannot disclose why there should not be exhibited the most perfect ideas of virtue.' Both virtue and vice must be portrayed unadulterated by any traits which are likely to qualify that admiration for virtue, and that disgust for vice, which it is the duty of a writer to arouse. Scarcely a year before, Fielding had laughed at the 'models of perfection' found in the works of some writers (*TJ*, X, i), but Fielding's realism and sense of humour did not prevent him from instructing his readers 'in this most useful of all arts, which I call the ART OF LIFE' (*Amelia* I, i).

The anxiety to instruct the reader, and the general lack of inhibition about portraying ideal characters, repeatedly led the novelists of this period to paint the portrait of a 'gentleman', and to argue heatedly about the qualities such a person ought to possess.

To this day the English language has found no word more expressive than *gentleman* to denote a person who embodies the various fine qualities that the society in which he lives associates with the character of an ideal man. In the eighteenth century, in particular, a number of writers attempt to reserve the term for their personal conception of the ideal man. Discussions about ideals of conduct and criticisms of false ideals and aspirations seem inevitably to converge on the gentleman, just as in the Renaissance they converged on the 'courtier' or the 'governour', and in medieval times on the knight, or alternatively, on the man of God.

Although they twisted the word *gentleman* into having a variety of connotations, not one of the novelists of this period ventured to portray an ideal gentleman as existing outside the wealthy, leisured class of society, that class which for generations had been the inheritor and transmitter of wealth and culture. Consequently, as the next chapter will show, when ideal heroes are portrayed in the novel, attention is focussed exclusively on the person who is a gentleman in the original meaning of the term, that is a man of 'good birth', 'a gentleman born', as Fielding calls his Booth (*Amelia*, V, v).

Since the eighteenth century novel is preoccupied with the concept of the gentleman, it provides rich material for ascertaining the ideals of character and behaviour which moralists and thinkers were seeking to establish during this first great period of the English novel. It makes vividly clear to us the reactions of a large and influential section of the nation to the manners, morals and social attitudes of the governing classes of contemporary society.

In the Preface to *Sir Charles Grandison* Richardson announces his intention of fashioning the ideal gentleman, and declares that in all his three novels his purpose is to criticise and warn those who flout the principles of morality and behaviour that should guide the life of the governing classes. In fact, as the following letter written to him shows, when Richardson embarked on another novel after *Clarissa*, what his friends expected of him was not so much a novel, as a courtesy book to end all courtesy books :

> I can't let Mr. Leak go to London, without desiring to know . . . whether we are like to see a Part of Ye Compleat English Gentleman next winter. I think since you have set Ye Ladies in Clarissa, so excellent a pattern, our sex have a demand upon you.[3]

Richardson was only too willing to meet such a demand. *Sir Charles Grandison* is a systematic attempt to devise every conceivable kind of situation in which an English gentleman may be called upon to display his gentlemanliness. At the end of the novel, Richardson appends sixty closely printed pages of an 'Index Historical and Characteristical to the Seven Volumes of This Work', in which he lists the variety of edifying topics, and predicaments of conduct and behaviour, which have been satisfactorily analysed by him in the novel. The Index is meant to serve the reader as a guide in his conduct and judgment of life.

In the 'editorial remarks' at the end of the first volume of *Pamela*, Richardson stresses that his portrayal of the fashionable libertine who reforms his ways provides 'an edifying lesson . . . for the use of such as are born to large fortunes'. In the second volume of *Pamela* which deals with the married life of Mr. B. and Pamela, Richardson has no story to narrate, and so sets about devising episodes which will enable him to discuss the conduct and bearing of an ideal gentleman and his lady in governing their household, tenants and servants, and in setting a noble example to the neighbouring gentry. The problem which receives the most detailed attention here is that of the education and upbringing of the children of gentlemen. Resorting to John Locke's *Some Thoughts Concerning Education* as a framework for the discussion, Richardson takes more than fifty pages to elaborate the problem which exercised the minds of parents and educationists in his time.

Fielding who could boast a better background and upbringing, was both amused and angered by the outsider Richardson's treatment of the subject. What irritated Fielding most was the prudential, commercial mentality which vitiates some of Richardson's work, particularly *Pamela*; moreover, Richardson's solemnity was of the kind that was bound to provoke Fielding's irony. But Fielding is as anxious as Richardson to examine the principles that should guide the governing classes in their conduct of life. No writer of the period presents more forceful and impassioned pictures of the ruthlessness with which the ignorant, selfish, coarse country gentleman exercised his authority, and the veneer of elegance underneath which the town gallant harboured the most degrading lust, hypocrisy and villainy. Against these vigorous pictures of brutality and depravity, Fielding places his characteristic heroes—Squire Allworthy, Dr. Harrison, Tom Jones, William Booth and Parson Adams—five different kinds of men, not one of them perfect, but each picturing quite clearly a few of the qualities their creator demands of an ideal person.

Smollett's passionate fulmination against the depravity, vulgarity and sycophancy of upper class life in London and Bath, produces not only some of the most forceful satirical portraits, but also, surprisingly, some of the most striking panegyrical portraits of gentlemen in the novels of this period. In his earlier books, *Roderick Random* and *Peregrine Pickle*, Smollett's insensitiveness to the brutalities he describes is a little too evident; the reader is disturbed by the coarseness of the writer's moral perception, especially in the characterization of the heroes who are meant to be prepossessing, but fail lamentably to be so. The desire of Roderick and Peregrine to establish themselves as 'gentlemen', furnishes several revealing examples of the contemporary idea of the gentleman.

In *Humphry Clinker*, after a transitional stage in *Sir Launcelot Greaves*, Smollett achieves an unexpected but nevertheless very assured understanding of the art of living the gentleman's life. Matthew Bramble, with his crusty exterior and great heart, who, like Goldsmith's 'Man in Black', talks like a misanthropist and acts like a philanthropist, is a significant contribution to the century's idea of the gentleman. In the portrayal of Matthew's friends, Mr. Dennison, Mr. Wilson and the unfortunate Mr. Baynard, Smollett makes a purposeful attempt to explore the ideal—to show how the gentleman can best do his duty by himself and by society.

It did not suit Sterne's temperament to fulminate against injustice and corruption like Smollett, 'the learned Smelfungus' who 'set out with the spleen and jaundice', so that 'every object he passed by was discoloured and distorted'.[4] Nor, with his playful, jesting, but highly sophisticated approach to novel writing, was it necessary for Sterne to avow anything so solemn as an intention to place before his reader ideals of life and conduct. Yet how important he thought it was to preach his philosophy of 'true Shandeism' which 'opens the heart and lungs' (*TS*, V, xxxii), the philosophy of 'dear Sensibility' permeated by the laughter that drives out the 'spleen', is evident in all his writings, not excluding his very appealing sermons. In *The Life and Opinions of Tristram Shandy, Gent.*, by creating 'my Uncle Toby's most whimsical character' (I, xxii) Sterne paid, as Hazlitt saw, 'one of the finest compliments ever paid to human nature',[5] and also succeeded in contributing to the gallery of 'men of feeling' its most artistically executed portrait. The ideal of true compassion and fortitude, of a sympathetic understanding and an unalloyed sweetness of temperament, of that true good breeding which manifests itself in complete forgetfulness of self, and needs not the least help from fashion or sophistication, is presented in Toby :

> ... but the sweet look of goodness which sat upon my uncle Toby's, assimilated everything around it so sovereignly to itself, and nature had moreover wrote Gentleman with so fair a hand in every line of his countenance, that even his tarnished gold-laced hat and huge cockade of flimsy taffeta became him (IX, ii).

Goldsmith resembles Sterne in his praise for the warm heart and guileless innocence, though his somewhat naive didacticism and folk-tale technique are very different from Sterne's subtle art. In *The Vicar of Wakefield* the desire to express a philosophy of life is reflected in two characters—the Vicar himself, and Sir William Thornhill, who assumes the disguise of the eccentric, impoverished gentleman, Mr. Burchell.

Henry Brooke's *The Fool of Quality*, first published in five volumes between 1767 and 1770, and republished as '*Henry, Earl of Moreland*, edited with retrenchments by John Wesley' in 1781, is frankly pedagogical in intention. It describes the education and upbringing of an ideal nobleman by his uncle, an ideal merchant-prince, who lives a retired life in the country, and is master of a fortune that even kings envy and fall back upon for loans. The chief aim of education, as Brooke sees it, is to develop a feeling heart and to give training in benevolence and in a truly Christian piety.

The extravagance of its plot, the lack of practicability of some of its suggestions, and the orgies of emotion in which the author's philosophy of sensibility involves the characters, give *The Fool of Quality* a touch of absurdity. Nevertheless, it is invaluable for an analysis of the idea of the gentleman, as it gives a detailed description of the mental and moral training recommended for an aristocrat by an author who had himself moved in fashionable London circles and been 'the darling of the Prince of Wales; beau, swordsman, wit, poet, courtier, the minion once of fortune',[6] had afterwards retired to a life of sensitive but over-emotional piety and charity, and then, late in life, had been captured by the educational doctrines propounded in Rousseau's *Emile*.

Henry Mackenzie's *The Man of Feeling* (1771) and *The Man of the World* (1773) bear titles which succinctly describe the ideal and the anathema of a popular school of contemporary literature and philosophy. Mediocre and banal though they may seem to most modern readers, Mackenzie's purposeful treatment of story, character and sentiment to illustrate an ideal of life makes these two novels more useful than the first-rate, sophisticated examples of the genre, as specimens for the study of an influential trend in the literature of the period.

Fanny Burney's *Evelina* (1778) and *Cecilia* (1782) provide the only feminine view of the gentleman. Her preoccupation with matters of good form, conventions of etiquette, and gradations of breeding—good-breeding, ill-breeding, low-breeding, 'under-breeding'—takes us to an atmosphere very different from Mackenzie's emphatically proclaimed distaste for 'the world'. Generally held to be the best novel between *Humphry Clinker* and *Sense and Sensibility*, *Evelina* is certainly an absorbing document for the study of the upper and middle ranges of the eighteenth century class structure. No other book furnishes such vivid evidence of the supreme importance attached by contemporary society to matters of form, manners and appearances.

With Fanny Burney's *Cecilia*, the first great period of the novel that opened with Richardson's *Pamela* comes to an end. In English literature, as well as in English cultural and social history, the four decades it covers coincide with the period when Samuel Johnson presided over the destinies of English literature and when a common ideal of conduct and manners, popularised by Addison and Steele in the second decade of the century, was shared by large sections of the leisured classes of society as well as by the aspiring middle class.

Addison and Steele, particularly through *The Spectator*, undoubtedly provided the most influential contribution to the idea of the gentleman in the eighteenth century. Published in periodical form from March 1711 to December 1712, *The Spectator* in volume form went through an extraordinarily large number of editions during the next hundred years. From 1740 to the end of the century as many as twenty-five editions were brought out, not to mention the spate of new essay-serials which aspired to nothing so much as a close imitation of *The Spectator*.

In addition to being marked out by a common attitude to culture and morality, this first great period of the English novel shows certain other common tendencies as well. The cult of sensibility in literature and in actual life which was encouraged by the ideals of certain philosophers and divines in the last decades of the seventeenth and the first decades of the eighteenth century, finds its most outrageous, as well as its finest, expression in the novels of this period.

In the sphere of religion and morality, this tremendous

upsurge of feeling gathered round the figure of John Wesley who, all throughout this period, was exciting a passionate religious fervour among hypnotised crowds of people especially from the middle and lower classes. Though Wesley succeeded in arousing only the scorn of representative writers like Fielding and Smollett, and had very little access to the upper circles of society, except through his disciples, the Countess of Huntingdon and 'psalm-singing Dartmouth' (the philanthropist, William Legge, second Earl of Dartmouth), Wesley's violent denunciation of the fashionable gentlemen and ladies whom he rebuked as a 'generation of triflers',[7] was bound to have a sobering effect on the idea of the gentleman in the popular mind.

In spite of Wesley and his band of enthusiasts, this is also the period in English history when an influential section of the leisured classes is attracted by the idea of the gentleman so strikingly illustrated by its most brilliant 'man of fashion', Philip Dormer Stanhope, fourth Earl of Chesterfield, in his personal life, as well as in those famous letters that he was writing to his son and godson from the beginning till almost the end of this period.

The first great period of the English novel derives a clear identity of its own from this variety of highly characteristic, though often dissimilar, attitudes. The novelists reflect this identity in all its many colourful facets, providing excellent material for a study of the ideals and aversions which give it its individuality.

2 The Importance of Being A Gentleman

A Dissertation Concerning High People and Low People ... and perhaps if the Gods according to the opinion of some, made men only to laugh at them, there is no part of our behaviour which answers the end of our creation better than this. (*JA*, II, xiii)

Few words in the English language have been the subject of such continuous debate as the word *gentleman*. Adopted into the language in its etymological sense in the thirteenth century to denote a man belonging to an 'ancient family', by the nineteenth century, even for so analytical a mind as Coleridge's, the word, especially when used 'emphatically', has come to have a 'sense ... which it is more easy to feel than to define'.[1]

During the eighteenth century, even after five hundred years of debate, the meaning of the term still remains a popular subject for controversy and satirical comment; yet, at the same time, a *gentleman* class, about the status and privileges of which there is no ambiguity, enjoys a prestige which makes membership of it a coveted distinction. In a society which has become more superciliously class-conscious than in earlier centuries, those already privileged to belong to the class, guard its frontiers with a fastidious sensitiveness to the subtleties of class distinctions; at the same time, an increasing number of new aspirants make attempts to climb into the privileged territory. Even as the circle grows bigger, a number of writers, some themselves not within the charmed circle, raise their voices to champion the cause of the gentleman, and to uphold the principle of 'subordination' which ensures him an uncontested position at the top of the social hierarchy.

A surprisingly large number of writers of varied antecedents and temperaments seem anxious to pronounce their decision on whether the word *gentleman* is to be regarded as a status term or a moral term; some contend that it can be used only to indicate a man of high birth; others apply it to a man enjoying a superior social status; still others, to any man who possesses considerable wealth, especially if it is invested in landed property. On the other hand, there are those who would like to reserve the term for a man whose manners are refined, or for one who has received a 'polite' education; yet others would confine it to a man of a high moral character and some would apply it only to one who is useful and beneficent to the community.

Several writers of this century feel that *gentleman* is a denomination which betokens such high reverence, that they attempt to dissociate it altogether from its etymological meaning, and to reserve it for the man who satisfies their personal concept of an ideal man. Early in the century, Richard Steele tilts at the class barriers and claims the title for the honest, upright, useful man, without any reference to his birth, education, occupation or social behaviour:

> The courtier, the trader, and the scholar, should all have an equal pretension to the denomination of a gentleman. That tradesman, who deals with me in a commodity which I do not understand, with uprightness, has much more right to that character, than the courtier that gives me false hopes, or the scholar who laughs at my ignorance ... The appellation of gentleman is never to be affixed to a man's circumstances, but to his behaviour in them. (*Tatler*, 207)

However, César de Saussure, who travelled in England from 1725 to 1729, registering the facts of usage with the curiosity of a foreigner, heard no moral overtones in the word, and recorded: 'The term gentleman is usually given to any well-dressed person wearing a sword' (*A Foreign View of England*, p. 212).

In the middle of the century, Johnson records four meanings for *gentleman* in his *Dictionary*:

(i) A man of birth; a man of extraction, though not noble.

(ii) A man raised above the vulgar by his character or post.
(iii) A term of complaisance : sometimes ironical.
(iv) The servant that waits about the person of a man of rank.

Though Johnson records the various hazy and subjective meanings that the term has acquired by his time, the following conversation in Boswell's *Life* shows that in his own mind the class and lineage connotations of the term were so prominent that, in a quite matter-of-fact tone, he could describe himself as not a gentleman. Defending the tradition of giving respect and deference to 'old families', he says to Boswell :

What is it but opinion, by which we have a respect for authority, that prevents us, who are the rabble, from rising up and pulling down you who are the gentlemen from your places, and saying, we will be gentlemen in our turn ? (*Life*, II, 153)

Adopted in English in the thirteenth century from Old French *gentilz hom*, in its original signification the word *gentleman* denotes a man belonging to a 'gens' or 'stock' (Latin *gentilis*). According to the *New English Dictionary*, in England the term was already used by the fourteenth century to indicate :

A man in whom gentle birth is accompanied by appropriate qualities and behaviour; hence, in general, a man of chivalrous instincts and fine feelings.

But probably the *NED* definition needs to be qualified by taking into account what Karl Bulbring says in his introduction to Defoe's *The Compleat English Gentleman* :

It is curious to observe here that in all the instances of medieval literature where the word gentleman is used, it either directly refers to a man of gentle birth, or it is accompanied by an analysis of a true gentleman's qualities.

As a designation, or as the title of a class that constitutes a separate social order, like that of knights, esquires, yeomen, husbandmen, etc., the term was not used in England till the beginning of the fifteenth century, when it was first adopted by the younger sons of *nobiles* who 'had no titles, and under the older system had no definite social status or designation pointing to their gentle birth'.

Early in the history of the word a debate begins whether a man of low degree can, by virtue of his achievements, claim the title of *gentleman*.

The anonymous writer of *The Institution of a Gentleman* (1555) concedes to men of low degree the right to raise 'their poore line', provided they, because of their creditable accomplishments, have been appointed to a 'great office', and have amassed money. To such he gives the designation *ungentle gentle*, differentiating them from the *gentil gentil*, who can boast both high birth and noble qualities, and the *gentle ungentle*, who are descended of 'noble parentage', but whose manners are 'corrupt and ungentle'. The children of the *ungentle gentle* are to be termed gentlemen.

By the time William Harrison gives his *Description of England* in 1577, the word has almost ceased to perform its function of indicating lineage; professional men and almost anyone else who has some wealth, and 'can live without manual labour, and thereto is able and will bear the port, charge and countenance of a gentleman' can make a claim to the title, by paying for a coat-of-arms, which by then had become the insignia of a gentleman.

Thus by the last decades of the sixteenth century, the most significant facts that separate the gentleman from his inferiors, are the non-performance of manual labour and the non-purveying of goods, except on a very large and profitable scale. According to Harrison, merchants are to be classed as citizens, but 'they often change estate with gentlemen, as gentlemen do with them by mutual conversion of one into the other.'[2] One notes that Harrison assumes that a gentleman loses caste when he becomes a merchant.

This 'mutual conversion' has remained a fact of the English class structure ever since the Reformation, establishing that system of 'removable inequalities' which Walter Bagehot in the nineteenth century noted as the characteristic feature of English social life.[3] By the end of the Elizabethan period, unthrifty gentlemen were being bought up by industrious yeomen; and merchant-adventurers and 'projectors', having made vast fortunes, were buying land and setting up a 'family'. This process was further accelerated under the Stuarts with the selling of honours and titles, for the Heralds granted coats-of-arms in the most casual manner to all aspirants supporting their request with money. Such indiscriminate grants of coats-of-arms are a frequent subject of satire in Tudor and Stuart plays. In *Every Man Out of His Humour* (III, iv) Ben Jonson shows Sogliardo triumphing in his new-found dignity :

> *Sogliardo* : I can write my selfe gentleman now; here's my pattent, it cost me thirtie pound, by this breath. . . it is your Bore without a head *Rampant*. . .
> *Carlo* : . . . Troth, I commend the *Heralds* wit, hee has decyphered him well; a swine without a head, without braine, wit, any thing indeed, ramping to gentilitie.

Henry Peacham, in *The Compleat Gentleman* (1622), speaks in a more grave and apprehensive tone about such ambitions among low-bred rustics, and defines nobility as, 'the Honour of blood in a Race or Linage'. Yet, even he feels constrained to condemn those among the 'nobly borne' who 'staine their stocke with vice' but 'disparage and disgrace those, who by their virtuous endeavours are rising' (pp. 1-8).

Attacks on the tendency to disparage the virtuous and industrious, and exalt the well-born, are much more emphatically worded in the homiletic writers and even in the poets of the middle ages; one often comes across Christian moralists who, feeling it to be their duty to evolve a theory of gentility which is independent of worldly goods and hereditary privileges, decide to recognize no other criteria of gentility except love of God and moral virtue. Two well-known passages in Chaucer assert that virtue alone confers gentility—the twenty-three line passage, which he inserted, in his translation of the *Roman de la Rose* (ll 2180-2203) and the sixty-two line passage in *The Wife of Bath's Tale* (ll 1109-70) which dismisses the arrogance of 'old richesse' as 'nat worth an hen'. In Gower's *Confessio Amantis*, there is a similar long passage (IV, 2200-90) which disputes the claims of 'richesse' and 'high Lignage', and declares that the 'verrai gentil man' is he who 'virtu suieth'.

This tendency to establish virtue and piety as the most important criteria of gentility, did not quite disappear even during the Renaissance, when the concept of the perfect gentleman was embodied in the graceful form of the all-accomplished, versatile courtier—learned, discreet, polished and courteous; poet, statesman, soldier and lover.

When the glory of the courtier and cavalier faded, leaving Cromwell and his 'fanatic faction' to set the standard, the pietistic tendency again gathered strength. Very popular in Puritan circles were two treatises by Richard Brathwaite—*The English Gentleman* (1630) and *The English Gentlewoman* (1631). Not surprisingly, instead of propounding the principles of polite conduct, these two treatises assert that the only criteria of true gentlemanliness are acts of charity and devotion.

After suffering a temporary set-back in the fashionable and frivolous society of the Restoration, this way of thinking received a fresh impetus from the evangelical revival of the eighteenth century, and was readily endorsed by the growing number of prosperous merchants and professional people—middle-class men, with a puritan background of industry, sobriety, piety and thrift who were climbing almost to the top of the social ladder. In 1726, the evangelist William Law gave *A Serious Call to a Devout and Holy Life* and maintained : 'it is the one only business of a Christian gentleman, to distinguish himself by good works, to be eminent in the most sublime virtues of the Gospels' (ch. X).

In spite of this repeated insistence through the centuries that the word *gentleman* should be used to indicate high moral character and not family antecedents, unlike its component part *gentle*, *gentleman* could not break loose completely from its original meaning. But it could not remain a purely status term either, unlike the corresponding word *gentlewoman*, which managed to avoid moral overtones more successfully, and continued, as long as it was used, to indicate a woman born into a certain class.

What is more, till at least the nineteenth century, many writers, some even among those who insisted on rejecting the lineage and status connotations of *gentleman*, harboured a sneaking feeling that there is some noble power in 'ancient blood', which itself endows a man with virtuous and 'gentlemanly' qualities of a kind which the low-born cannot possibly manifest. Indeed none of the novelists discussed here are able to rise genuinely above class prejudice—not even those who are scathingly severe in ridiculing the snobbery and exposing the degeneration of the upper classes, not even those who emphatically assert that worth alone entitles a man to respect, and that worth can be found in a beggar as well as a lord. Quite often after having demonstrated through a whole novel the fine feelings and generous actions of a low-born hero, they cannot end without discovering gentle blood in the veins of their good churls. Henry Brooke's *The Fool of Quality* affords a striking illustration.

A genuine sympathy for the poor and a genuine faith in Christian teaching repeatedly prompt Brooke to assert that all human beings are equal and that riches and rank have a corrupting influence particularly upon children. Conscious of offering a revolutionary challenge to accepted class theories, he disputes the validity of the theory that superior talents, nobility of temperament and a distinguished personal appearance are indications of high birth and noble ancestry. Ned, the beggar boy, who becomes the dear companion of Harry, 'the fool of quality', is a fine, talented and amiable boy. Mr. Clinton, Harry's wise and benevolent uncle, finding Ned so well-endowed by nature, can hardly bring himself to believe that a boy of his extraordinary genius should be 'no other by birth than a beggar's brat' (ch. X). Commenting on Mr. Clinton's attitude the 'Author', in a dialogue with his 'Friend', asserts that a beggar's child may be as well-endowed by Nature as a king's :

> *Author* : . . . I conceive that an infant begot on a dunghill, brought forth in a pigsty, and swathed with the rotten remnant of the covering of an ass, may have talents and capacity above the son of an emperor. (ch. X)

However, the author's declared convictions do not save him from succumbing to the beliefs of the gentleman-oriented culture in which he lives. Ned, the beggar boy, is finally discovered to be the long-lost son of the respectable Mr. and Mrs. Fielding; gentleman's blood flows in his veins; the puzzle of his noble appearance and impressive talents is solved; orthodox opinion is vindicated. What is most surprising is that by the time the author makes the discovery about Ned's birth, he has quite forgotten the brave fight he has put up only a few pages before.

Not only in Brooke's sentimental novel does the fight against the prejudices of the gentry thus fizzle out. In both *Joseph Andrews* and *Tom Jones*, Fielding ostensibly sets out to demonstrate that worth and talents are not the monopoly of the high-born. In *Joseph Andrews*, in particular, Fielding seizes every opportunity to emphasize the argument that though Joseph is born in a family of servants and bred in a stable, in his appearance, manners, character, mind and feelings, he is essentially more refined and noble, more truly 'genteel', than the 'born' gentlemen and ladies. In the second chapter of the novel Fielding flings a challenge at the reader, asserting the right of the low-born lad to display heroic and noble virtues :

> But suppose, for argument's sake, we should admit that he had no ancestors at all . . . Would not this *autokopros* have been justly entitled to all the praise arising from his own virtues ?

That Fielding's challenge is offered more than half in jest (he is parodying Richardson who ventured to allow the base-born Pamela to rise and acquire 'honour'; and, quite probably, he has already decided how to bring the story to a conclusion), is itself a revealing indication of his attitude towards this question. But it is in a far from jesting tone that he describes the revolting brutality of the country gentlemen who are hunting the hare, and who turn with more zest to hunt Parson Adams and Joseph. His disgust and revulsion are obvious, as he draws a startling picture of the utter degradation of the lives of the gentry—their revolting attitude towards women, their propensity to turn virtue and wisdom into ridicule, their contempt for religion, their drunkenness, debauchery and cowardice, their stupid, brutal and cruel diversions, and their fatuous jokes (III, vi-vii).

Yet after satirizing so powerfully the despicable character of the scions of ancient families, Fielding betrays a disappointing conformity with class prejudice. Joseph can be permitted to demonstrate refinement and true gentility, even though Gaffar Andrews has spent but sixpence a week on his education for a few years and then sent him to work as a stable-boy, but the taint of non-genteel parentage is quite another matter. Goodman and Goody Andrews must give place to Mr. and Mrs. Wilson. The refinement and gentility Joseph has displayed must not, even by a freakish quirk of nature, be lodged in an 'autokopros', but must flow from the veins of a gentleman (Fielding defines *autokopros* as 'sprung from a dunghill'—I, ii).

Such an appraisal of Fielding's idea of the gentleman may seem to be a distorted interpretation, or an overstatement of the case, were it not for the somewhat similar pattern in his next novel also, which ends with a similar trick solution. Tom Jones, the attractive, handsome foundling, with the fine, brave, generous instincts, is discovered at the end of the novel to be of gentle birth, son of Bridget, daughter of the distinguished Allworthy family, and of Mr. Summer, son of a clergyman friend of Allworthy's. In marrying off Tom to Sophia, his illegitimacy seems to matter not a jot; this, as has been pointed out,[4] is typical of an aristocratic way of thinking, to which blood, not the sacrament of marriage, is important. Though illegitimacy is of no account, Tom, whatever his merits, could never have married Sophia, if he were the son of Jenny Jones and Partridge, as he is supposed to be all through the novel.

The story-pattern which is followed in both novels cannot be dismissed as a traditional romantic story-pattern, or as a burlesque of the stock recognition endings of romances and dramas like *Oedipus*.[5] Rather, as Ian Watt notes:

> [The discovery of gentle blood in Tom] is not wholly a surprise to the perceptive reader, for whom Tom's eminent 'liberality of spirit' has already suggested his superior pedigree; the recent Soviet critic, therefore, who sees the story as the triumph of a proletarian hero is neglecting, not only the facts of his birth, but its continuing implications for his character.[6]

Fielding was no socialist, or as the eighteenth century called the tribe, no 'leveller'. He may draw scathing pictures of the depravity of the privileged classes of society; he may show with fierce indignation the injustice, tyranny and oppression which was the result of concentration of power in a few hands; but the necessity and logic of the class structure itself are never questioned by him. The purpose of the harsh satire is to recall the privileged classes to their duties and obligations, not to summon the down-trodden to seize and share the privileges.

That a writer like Fielding, with his penetrating intellect, generous instincts and deep humanity, should show no inclination to question the validity of such theories of inequality, is a significant indication of the ethos of the times. No other writer of the century shows so genuine an appreciation of the vigour, variety and interest of 'low' life as Fielding. No other writer asserts with more conviction that a poor postillion, or a poor pedlar, 'low' fellows according to the world, may often have more humanity and generosity than a rich and 'polite' gentleman. No one ridicules more often, and with keener zest, the snobbery which infected every stratum of the class-conscious society of the time. He himself could laugh at 'the high blood of ancestors' as 'blood made of rich sauces and generous wines' (*TJ*, I, xi).

About the fairness of the legal system which safeguarded this class-structure, Fielding did not have any illusions; nor did he wish to conceal from his readers the crass iniquity of a system which gave quite arbitrary power to the 'high'; which enabled them to punish the 'low' for trifling faults, while they themselves escaped punishment for much graver sins. In fact, a modern reader finds it difficult to understand why Fielding never arrives at the point where he is willing to question the validity and morality of the stratified class system, when he can lay bare all its deficiencies with such clarity of vision. In fact the total artistic effect of Fielding's novels suffers precisely because he sees the faults of the class system so clearly, and exposes them so fiercely. That hardly any critic has found the happy ending of *Amelia* acceptable is largely due to the fact that it is totally at variance with the tone of the social criticism which, right through the novel, has tried to establish that in a society as unjust and corrupt as that of contemporary England, it is impossible for a good gentleman to prosper, or for his virtuous lady to escape unmolested. The sudden discovery of a legacy that enables the Booths to settle down in bliss as country gentleman and lady is a glib solution obtained only by the author's shutting his eyes in despair upon the facts he has seen with such concern through six hundred pages.

If an extremely clear-eyed perception of the defects of the class system does not provoke Fielding, who belongs to the patrician class, to be a 'leveller', neither do inferior birth and a typical middle class tradesman's Puritan disapproval of the morals of the upper classes prevent Richardson from giving staunch support to the sacred principle of 'subordination'. As in all other matters, so in this matter of social and economic theories, Sir Charles Grandison's conduct is meant to show the true path :

> He . . . is most likely to resemble him [Sir Charles] who has an unbounded charity and universal benevolence to men of all professions; and who, imitating the divinity, regards the heart, rather than the head, and much more than either rank or fortune, though it were princely; and yet is not a leveller, but thinks that rank or degree entitles a man, who is not utterly unworthy of both, to respect. (IV, liv)

The fact that in Richardson's first novel the servant girl Pamela, daughter of Goodman and Goody Andrews, vindicates her right to marry the great gentleman in whose house she works as a servant, is not to be taken as an assertion that the classes should mix, mingle and perish. Richardson, in the person of his Pamela, emphatically disclaims any such liability (II, xxxii).

There is an interesting passage in Boswell's *Life of Johnson* on this problem of *mésalliances*. Like Richardson, Johnson, who was of equally obscure extraction, was a fierce supporter of the hierarchical system. So was Boswell, more understandably, in his pride as a Scottish laird. Recording an argument between Johnson and Mrs. Thrale about the attitude to be adopted by her relations towards 'a young lady who had married a man much her inferior in rank' Boswell rejoices that though Mrs. Thrale 'was all for mildness and forgiveness', Johnson would not yield :

> JOHNSON : . . .Were I a man of rank, I would not let a

daughter starve who had made a mean marriage... I would support her only in that which she herself had chosen; and would not put her on a level with my other daughters... it is our duty to maintain the subordination of civilized society; and when there is gross and shameful deviation from rank, it should be punished so as to deter others from the same perversion. (*Life*, II, 328-9)

Faith in this principle of 'subordination' received intellectual support from the prevalent philosophical doctrine of 'the great Chain of Being'. This neo-Platonic theory saw the cosmos as composed of an innumerable number of links fitted together in hierarchical order, each link 'Alike essential to th' amazing whole':

> Vast chain of being, which from God began,
> Natures aethereal, human, angel, man,
> Beast, bird, fish, insect!
> (*An Essay on Man*, I, 237-9)

It was easy to fall back on this hierarchical theory to justify social inequalities and prove that in the social order, as in the cosmic, 'Whatever IS, is RIGHT'. For, if the insect in the grass trod upon by man's foot was essential, so was the impoverished peasant on the rich man's estate.

Though Johnson staunchly supported the principle of hierarchical gradation in society, he attacked the theory of the Chain of Being and the currently fashionable philosophical optimism to which it led. Nor is the sturdy independence of Johnson to be talked of in the same breath as the tedious concern with birth and status and wealth in an upholder of 'subordination' like Richardson. In *Pamela*, in particular, Richardson's powerful and dramatic presentation of the social and psychological conflict between the virtuous, oppressed, 'low-born cottager', Pamela, and the licentious, selfish, all-powerful, 'fine gentleman', Mr. B., is vitiated by his servile shop-keeper propensity to be dazzled by the might and splendour of the high-born. Richardson is both awed and appalled by the magnificent licentiousness of aristocratic attitudes.

A Puritan zeal to expose the profane libertinism and the 'sinful pride of a high estate', incites Richardson to draw a fierce picture of the arrogance, selfishness, cruelty and corruption of the gentry and aristocracy. In the middle sections of the first volume of *Pamela*, the conflict between the classes is presented with great power and emotion and a keen sense of the implications of social and economic inequality. Because of their economic dependence on Mr. B., and great deference to his exalted social position, Mr. B.'s kindly old steward, his saintly housekeeper and the young clergyman who looks to him for patronage are all almost paralysed in their will to protect the defenceless Pamela. Richardson's sympathy for the plight of the harassed Pamela, utterly exhausted in body and spirit by her prolonged struggle to defeat the power of her master and oppressor, finds expression in scenes of great dramatic intensity. The reader is therefore naturally disturbed to find that in spite of all his vehement disapproval of the conduct and values of the upper class, Richardson cannot find any more appropriate 'reward' for his heroine's virtue, than to marry her to the great gentleman who has so harassed and bullied her.

The reader is even more disturbed by the obsequious manner in which Mr. B.'s 'condescension' in marrying Pamela is treated. When Pamela announces to her father that Mr. B. has proposed marriage, the following dialogue is reported :

'... and you'll see, from the depth of misery, what God has done for me.'—'Blessed be his name', said he; 'but, do you say he will marry you ? Can such a brave gentleman make a lady of the child of such a poor man as I ? O the Divine goodness !' (I, Pamela's Journal)

The promise to undergo the ceremony given, the 'once naughty assailer of her innocence', becomes the 'generous good gentleman' with the 'rich mind'. Their daughter's marriage with a man who has given so many proofs of his ungovernable passions and tyrannical egoism, gives hardly any uneasiness to Pamela's parents. Henceforward they live in untroubled happiness and perfect security on the little estate on which Mr. B. sets them up.

In a letter to Dr. George Cheyne (31 Aug 1741), who had admonished him about his treatment of certain situations in *Pamela*, Richardson tried to justify the 'gratitude' of Pamela and her parents. The justification makes quite clear to us the writer's own attitude towards the relationship between the classes:

> But the Gratitude of her Parents, and herself to their Benefactor, I own I have carried *intentionally* High, on their Parts . . . By which means I intended a *double* example; one for the Obliger, and the other for the Obliged. And when it is consider'd, that between Mr. B. and Pamela's Father and Mother, there lay only an *accidental*, not a *natural* Relation; perhaps it will not be thought so much amiss, that the good old Folks endeavour to conduct themselves in such a Manner as they would have done, had there not been that *accidental* Relation . . .

Pamela herself is so overwhelmed by the 'obligations' Mr. B. has heaped on her that, even after she becomes his wife, she frequently throws herself at his feet to thank him and utters the most extraordinary expressions of gratitude:

> 'O but, Sir,' said I, 'I have seen God's salvation' and if anybody ever had reason, I have, to say, with the blessed Virgin—My soul doth magnify the Lord; for he hath regarded the low estate of his handmaiden, and exalted one of low degree. (I, Pamela's Journal)

When Richardson is not consciously contrasting the virtue of the poor with the vices of the rich, we catch him slipping into the habit of associating rank and fortune with goodness. In *Clarissa* even the heroine, a young lady 'so noted . . . for prudence, for *soul* (I will say, instead of *sense*), and for virtue' (II, xliv), confuses issues.

However, *Clarissa* is not marked by the obsequious respect for the upper class that is so noticeable in *Pamela*; or rather, the situation does not give occasion for it, since Lovelace and Clarissa, unlike Mr. B. and Pamela, are not separated by a social gulf that would normally make it impossible for them to marry each other.

Both Lovelace and Clarissa belong to the very wealthy but untitled gentry, and both can claim connections with the peerage on the mother's side. Clarissa's mother, however, is the daughter of a mere viscount, whose line is extinct; while Lovelace's uncle, Lord M., is a very rich and influential earl who controls three or four parliamentary boroughs. Lovelace himself, though only a sister's son, is heir presumptive to Lord M., and his relations hope to secure for him his lordship's title which would otherwise become extinct after his death. On the other hand, the relations who are most closely associated with Clarissa, are her two mercenary merchant uncles, who have made their pile from East India traffic and from mining. Nevertheless, it would be distorting Richardson's viewpoint and purpose if, with some recent critics[7], we regard the novel as presenting a conflict between two antagonistic social classes sharply differing in morals and mores—between the liberal-minded but licentious aristocracy, and what is called 'the rising middle class', with its puritanic and individualistic outlook. The Harlowe brothers, after all, have adventured into trade like many younger sons of very respectable gentry. It is true that Lovelace often speaks slightingly of Clarissa's family as being much inferior to his; but Lovelace's titled aunts, his friend Belford, and Lord M. himself do not consider an alliance with the Harlowes unworthy.

It is not as representatives of two social classes, but as two individuals with antagonistically different moral convictions, that Clarissa and Lovelace clash and destroy each other. The Harlowes are nowhere depicted as Puritans, punctilious in the performance of their religious or moral duties; and, as far as sexual lapses are concerned, the men of Clarissa's family are far from innocent, though they manage their peccadilloes more surreptitiously, and somewhat less unscrupulously, than Lovelace.

Not class antagonism, but the fanaticism and unhappiness that are generated by social ambition and avarice, is Richardson's subject in his delineation of the Harlowes. The family's sense of values and moral perspective are destroyed by the single-minded desire to climb higher up the social scale and obtain a peerage. Clarissa often speaks with despair of 'the family fault': 'the darling view some of us have long had of *raising a family* as it is called' (I, xiii). The malice and extreme cruelty with which her brother and sister treat Clarissa, and which is the initial cause of her tragedy, is largely due to the fact that Clarissa's paternal grandfather has bequeathed to her a large part of his vast wealth, passing over the claims of his own sons as well as his other grandchildren—Clarissa's brother, James, and her sister, Bella. In addition to this cause for jealousy, James fears that if Clarissa marries Lovelace, and has chances of becoming 'a peeress of Great Britain', his two bachelor uncles, in their hope of relating the family to the peerage, would try to better her chances by bequeathing a large part of their wealth to her, though already 'there is not a finer fortune in the country'. To prevent this, James contrives that in place of the dazzling Lovelace, the family should decide on the repulsive Solmes as husband for Clarissa. Vastly rich, Solmes is ugly in body, mean in mind and impelled in all his actions by what Clarissa describes as a 'diabolical parsimony'. 'The captivating proposals' Solmes makes regarding the marriage settlements, are an irresistible temptation not only to James, but to Clarissa's father and uncles who believe that 'the family views will be promoted by the match'. For not only is Solmes immensely rich, but his estate is very conveniently situated next to Clarissa's own, and Solmes does not mind agreeing to make over to James the 'reversionary' rights to his and Clarissa's joint estate, in the event of his dying childless.

Meanwhile, on his side, the despicable Solmes has satisfied himself about the advantageousness of the marriage. Though his prospective bride has repeatedly stressed that she has an 'aversion' to him, he remains unperturbedly constant in his offer of love and marriage, for he knows that Clarissa's estate lies next to his own, and will 'double the value' of his; besides, marriage with her will be 'an alliance which would do credit to his obscurity and narrowness' (I, xxxii).

As we thread through all the ramifications of these complicated and far-reaching schemes for 'aggrandizing the family', we feel the force of the concentrated passion with which Richardson exposes the rapacity and ambition of the Harlowes.

Having chosen as one of his major themes the censure of such ambitions among the upper and upper-middle classes, in this novel Richardson escapes the danger of falling into that attitude of obsequious deference which marks his approach to superior social status in *Pamela*. Similarly, in *Sir Charles*

Grandison, the danger is obviated because the lower classes do not intrude into the select circle of baronets and counts and ancient families. But in *Pamela*, the petty concept of innocent virtue finding its reward in stepping up the social ladder and marrying into the gentry, vitiates the development not only of the main theme, but affects the treatment of even the minor details and incidental problems. The confused attitude, which consciously criticises, but subconsciously accepts, the notion of the superiority of the gentleman, can be illustrated from almost any part of the novel; it colours even the philosophy of education that Pamela is made to propound. Commenting on the 'great distance Mr. Locke enjoins to be kept between children and servants', the former servant-girl begs to differ from the philosopher. No danger is to be feared if the morals of servants have been carefully supervised by the master and mistress, especially as there is no likelihood that if they play in the company of their inferiors, the awe and respect due to young gentlemen and ladies will be diminished:

> I have observed, before now, instances of this, in some of the families we visit, between the young Masters or Misses, and those children of lower degree, who have been brought to play with them, or divert them. On the Masters' and Misses' side I have always seen, they lead the play and prescribe the laws of it . . . while, on the other hand, their lower-rank play-fellows have generally given in to their little humours, though ever so contrary to their own; and the difference of dress and appearance, and the notion they have of the more eminent condition of their play-fellows' parents, have begot in them a kind of awe and respect, that perhaps more than sufficiently secures the superiority of the one, and the subordination of the other. (II, xciv)

The gentleman, it seems, will always be the natural leader, even among playmates.

The fact that even a much-acclaimed novelist who sought to assert the claim of a waiting-maid to marry a gentleman by right of her virtue and accomplishments, could put so much trust in the power of high birth, 'dress and appearance' to confer distinction upon a man, made it imperative for later writers like Thomas Day to reiterate, on almost every page of their books, that in a natural and just society the intelligent, skilful, resourceful and intrepid man would become the leader.

The principal object of Thomas Day in his *Sandford and Merton* is to criticize the contemporary idea of the gentleman. The book dismisses with contempt the claim to social deference made by the gentleman, and exposes in forceful satirical pictures the folly and falsity of his assumptions about his own superiority. Episode after episode is devoted to proving that a class of men who are idle, selfish, cruel and effete can have no claim to deference from the rest of mankind, in any reasonable, well-ordered, 'natural' society. Day refers with great scorn to the popular idea of the gentleman as a person who is distinguished from the vulgar by being able to live as a parasite on the labour of others. In a state of nature, or when cast by fortune upon a desert island, it is not the gentleman who is selected as leader. Then the most resourceful and courageous are elected leaders, while the gentlemen, who are not used to work, perish—an idea which, more than a century after Day, James Barrie used in *The Admirable Crichton*.

Sandford and Merton is far more radical in its attack on the gentleman-centred class structure than any other book of the period. Its principal character is Tommy Merton, a vain, fretful, unhealthy and timorous young gentleman of sixteen, who has imbibed all the set ideas about the superiority of the gentleman and the disreputability of labour. These smug and complacent notions about the superiority of his class are so deeply ingrained in Tommy that even after months of training under the radical priest, Mr. Barlow, he continues to mouth them. Mr. Barlow has to contrive numerous episodes, and devise many stories, to prick the bubble of Tommy's pride. The chief lesson that Tommy is made to learn is that the poor, the black people and the representatives of primitive races are superior to him in skill, knowledge, courage and generosity. Day stresses that it is wrong to accuse the lower classes of grossness and indelicacy. His poor invariably have an essential refinement, while his rich are despicable. In his book, *gentleman* has become an almost opprobrious term.

However, the society that Day portrays has not felt the influence of Jacobinism. The poor placidly accept their lot in the existing social and economic framework, and give willing deference and ungrudging service to the gentleman. Young Tommy is appalled when he discovers that his mother throws away on an opera ticket a sum which represents a whole week's income for farmer Sandford; but the honest farmer accepts the situation and says he must 'thank the great and wise God that our condition is no worse' (p. 176). However, the writer's own voice is far more angry and bitter as he protests against the existing social conditions in which only parasites are allowed to flourish. In fact, Day is more single-minded in asserting that birth and rank confer no superiority, and in his praise of primitive peoples, than even Rousseau whom he venerated as 'the first of human kind' in his dedication to the third edition of his anti-slavery poem, *The Dying Negro*.

Rousseau's whole system of education is based on the assumption that education has destroyed the capacity to think among the upper classes. Yet he affirms :

> People who spend their whole life in working for a living have no ideas beyond their own work and their own interests, and their mind seems to reside in their arms ... a cultivated mind alone makes intercourse pleasant ... It is hard to find in the lowest stratum of society a woman who is able to make a good man happy. (*Emile*, bk. V)

So, ultimately, society divides itself into two classes—the class of the gentleman and the class of the working man.

It is not as if in the scheme of education that he propounds, Rousseau makes a place for the education of the poor and envisages a consequent possibility of their becoming pleasant companions. He is quite content to accept the situation around him and assume that the poor need not be provided with education. So he proceeds to his corollary that the poor are unthinking and incapable of bringing up 'intelligent or pleasing children'. In fact even 'good birth' is an essential component in his conception of an ideal man :

> Yes, I maintain, and I am not afraid of the testimony of experience, a youth of good birth, one who has preserved

his innocence up to the age of twenty, is at that age the best, the most generous, the most loving, and the most lovable of men. (bk. IV)

So when, in the final sections of *Emile* Rousseau depicts the ideal life of the ideal man living close to nature, the reader should not be too surprised to find a picture not very different from the scores of pictures of ideal country gentlemen painted by conservative poets and novelists throughout this century.

If even the father of liberty, equality and fraternity can find the highest manifestation of the ideal only in the gentleman class, it is not surprising that Henry Brooke, who heard Rousseau's call for the natural life and the natural education, should select the son of an earl to try out the new scheme of education. Yet a feeling for egalitarian ideas and a spirit of Christian charity compel Brooke to assert that the best and noblest man can be found in any class of society. But he finds that 'gentleman' has come to be the most coveted of all titles; consequently he feels obliged to seek that very title for his ideal man. This puts him in a dilemma which tortures him all along and constantly makes him fret about the meaning of the term *gentleman*. Unlike the radical Thomas Day, he does not regard it as an opprobrious term, to be used only to ridicule or chastise the upper classes. Nor can he allow it to be a mere technical term indicating birth and status. One of the principal objects of Brooke's novel is to define and explain the term afresh from his own point of view. Describing it as the 'most venerable of all titles' and 'the most exalted of all characters', Brooke devotes numerous sections of his novel to an examination of the meaning of the word. In a dialogue (ch. XI) between the 'Author' and his 'Friend' he enumerates 'the qualities that entitle a man to this supreme of denominations'. A warm and sensitive heart, deep affection, humanity, patriotism and piety are selected as the qualifying attributes; in later paragraphs Brooke adds charity and 'a delicacy of behaviour towards women'. But birth, rank, status, sophistication and elegant manners have no place in his conception of the term.

Like Thomas Day, Brooke registers a sharp protest against the commonly accepted notion that the term *gentleman* is to be used for one who does no work, and that gentlemanly activities are characterized by their non-utility, an absence of monetary returns. Reacting violently against the values of such a mandarin culture in which men are despised for being of use to others and work is regarded as something intrinsically base. Brooke takes up an extreme position and pronounces: 'Nothing is truly estimable save in proportion to its utility' (ch. IV). In the earlier chapters of his novel, Brooke satirizes the prevailing notion that a gentleman loses caste if he engages in trade. Henry Clinton, younger son of Richard, Earl of Moreland, has been apprenticed to a tradesman after his father's death. His elder brother, the second earl, a gay young dog who keeps company with my Lord Rochester and with the merry monarch himself, has 'the utmost contempt for all cits and traders'. His brother's association with trade he considers such a stigma upon the family name, that he concludes that Henry has been 'deprived of all title to gentility', and summarily lops him off as 'a branch cut off from the family tree'. Yet, having run through his fortune, he himself goes to the 'city' for a wife, as indeed many of the nobility did. The cit's daughter wants a title, and he wants her portion of £ 100,000; both are thus happily accommodated. This sort of marriage of convenience, as is seen from the caption which Hogarth gave to his famous series of engravings (completed 1745) depicting the mercenary union of an earl's son with an alderman's daughter, was becoming the *marriage a la mode.*

Though aristocrats did not scruple to marry into the 'city,' and though the number of 'citizens turned gentlemen'[8] increased as fresh opportunities for large profits in home and foreign trade enabled a new affluent class of tradesmen to buy land, contempt for trade seems to have increased rather than diminished during the course of the century. The society portrayed by Fanny Burney in the eighties, and by Jane Austen at the turn of the century, seems to be even more fastidious about the source of large fortunes, and seems to regard trade as an even darker taint, than the society portrayed by Addison and Steele in the first two decades, or by Richardson and Fielding in the fifties. However, as contempt for the merchant increased in certain quarters, some of the most representative writers took up his cause. The inevitable butt of ridicule in the comedies of the Restoration period, the merchant now came into his own in literature. Addison and Steele both played an important part in setting the trend.

It was Addison's ambition to make *The Spectator's* campaign for good breeding and for 'wit tempered with morality' (no. 10), effective among all the different sections of a rapidly growing middle class, as well as among the established upper class. For the first time a writer took it upon himself to write for the whole reading population, catering at one time for court, 'town', 'city' and country gentleman, resolving the long-standing conflict between these traditional antagonists. In such a situation, the country gentleman and the merchant, who had both been subjected to much banter and contempt in previous literature, had to be vindicated, and the conventional subjects of satire had to be changed. Addison is quite conscious of the change in tone he must introduce if he is to succeed with this new and heterogeneous audience :

'In short', says Sir Andrew, 'if you avoid that foolish beaten road of falling upon aldermen and citizens, and employ your pen upon the vanity and luxury of courts, your paper must needs be of general use.' (no. 34)

Thus it is that Sir Andrew Freeport, 'a merchant of great eminence in the city of London', is given a distinguished place, and the most balanced, useful and pleasant role, among the members of the Spectator Club. With perceptible defiance in his tone, Steele flings the challenge on behalf of the merchant : 'A general trader of good sense is pleasanter company than a general scholar' (no. 2). The several debates in which Sir Andrew contends with Sir Roger are directed at proving that the role of leader and benefactor which the landed gentleman hitherto considered his monopoly is more truly the merchant's. Here one finds perceptible changes in the attitudes towards the traditional ideals of magnanimity, beneficence and refinement —changes of a kind that will enable this new class to assert itself. Similarly, a new ideal of glory, patriotism and power, in sharpest opposition to the chivalric and courtly ideal, is given definition. Here again, the merchant's characteristic qualities will make him the most successful contender for the highest place. Sir Andrew 'is acquainted with commerce in all its parts, and will tell you that it is a stupid and barbarous way to extend dominion by arms, for true power is to be got by arts and industry' (no. 2).

A decade later, in *The Conscious Lovers*, Steele again takes up the cudgels for the commercial classes against the established aristocracy and gentry. For the first time in an English comedy, an English merchant, instead of being an unsympathetic, greedy miser, a clumsy, gross object of ridicule, is offered as the norm—the good-hearted, balanced, urbane character, round whom circle the eccentrics, and the oddities and the lovers. The question of the merchant's claim to be classed as *gentleman* is deliberately taken up in the second scene of the fourth act. Mr. Sealand, the merchant, addresses Sir John Bevil, who is anxious to get the merchant's fortune for his son, but is reluctant to form an alliance with a trader's family:

> *Sealand*: . . . We merchants are a species of gentry that have grown into the world this last century, and are as honourable, and almost as useful, as you landed folks, that have always thought yourselves so much above us; for your trading, forsooth, is extended no farther than a load of hay, or a fat ox.

Sealand is not one of those many merchants who, having made their pile in trade, have bought estates and settled down to being gentlemen; he still buys and sells; the taint of trade still lies deep and clear on him.

We cannot say that Steele's campaign for this new 'species of gentry' who 'do something' has much effect on the novel, though the essay-serials written in imitation of *The Spectator* frequently stress the respectability of the mercantile life. Steele's Sealand does not, after all, become the precursor of many merchant heroes in the fiction or drama of the eighteenth century. What is more, even Sir Andrew Freeport, as Addison announces (no. 549) when taking leave of the members of the Spectator Club, decides to retire from business and buy a large estate, so that he can settle down as an ideal country gentleman and perfect landlord. Henry Brooke writes paeans in praise of the merchant, but his merchant-prince, Mr. Clinton, is after all the scion of a noble family; besides, though for a while he is so proud of being a trader, he has sold his business even before he comes upon the scene and, throughout the action of the novel, is absorbed only in thoughts of benevolence, charity and the new education.

Henry Mackenzie, like Brooke, breaks away from tradition in many matters, yet cannot quite overcome the traditional aversion to trade. Though he goes out of his way to present a few good tradesmen in minor roles, in other parts of his novels there is a suggestion that the practice of trade, especially if it brings large profits, has a demeaning influence and is impossible for the ideal 'man of feeling'. The hero of *The Man of the World*, the good Mr. Annesly, is portrayed (I, i) as rebelling against the narrowing and oppressive environment of trade, to which his father, a wealthy merchant, worth £ 30,000, wishes to confine him. Mild and gentle though he is, on this point he is willing to go so far as to break with his father.

Mackenzie's extremely sympathetic biographer, H. W. Thompson, reveals that Mackenzie himself was not above that species of foppery which considered it beneath the dignity of a gentleman to write in return for money:

> [Before 1808] Mackenzie received next to nothing for his writings.... Part of this situation resulted from the snobbish pose of being a gentleman—the attitude which later made Thomas Carlyle rage, 'we have no more writers but only writing gentlemen'.[9]

Among the major novelists, Richardson, perhaps naturally, is the one who is most dissatisfied with the disdainful attitude towards the tradesman. A characteristic scene in *Sir Charles Grandison* shows the perfect woman, Harriet Byron, wife to Sir Charles, remonstrating with his sprightly sister Charlotte, Lady G. Her impoverished cousin, Mr. Grandison, has married the widow of a city merchant who, in the first month of marriage, has 'already presented him with 25000 pounds'. Harriet is shocked because Charlotte insists on referring to Mr. Grandison's wife as a 'widow cit' (VII, iv).

Richardson makes the gentleman born to 'ancient riches' instinctively express revulsion at being put on the same level with those who have been at pains to gather wealth. The aristocrat Lovelace lays scornful stress on the '*acquired* fortunes' of Clarissa's uncles, underscoring 'acquired', as he writes to his friend (II, X), though Anthony Harlowe is proud of his having himself amassed an independent fortune. Mr. B. finds even the title of baronet beneath his dignity, because traders have managed to climb into the order (II, xxix).

Though Richardson thus occasionally thought it necessary to register a mild protest against the supercilious attitude towards trade, he himself did not deign to make a tradesman the hero of any of his novels. Instead of portraying the life he knew intimately, he chose to moralize about Lord A. and Lady B. and the Countess of C., providing an opportunity to aristocrats like Horace Walpole to ridicule his tradesman's concept of upper class life as 'pictures of high life as conceived by a book-seller' (*Letters*, 20 Dec 1764).

It was not even as if Richardson himself always felt comfortable about dealing with a social milieu unfamiliar to him. A letter addressed to Lady Bradsaigh when he was writing *Grandison*, shows he was quite conscious of his limitations : 'How shall a man obscurely situated . . . pretend to describe and enter into characters in upper life ?'

Even more curious than Richardson's case, is that of another outsider, Daniel Defoe (de Foe), the self-taught son of a tallow-chandler, James Foe. He had stood behind the counter, and in the pillory, but undertook, alongside a variety of other literary ventures, to draw the image of 'the Compleat English Gentleman'. Demonstrating with considerable sarcasm that the 'bred' sons of wealthy merchants are often much more refined and worthy than the sons of gentlemen, Defoe announces (pp. 256-8) his intention of proposing a 'fund for the increase of our nobility and gentry in English, being the beginning of those we call Bred Gentlemen'.

We find Defoe recording the emergence of a new open society. He points out the changes that have taken place in the composition of society in 'these last ages' because of the 'abundance of modern advantages and private ways of getting money'. Numerous opportunities have opened out in law, trade, navigation, 'improvement of stocks', to amass money and found estates and 'families'. On behalf of the sons of these new men, who were often given a liberal education, Defoe puts up a strong fight against the 'born gentlemen'. Such 'bred' and wealthy men have a far better claim to the title of *gentleman*, than the ignorant, boorish squires who are found all over the countryside, riding, hunting and drinking. These sons of merchants have learning and good breeding, and they have also 'the grand essential, the great fund of families, the money';[10] how then can gentlemen refuse to admit them into their class?

But though Defoe fights for the claims of the sons of merchants, he refuses to allow the merchant himself to intrude into the fold, even if he has retired from trade and settled down upon vast landed estates; for he feels very strongly that the 'first money getting wretch' will never be able to rise above the meanness, greed and low tastes of his trading career.

Much as he emphasizes education and good-breeding, it never occurs to Defoe to plead the case of a 'bred' poor man, however refined and learned he may be. For him the characteristic and indispensable attribute of the gentleman, 'the grand essential', is money. One remembers that great realist, Sancho Panza, and his appraisal of the matter:

> ...for so much thou art worth as thou hast, and so much thou hast, as thou art worth. There are but two lineages in the world, as my grandmother used to say: 'the Haves and the Have-nots', and she stuck to the Haves... An ass with golden furniture makes a better figure than a horse with a pack-saddle. (*Don Quixote*, II, xx)

Smollett's *Roderick Random* provides a vivid exposition of this philosophy of the indignity of labour. Roderick's grandfather, a haughty, wealthy Scottish judge, has never looked upon him with much favour, not having approved of the marriage of Roderick's father, his younger son, with a poor relation living in the house. When Roderick is thirteen, Tom Bowling, his dead mother's brother, a not very prosperous lieutenant in the navy, and a man of little education, arrives on the scene, and rebukes the judge for his 'unchristian' neglect of Roderick. The old gentleman feeling somewhat guilty about his treatment of the young lad, promises to 'bind him apprentice to some honest tradesman or other'. 'The honest tar, whose pride and indignation boiled within him', spurns this offer, taking it as an insult. 'Muttering curses all the way against the old shark', he takes Rory away and, poor as his condition is, gives him a liberal education at a Scottish university for three years, as befits his dignity as the son of a gentleman (I, iii).

Through the greater part of the novel we find the penniless Roderick making desperate attempts to find a means of living consistent with his status as gentleman. Most gainful labour, he finds, involves a loss of status. The faithful Strap, his life-long companion and servant, finding Roderick has lost his last shilling at the gaming table, bursts into tears :

'On my own account', said he, 'I am quite unconcerned; for while God spares me health and these ten fingers, I can earn comfortable subsistence anywhere; but what must become of you, who have less humility to stoop, and more appetites to gratify?'

A succinct résumé, indeed, of the difference between a gentleman and a non-gentleman.

The disdain for trade and other monetarily rewarding activities, takes its most extreme form in the two women novelists of the end of the century, Fanny Burney and Jane Austen. In quite a few of her novels Jane Austen ostensibly intends to satirize and condemn this kind of snobbery. But the beloved heroines of both novelists, Fanny Burney's Evelina and Jane Austen's Emma, and sometimes the novelists themselves, take up an almost vindictive attitude towards tradesmen and such other 'low' people. The grotesque pride and class-consciousness of Lady Catherine de Bourgh in *Pride and Prejudice*, and of Sir Walter Elliott and two of his daughters in *Persuasion*, are castigated in some of Jane Austen's sharpest satire, but the concentrated attention that Emma Wodehouse gives to the study of family antecedents and social status, her unrelenting insistence on observing all the subtleties of class distinctions, are dealt with in a somewhat different tone, which makes it at times difficult to determine the writer's own attitude. Describing Frank Churchill's off-hand attitude in arranging a dance that involves a most inconvenient mixture of classes, Emma is made to reflect :

...even when particulars were given and families described, he was still unwilling to admit that the inconvenience of such a mixture would be anything, or that there would be the smallest difficulty in everybody's returning into their proper place the next morning...Of pride, indeed, there was, perhaps, scarcely enough; his indifference to a confusion of rank bordered too much on inelegance of mind. (ch. XXIV)

In such passages the tone is not completely accounted for by the fact that Jane Austen is narrating the story largely from Emma's point of view, and one wonders whether the writer is satirizing her heroine's fastidiousness, or revealing her own sentiments. Emma, with her intransigent attitudes towards class distinctions, would not have got off so lightly if the novelist had not, at least in her youth, felt similar qualms about tradesmen. The almost inimical attitude that Emma adopts towards the respectable Mr. Martin who, though a farmer, presumes to fall in love with her friend Harriet, and her resolution to teach a lesson to the quite amiable Cole family for presuming to invite her to dinner, forgetting that they made their fortune in trade, are treated with affection as a fastidiousness quite natural in a high-spirited and very superior young lady.

Fanny Burney's antipathy to trade and 'low connections' is more clear. Though in the manner of most novelists of her day, she satirizes snobs and 'Court Calendar bigots' (*Evelina*, III, iii), she finds it difficult not to feel revolted by the social inadequacy of the trading classes. Their futile efforts to imitate their social superiors strike her as appallingly vulgar. The embarrassment to which her heroine, Evelina, is subjected because of the trades-people who are her relatives greatly distresses both heroine and author. Both feel the humiliation when the heroine has to confess to staying at so unfashionable an address as Holborn.

This antipathy to the trading classes inspires Fanny Burney to write satire that is a merciless, but brilliantly vivid and vivacious exposure of their shallowness, crudity and pretensions. In passages of inspired malice she depicts their self-conscious efforts to appear 'genteel', to dress, talk, eat and entertain like the 'quality', which turn their lives into a grotesque parody of aristocratic behaviour. She mimics their silly conversation and gauche behaviour; the flutter in their hearts when they see a real lord; their naive ambition to appear in the company of 'gentlemen', and if that cannot be achieved, at least to sit and gaze at them passing by their shop. Clever fun is frequently made of the determination of Polly and her kind who 'would ten times rather die an old maid, than marry any person but a gentleman' (*Evelina*, II, 21).

It is not that Fanny Burney's satire of those moving in the inner circles has a less sharp edge. The pedigree-conscious snobs of the fashionable world are ridiculed in trenchant words. But there is a bias in her outlook which makes the worst enormities of the fashionable gentlemen and ladies seem somewhat less distasteful, because of the surface sheen upon their manners, than the clumsiness of the common folk. Obviously, the rift in society which Addison perceived at the beginning of the century has not healed. In 1711 Addison had lamented in *The Spectator*:

> When I consider this great city in its several quarters and divisions, I look upon it as an aggregate of various nations distinguished from each other by their respective customs, manners, and interests...In short, the inhabitants of St. James's are a distinct people from those of Cheapside, who are likewise removed from those of the Temple on the one side, and those of Smithfield on the other. (no. 403)

Whenever Fanny Burney portrays the inhabitants of Cheapside the most biting edge of her vivacious satire comes into play; yet no writer at this date could quite dismiss the worth and importance of the city. At least twice in *Cecilia*, she feels compelled to recognize the rising standards of 'elegance and liberality' in the city. Unlike the plot of *Evelina*, much of which is evolved from the embarrassments caused to a young lady by relations who are low trades-people, the pivot on which the far more complicated plot of *Cecilia* turns is the fanaticism and unhappiness that is generated by the Delvile family's insensate pride in their long pedigree, and the equally insensate prejudice which has made Cecilia's uncle specify in his will that the man who marries her—and her estate of three thousand pounds per annum—should take her surname and renounce his own. At the end of the novel (X, x) one of the characters is made to stress how they 'owe all their miseries to PRIDE and PREJUDICE'; it is undoubtedly from here that Jane Austen got the inspiration for the title of her novel.

Cecilia Beverley's pedigree is reflected upon by others, as well as by herself, in various revealing phrases. We hear of 'the brevity of her genealogy' (IV, xii), of 'her birth, which though not contemptible, was merely decent, and which, if traced beyond her grandfather, lost all title even to that epithet' (VI, iii). The Delviles, with whose son Cecilia falls in love, are a very old race, extremely proud of their family history. 'They count on each side Dukes, Earls, and Barons in their genealogy' (III, X); however, the family fortunes are sadly depleted, and it is essential that young Delvile should marry a magnificent fortune.

The arrogant solemnity with which Delvile senior parades his awesome ancestry is ridiculed all through the novel. The miserly but delightfully portrayed Mr. Briggs is often used to tell him off:

'Why all the old grandfathers and aunts you brag of; a set of poor souls you won't let rest in their coffins; mere clay and dirt'...Who cares for dead carcasses? nothing but carrion. My little Tom's worth forty of 'em'. (V, ix)

Not that the author herself would ever equate 'little Tom', the errand-boy, with forty Delviles, except to twit pomposity. The 'famous Tom Paine' called forth only her scorn and anger when he started propagating 'his pernicious doctrines' (*Diary*, May 1792).

In spite of their pride, the Delviles, especially the haughty but very noble Mrs. Delvile, and the son Mortimer, do not object to Cecilia's birth, since she is not only extremely rich, but also superior to every other woman they know, in character, manners and appearance. However, their sense of duty to their family makes the clause in Cecilia's uncle's will an absolutely insuperable obstacle. When Mrs. Delvile sees love triumphing in Mortimer over 'duty, spirit, and fortitude' (VI, vii), she falls down in a fit from which she never recovers completely (VIII, .ii)

Ultimately the difficulty is resolved only by Cecilia's renouncing her enviably large fortune which the impoverished Delvile estates need so badly.

Class prejudice is delightfully ridiculed by Lord Chesterfield in an essay in *The World* (March 6, 1755) :

> The Vulgar distinction between people of BIRTH and people of NO BIRTH will probably puzzle the critics and antiquaries of the thirtieth or fortieth centuries, when, in their judicious and laborious researches into the customs and manners of these present times, they shall have reason to suppose, that in the sixteenth, seventeenth and eighteenth centuries, the island of Great Britain was inhabited by two sorts of people, some BORN, but the much greater number UNBORN . . .
>
> BIRTH singly, and without an epithet, extends, I cannot positively say how far, but negatively it stops where useful arts and industry begin. Merchants, tradesmen, yeomen, farmers, and ploughmen, are not BORN, or at least, in so mean a way as not to deserve that name; and it is perhaps for that reason that their mothers are said to be *delivered*, rather than *brought to bed* of them.

On one occasion Chesterfield amused fashionable London by putting the heads of Adam and Eve among the portraits of his ancestors to poke fun at the pedigree mania. Horace Walpole thought 'the ridicule admirable' (to Sir Thomas Mann, 1 Sept 1750).

Though aristocrats like Chesterfield and Walpole at times found amusement in poking fun at their class-and-genealogy-conscious contemporaries, they themselves would certainly not have been content to rub shoulders with the plebs. Fielding's gloss in *The Covent Garden Journal* (14 Jan 1752) for the word *NOBODY*—'All the people in Great Britain except about 1200', would have amused them, but they would not have been embarrassed by the fact that their own exclusiveness gave a practical demonstration of the meaning that Fielding gave to the term.

Even the not quite so well-born Smollett, through the mouth of Matthew Bramble in *Humphry Clinker*, shows disgust at the promiscuous mingling of patrician and plebian in the supposedly fashionable society of London and Bath. Matthew feels that 'the mixture of people' is 'destructive of all order and urbanity', and will bring far worse disrepute 'than debasing the gold coin of the nation' (30 April, by Jeremy). Though Smollett's satire in this last novel is balanced and genial enough to enable him to express amusement about old Matthew's aversion to the multitude through the mouth of his nephew Jeremy, the strikingly forceful and trenchant words given to Matthew, make us feel that Smollett is expressing his own revulsion at the 'preposterous coalition' in which all sorts of social climbers, 'impudent plebians', jostle against the 'genteel people'.

If people like Matthew Bramble and Emma found the 'confusion of rank' revoltingly objectionable, there were others who felt offended by the new Christian preachers who had the temerity to place sinful aristocratic hearts on a level with sinful plebian hearts. The Duchess of Buckingham, illegitimate daughter of James II, wrote in protest to Selina, Countess of Huntingdon, disciple of John Wesley :

> ... These doctrines are most repulsive and strongly tinctured with impertinence and disrespect towards their superiors, in perpetually endeavouring to level all ranks ... as it is monstrous to be told that you have a heart as sinful as the common wretches that crawl on the earth.

Class-conscious though society was, even dukes and duchesses not infrequently poured pollution into ducal veins :

> His Grace the Duke of Shandois married an innkeeper's maid ... the Earl of Salisbury his steward's niece—Miss Keate, daughter to a barber and shewer of the tombs in Canterbury, and the Earl of Bristol, his late wife's maid. And the Duke of Bridgewater his tutor's niece.[11]
>
> The present Duchess-Dowager [of Ancaster] was natural daughter of Panton, a disreputable horse-jockey of Newmarket; and the new Duchess was some Lady's woman, or young Lady's governess. Fortune was in her most jocular moods when she made all these matches, or had a mind to

torment the Heralds' Office. (Walpole to Sir Horace Mann, 9 July 1779)

Not less tormenting to the heralds' office must have been the continuous series of West Indian planters, returning with the profits of sugar and slave labour, and 'nabobs' returning with booty plundered while fighting for the prosperity of the East India Company. Many of these easily found room at the top, though they had left the country, because they could not find room even on the lowest rung of the ladder. A remark from Horace Walpole's letters illuminates the social scene :

The Lord Advocate of Scotland, who has sold himself over and over, is prosecuting Sir Thomas Rumbold for corruption at Madras ! This Rumbold was a waiter at White's. There are two or three of like origin, who have returned from Bengal incrusted with gold and diamonds. (Walpole to Sir Horace Mann, 30 April 1783)

Natural sons and daughters—in whom the 'high' blood of gentlemen, and of aristocrats, and of kings, is mixed with very doubtful blood indeed—recur constantly in the novels of the period. In real life, if not in fiction, most of these natural children remained abandoned and neglected. But some, like Chesterfield's Philip, and, of course, most of the illegitimate of royal blood, made their way into the inner circle, even if some sticklers, or political enemies of the fathers, at times refused them social recognition and distinguished positions. The fastidious Henry Peacham, who so carefully weighs the claims of every class and profession to be admitted among 'nobility and gentry', and refuses entry to so many, 'willingly' produces examples 'to confirme our custome of ennobling' illegitimate children (pp. 9-10). But Boswell, who fathered at least two illegitimate children, disapproves 'of confounding the distinction between lawful and illicit offspring, which is, in effect, insulting the civil establishment of our country, to look no higher' (*Life*, I, 266).

Though the question of admitting illegitimate children into society remained controversial, most people did not doubt that 'low' characters could not be admitted into novels and plays.

As Goldsmith's Vicar noted, 'every reader, however beggarly himself, is fond of high-lived dialogues, anecdotes of lords, ladies and knights of the Garter' (ch. XI).

Not beggarly readers alone sought such fare to compensate for their frustrations. David Hume, in his essay on *Refinement in Writing*, postulates the aesthetic theory that proves the correctness of shunning 'low men' as fictional characters:

> Sentiments which are merely natural affect not the mind with any pleasure, and seem not worthy of our attention. The pleasantries of a waterman, the conversations of a peasant, the ribaldry of a porter or hackney coachman, all of these are natural, and disagreeable. Nothing can please persons of taste, but nature drawn with all her graces and ornaments, *la belle nature* ...[12]

Asked by a correspondent to single out 'the chief qualification of a good poet, especially one who writes plays', the 'Spectator' replied unhesitatingly in one pithy sentence: 'To be a very well-bred man' (no. 314). Dryden pointed out why Shakespeare and his contemporaries deserved to be less popular than their successors:

> ... the language, wit and conversation of our age are improved and refined above the last ... the wit of our predecessors ... was not that of gentlemen ... I cannot find that any of them had been conversant in courts, except Ben Jonson ... Gentlemen will now be entertained with the follies of each other; and though they allow Cob and Tib to speak properly, yet they are not much pleased with their tankard or with their rags. ('Defence of the Epilogue to the second part of *The Conquest of Granada*')

In *The Fable of the Bees* Mandeville's shrewd satire hits out at this squeamish taste as brilliantly as at all the other complacent, hypocritical attitudes which seek to gloss over uncomfortable facts:

> *Cleo*: Look upon that Dutch Piece of the Nativity ... What a Fool the Fellow was to draw Hay and Straw and

> Cattle, and a Rack as well as a Manger : it is a Wonder he did not put the Bambino into the Manger.
> *Ful*: The Bambino ? That is the Child, I suppose; why it should be in the Manger; should it not? ...
> *Cleo* : Pray, Cousin, say no more in Defence of your low Taste; The Painter has nothing to do with the Truth of the History; his Business is to express the Dignity of the Subjects .... (II, 32-5)

It was because of such ideas of dignity that the novel, the new form which was created to cater for the entertainment and instruction of the non-aristocratic classes, as a rule appointed only well-born people as heroes and heroines. Defoe, branching out into the 'new species of writing', had selected the street girl, Moll, as his heroine; however almost every English novel published in the half-century that followed, besides selecting as hero and heroine a gentleman and lady who, at least at the end of the novel, settle down to a life of leisure 'on a considerable estate', threw in for good measure one or two earls and countesses—an amazing feat indeed, if one remembers that during this period the total number of earls, viscounts and barons at any one time in the whole kingdom seldom went beyond one hundred and fifty.[13]

So strong was the pull of the 'genteel' life that Smollett, in spite of his relish for 'low' life, feels compelled to make even his 'picaro' heroes belong to the gentleman class. Henry Mackenzie feels he deserves a pat on the back for making Edwards, an old, destitute farmer, the hero of one of the important episodes in *The Man Of Feeling* (the principal hero is Mr. Harley, a gentleman of an ancient family):

> Heroes amidst the blaze of war, or the glare of courts, have been in every one's hands ... I have found [one] in a simple farm-house; yet, I flatter myself, he is not the less a hero. The world thinks otherwise .... (to Miss Betty Rose, 12 Feb 1770)

Mackenzie was not being unfair to 'the world'; the delightful bailiff scene in Goldsmith's *The Good-Natur'd Man*, was hissed off the stage by 'the world', since its refined taste was outraged by the 'low' characters. In *Tom Jones* Fielding satirizes this aversion of the public to 'low' characters, by describing how even the 'gentlemen's gentlemen' sitting in 'the footman's gallery' damned *The Provoked Husband* for introducing 'a parcel of servants', including a coachman, on the stage (XII, v). As far as the reading public and the theatre-goers were concerned, Burke raised the alarm a little too early when in 1770, two years after Goldsmith's bailiffs were hooted off the stage, he lamented : '. . . rank, and office, and title, and all the solemn plausibilities of the world, have lost their reverence and effect.'[14]

'Rank, and office, and title'—as yet, everywhere, they made all the difference in the world. Their effect was still powerful and practical. To rank and title, even to felons of rank and title, the law of the land itself still guaranteed privileges.[15] The flagrantly unjust game laws are not the only example. During the period that Burke wrote, astounding instances are recorded of privileges claimed and granted. In 1760, Lawrence Shirley, fourth Earl of Ferrers, notorious for his life of drunken brutality, was accused of murdering his steward in an extraordinarily barbarous incident. Sentenced to death, he pleaded that, in consideration of his rank, he should be beheaded and not hanged; the plea was not granted; but his second petition that he should be hanged with a silken rope is said to have been complied with. Nor could he be made to ride to Tyburn in the felon's cart. Dressed in his wedding clothes, he travelled to the gallows in a landau drawn by six horses. In 1776, Elizabeth Chudleigh, Duchess of Kingston, was put on trial for bigamy before her peers in Westminster Hall. The imposing proceedings, every one knew, were nothing but a spectacular farce and that even if she was found guilty, no penalty could be imposed upon the Duchess; she would 'claim her peerage' and be discharged. Then she would make a curtsey to their lordships and they would return the compliment with a bow.[16]

If the law itself was helpless against rank and title, they acted like a charm upon the ordinary man. Nor was it necessary to be a peer of the realm; to be a gentleman, even though a penniless one, was enough to exact homage and service. The common man knew the rights of his betters, and willingly conceded them. He permitted the gentlemen to break down his hedges, to ride over his corn, to evict him and his family, to shoot his inoffensive dogs and to send him to gaol for killing a rabbit or cutting a tree. It was theirs to make him happy or miserable. Most of them did not make him miserable. He was glad to get the left-overs from their tables and drink their small beer. He touched his cap to them as they rode by on their horses and in their carriages, and gossiped, grumbled or laughed about them after they had passed. His privilege of fleecing them he exercised whenever he could. But he knew his distance and he kept it. And he kept his awe and veneration for the position and title of gentleman.

Not all who belonged to his class acted as unselfishly and loyally as Strap did with Roderick Random, but most acted just as respectfully. Though Roderick has but a few guineas in the world, and Strap has more, earned by doing hard work, knowing Roderick to be a gentleman, Strap will not allow him to carry his luggage, and offers to do it for him all the way from Newcastle to London (I, viii). Roderick gambles away all his money, and Strap offers him his purse. Roderick tries to return it:

> He absolutely refused my proposal, and told me, it was more reasonable and decent that he should depend upon me, who was a gentleman, than that I should be controlled by him. (I, xvi)

The droll Timothy Crabshaw will not say he is sane, if his master, Sir Launcelot Greaves, is mad:

> ...when your honour is pleased to be mad, I should be very sorry to be found right in my senses. Timothy Crabshaw will never eat the bread of unthankfulness—it shall never be said of him, that he was wiser than his measter. (ch. VII)

Sophia Western's pert waiting-maid, Mrs. Honour, knows how it is; the difference between her and the gentleman—it does not exist, and yet it is very much there. She must be given the last word on the subject:

> 'Yes Ma'am...that he is, the most handsomest man I ever

saw in my life...and, as your ladyship says, I don't know why I should be ashamed of loving him, though he is my betters. To be sure gentle-folks are but flesh and blood no more than us servants. Marry, come up!...thof his skin be so white, and to be sure, it is the most whitest that ever was seen, I am a Christian as well as he...and as for abusing Squire Jones, I can call the servants of the house to witness, that whenever any talk hath been of bastards, I have always taken his part : "for which of you", says I to the footmen, "would not be a bastard, if he could, to be made a gentleman of ?"" (IV, xiv)

3 Fashioning the Gentleman

Every man of any education would rather be called a rascal, than be accused of deficiency in *the graces*. —Johnson.[1]

I would have every one...set his helping Hand to promote every where that Way of training up Youth, with Regard to their several Conditions, which is the easiest, shortest and likeliest to produce virtuous, useful, and able Men in their distinct Callings, tho' that most to be taken Care of is the Gentleman's Calling. For if those of that Rank are by their Education once set right, they will quickly bring all the rest into Order. (Locke, *Thoughts*, Epistle Dedicatory)

This call summoning 'every one' to give serious attention to the problems of education and to concentrate in particular on the education of the gentleman, he being indisputably the pivot on which all things turn, was given in 1693 by the philosopher John Locke in *Some Thoughts Concerning Education*. It found eager and repeated response from a variety of writers throughout the century that followed, not the least eager to respond being the novelists. The century was prolific in books on education and 'courtesy' designed to fashion and 'compleat' the gentleman by giving him the right proportion of the right '*Virtue, Wisdom, Breeding, and Learning*', the four heads under which Locke saw the problems of education (*Thoughts*, sec. 134). The periodical essay, perhaps the most characteristic literary form devised by this century, found its most popular subject in disquisitions on education, manners and deportment.

The belief in the perfectibility of man and society by means of the right education was one of the fundamental creeds of the century. Once again it was Locke who struck the keynote.

Though at one place in *The Conduct of the Understanding* Locke concedes that there is 'great inequality of Parts' among men (Sec. 2), in both *Some Thoughts* and *An Essay Concerning the Human Understanding* he tends to attach more importance to nurture than to nature, asserting :

> The Difference to be found in the Manners and Abilities of Men is owing more to their *Education* than to anything else...nine Parts of ten are what they are, good or evil, useful or not, by their Education. 'Tis that which makes the great Difference in Mankind. (*Thoughts*, sec. 32 and sec. 1)

This view finds vivid expression in two well-known images in the two treatises; the reference to the child who ought to be 'considered only as white Paper or Wax, to be moulded and fashioned as one pleases' (*Thoughts*, sec. 217) and the comparison of the mental condition at Birth to 'white Paper, void of all Characters' (*Human Understanding*, II, i, 2).

John Locke is one of the focal points of the attack Rousseau made on the education that the civilization of the Enlightenment gave to the gentleman, but the stress Rousseau lays on the overwhelming importance of education in moulding the personality is just as emphatic as Locke's, though it is expressed from a very different point of view :

> God makes all things good; man meddles with them and they become evil. He forces one soil to yield the products of another, one tree to bear another's fruit...All that we lack at birth, all that we need when we come to man's estate, is the gift of education. (*Emile*, I)

The century's faith in the importance of the part played by education in life is directly reflected in three of its novelists, Richardson, Mackenzie and Brooke. Others, like Fielding and Sterne, glance ironically at the prolix preoccupation of their fellow novelists with such problems, but subtly contrive to convey their own views. Fielding's ironically grandiose heading to book three of *Tom Jones* makes fun, in all probability, of the long discussions on education in his favourite butt. *Pamela* :

FASHIONING THE GENTLEMAN

IN THIS BOOK THE READER MAY PICK UP SOME HINTS CONCERNING THE EDUCATION OF CHILDREN

After making this offer in the heading, Fielding leaves the reader to form his own judgment about educational problems from the few deft strokes which he employs to satirize 'that singular plan of education' (III, v) which Squire Allworthy hits upon for bringing up young Blifil and Tom. Similarly, at the end of the famous incident of Toby and the fly, from which, Tristram tells us, he learnt much more than all his 'study of the *Literae humaniores*' and all 'the other helps of an expensive education... both at home and abroad', we read the comment: 'This is to serve for parents and governors instead of a whole volume upon the subject' (II, xii).

The least inclined of the novelists to give credit to the role of education in moulding character is Fielding. His views on the current controversies about the nature of man and his 'natural' goodness are quite unlike those of Richardson who shows tremendous faith in the power of education to determine a man's 'future life of Morals' (*Pamela*, II,xci), and who places the blame for the self-willed temper and corrupt morals of the upper classes squarely on their education. Henry Brooke and Henry Mackenzie are led to write novels directly because of their faith in the power of education to produce a change of heart in the upper classes of society.

As is to be expected the stand taken by the novelists on educational issues is conditioned by the current trends in educational as well as moral and social philosophy. It is therefore necessary to give some account of these trends here.

Richardson's ideas are mainly conditioned by Locke's *Some Thoughts Concerning Education*. More than fifty pages of the second volume of *Pamela* are devoted to a systematic discussion of Locke's treatise (II,lxiii-ci); in *Grandison* Locke's pronouncements are once again used as a basis for a drawing-room conversation on education (I, xii-xiii). As will be seen later, Fielding owes a great deal to the Latitudinarian divines and to Shaftesbury. Brooke and Mackenzie, who turn away almost with revulsion from the contemporary modes of fashionable education, find a mentor in Rousseau; but they also are considerably influenced by the sentimental philosophy of the school of Shaftesbury. Smollett, however, dismisses Shaftesbury with contempt, calling him a 'frothy writer' (*PP*, I, xliii), and ridicules his theories in an uproarious scene in *Peregrine Pickle* (I, lvii).

Ironically, the person responsible for the education and upbringing of Anthony Ashley Cooper, third Earl of Shaftesbury, was John Locke. *Some Thoughts Concerning Education* was largely the result of Locke's reflections during the period he resided as tutor in the house of Shaftesbury's grandfather, Dryden's 'Achitophel'. Shaftesbury's collected works were published in 1711 as *Characteristicks of Men, Manners, Opinions, Times*. Francis Hutcheson, the Scottish philosopher who became his disciple, did much to popularize his works, especially in Scotland where Mackenzie came under his influence.

The sentimental school of Shaftesbury declared its belief in the natural goodness of man. In this it stood in radical opposition to both the cynic philosophers of the school of Hobbes, as well as to Christian theologians who stressed the corruption of unregenerate human nature, and kept man virtuous by hopes of future rewards and threats of future punishments. In some ways it anticipated Rousseau's idealization of 'natural' man.

According to Shaftesbury and his followers man is endowed with 'moral sense', a faculty which enables him to distinguish between right and wrong, and instinctively to prefer the right. Unless depraved by the wrong kind of education, man will pursue virtue, drawn towards it by a natural attraction. Not love of praise, nor fear of man and God, nor self-interest, compels man to lead the virtuous life, but the natural attraction of virtue itself. Man finds virtue beautiful; in fact, beauty and goodness are one and the same. Consequently man's highest happiness lies in exercising his instincts of pity, love, gratitude and benevolence. On the other hand 'by having self-passions too intense or strong, a creature becomes miserable' (*The Moralists*, II, ii). What is necessary, therefore, is to educate the instincts, to train the feelings, to cultivate good taste, so that man may pursue what his 'moral sense', when allowed to develop 'naturally', recognizes as right.

For Shaftesbury, there can be no conflict between the

interests of an individual, i.e. self-love, and the interests of society:

> [it is] the private interest and good of every one, to work towards the general good, which if a creature ceases to promote, he is actually so far wanting to himself and ceases to promote his own happiness and welfare.... And, thus Virtue is the Good and Vice the Ill of every one.
> (*Enquiry Concerning Virtue*, II, ii)

Pope gave pithy expression to the doctrine in the *Essay on Man*:

> ... God and Nature link'd the gen'ral frame,
> And bade Self-love and Social be the same. (iii, 317-8)

The 'inward rapture' to be obtained from exercising this instinct of social love by performing benevolent deeds was soon to become one of the commonplaces of literature.

For Shaftesbury and his disciple Hutcheson virtue is synonymous with good taste; vice is an aesthetic defect. The properly educated man, the 'virtuoso', as Shaftesbury called him, is a man with a highly cultivated taste, as well as a virtuous man : '... 'tis not merely what we call principle, but a Taste, which governs men' (*Reflections*, III, ii). Since 'virtue' is the perfect development of aesthetic sensibility, it is the hall-mark of the gentleman : 'The *TASTE* of Beauty and the *Relish* of what is decent, just and amiable, perfects the *Character* of the GENTLEMAN and the PHILOSOPHER' (*Reflections*, III, i).

Shaftesbury does not refuse to recognise the existence in man of the self-regarding instincts which he classes as the 'self-affections', nor even of those instincts which are not 'tending either to any good of the public or private', which he calls the 'unnatural affections' (*Enquiry Concerning Virtue*, II, ii); but he decides that the man who allows himself to be dominated by the 'unnatural affections' is lacking in good taste, just like the man who prefers an ugly painting to a beautiful one.

As has been shown by Shaftesbury scholars, though the

phrase 'Beauty is Truth, Truth Beauty' has now come to be associated with Keats, numerous variations of the phrase can be found in the eighteenth century poets of the Shaftesburian school. For the Shaftesburian deist the contemplation of nature 'supplied the place of formal religious devotion'. 'Sensibility' led Mackenzie to describe the effects of nature in a way which anticipates Wordsworth's poetry.

Though Shaftesbury's own conception of virtue was 'chaste and austere', his theories were open to a variety of misinterpretations. Belief in the essential goodness of man can too easily lead to a contempt for the restraint of reason over the feelings. By an easy transition it can develop into the cult of primitivism, though nothing could be more remote from Shaftesbury's idea of the cultured virtuoso than the idealization of the noble savage.[2] The Shaftesbury school of philosophy was to a large extent responsible for the mawkish cult of sensibility and the masochistic desire to see and experience misery, that we find in the sentimental comedies and novels of the century.

But Shaftesbury was also an important influence for good. The doctrine which attempted to prove that there is no conflict between self-love and love for humanity, which asserted that happiness can be found only in the exercise of benevolence, was naturally a powerful incitement to humanitarian action. When compassion comes to be recognized as the perfection of the 'natural temper' and also as the most characteristic mark of the well-bred gentleman, it is bound to have a humanizing effect on society. Shaftesbury's doctrines challenged not only the cynicism and egotism of Hobbes and Mandeville, but also the complacency and callousness of the Church.

Though some modern scholars ascribe Fielding's insistence on 'good nature' as the most glorious among the virtues to the influence of the Latitudinarian divines only, the influence that contemporaries noted was that of Shaftesbury. Describing the morality preached in *Tom Jones* as one that exalted 'good affections' over moral obligations and Christian principles, Sir John Hawkins frowned upon it as 'that of Lord Shaftesbury vulgarized'.[3] In any case, the theories of the Latitudinarians did not differ fundamentally from those of Shaftesbury, so that the popularity of Shaftesbury and his school in England and

Scotland helped to reinforce the influence that the teachings of the Latitudinarians had wielded from about 1660 to 1725.

Consciously striving against the stoic stress on insensibility, the Latitudinarian preachers disseminated a creed of sensibility, advocating that the tender emotions, far from being suppressed, ought to be cultivated, they being the distinguishing marks of a genuinely good man. Central to Latitudinarian teaching was an emphasis on the emotional satisfaction and keen pleasure that man, being naturally benevolent, obtains by commiserating with the wretched and helping them. This satisfaction is to be derived even from the sorrow that man feels in looking upon scenes of misery, for such sorrow is 'a kind of agreeable Discharge... a sort of pleasing Anguish, that sweetly melts the Mind, and terminates in a self-approving Joy'.[4]

The Latitudinarian divines and Shaftesbury and his disciples laid so much emphasis on the reality of the altruistic instincts in man, and on the pleasure to be obtained from compassionate feelings and acts of benevolence, because of their distaste for Puritan and Calvinistic doctrines, and even more because of the urgent need they felt for combating the pernicious influence of the school of thought led by Thomas Hobbes, which asserted that the 'naturall Passions' of men are selfish and cruel and his actions are prompted by self-interest alone. In 1651 Hobbes had declared:

> For the Lawes of Nature (as *Justice, Equity, Modesty, Mercy* and (in summe) *doing to others, as wee would be done to,*) of themselves, without the terrour of some Power, to cause them to be observed, are contrary to our naturall Passions, that carry us to Partiality, Pride, Revenge, and the like. (*Leviathan*, ch. XXII)

The Hobbes school found a brilliant exponent in Bernard Mandeville who, in *The Fable of the Bees or Private Vices, Public Benefits*, sought to demolish the arguments of the Shaftesbury school by means of a trenchant raillery and an ingeniously cynical dissection of the motives of men. Impatient with philosophers who insisted that the fundamental human instincts were pity, love, benevolence and solicitude for others, Mandeville set out to demonstrate that all human actions are motivated by pride, fear, envy, shame or love of self. Since these passions are generally regarded as vicious, all human actions must be regarded as vicious. For actions, says Mandeville, ought to be pronounced upon according to their motives, not according to their effects. The difficulty is that actions motivated by what may be termed vices in an individual, contribute to the public good. No prosperous society can exist without such vicious activity. Therefore we are faced with a paradox; 'private vices' are 'public benefits'. In the short verse satire, *The Grumbling Hive, or Knaves Turn'd Honest*, which forms the preliminary part of his book, Mandeville shows the foolishness and futility of attempts 'To make a Great an Honest Hive' (1. 36).

The verse satire tells the story of a bee-hive. The proud, avaricious, corrupt and hypocritical bees in it were always busy gathering honey. The hive was strong and prosperous. One day the bees began to condemn the vices flourishing in the hive and to pray for honesty and virtue. Jove granted their prayer. The result was that nobody envied his neighbour any more, or wished to be better than him. Naturally, therefore, wants began to decrease. Trade came to a standstill. Poverty, decay and utter ruin turned out to be the punishment which fell upon the hive for giving up its vices.

This short verse fable is followed by a series of 'Remarks' numbered A to Y, and a number of essays, all meant to be regarded as annotations. It is in these remarks and essays which form the major portion of the book that Mandeville expounds his theory of human nature.

All human actions and even all human impulses, including the seemingly most altruistic, have their origin in self-love. Men give money to beggars 'from the same motives as they pay their corn-cutter, to walk easy'. By an examination of the nature of society, Mandeville attempts to prove that civilization and civilized institutions would not exist if politicians did not cleverly exploit man's instincts of pride, vanity, shame, avarice and luxury. He proceeds to demonstrate that it is not the love of virtue, but a sense of shame or pride, that keeps man from vice. A good woman will murder an illegitimate child, but a

FASHIONING THE GENTLEMAN

whore seldom does, not because she is less cruel, but because she has lost her sense of shame to a greater degree.

By cleverly marshalled arguments, Mandeville shows that the man whom society recognizes as a great leader, or a perfect gentleman, is one who has understood all the failings and frailties of men and has acquired mastery over the art of using these as tools. Civilized and pleasing manners are nothing but the art of soothing other people's vanity while concealing one's own. 'In all Civil Societies Men are taught insensibly to be Hypocrites from their Cradle.'

Mandeville's cynical appraisal of man and society provoked bitter opposition not only from Shaftesbury's disciple Hutcheson, but also from other prominent leaders of public opinion like the leading philosophers, Bishop Butler and Bishop Berkeley, and the influential religious leaders, William Laud and John Wesley. But Johnson, though he would not have concurred with Mandeville's extreme statements, appreciated the value of the book : 'I read Mandeville forty, or I believe, fifty years ago . . . he opened my views into real life very much' (*Life*, III, 292).

If even Johnson found him instructive, the rationalist and sophisticated sections of Enlightenment society were completely convinced by the force of the Mandevillean school of thought. Self-interest enlightened by reason, and prudently directed into profitable and reputable channels, came to be recognized as the best and highest principle man could follow. It was this doctrine of enlightened self-interest that Chesterfield preached to his son in those letters which many parents of the time put into the hands of their children as the book of wisdom.

Between the years 1737 and 1768, the acknowledged leader of fashion and wit, Philip Dormer Stanhope, fourth Earl of Chesterfield, wrote well over four hundred letters to his natural son, Philip Stanhope, in order to educate him in the art of getting on in the world. Chesterfield's declared intention was to make his son '*un homme universel*' (*Letters*, 27 May 1752); to 'unite all the knowledge of a Scholar with the manners of a Courtier' in him (*Letters*, 10 May 1748), in order to make him the most brilliant statesman and the most admired gentleman of his times.

Though Chesterfield's advocacy of gallantry, his insistence

on 'the graces' at the expense of the more orthodox virtues, and his recommendation that expediency should be the test of every action, aroused much outraged criticism when the *Letters* were first published in 1774 after his death, there is no doubt that they reflect the prevailing temper of an important section of the English and European society of his time. Voltaire declared: 'I am not certain but that it is the best book on education which has ever been written.'[5] Even Samuel Johnson, though he harboured no friendly feelings for Chesterfield, pronounced: 'Take out the immorality, and it should be put into the hands of every young gentleman' (*Life*, III, 53). On another occasion however the 'immorality' proved too much for him and he vehemently condemned the *Letters*: 'They teach the morals of a whore, and the manners of a dancing master' (*Life*, I, 266).

It is significant that the 'Advertisement to the Original Edition' of the *Letters* recommends the book as 'a complete system of education', and stresses its value as an educational guide 'for gentlemen, orators, and diplomats'. By the end of the century several editions and selections had been published and, in spite of the wrathful protests and amused satire directed at it by writers of varying temperaments, it had become a popular handbook of etiquette for the gentleman.

If any one book is to be selected to discuss ideas diametrically opposed to those of the Chesterfieldean system of education, the choice must fall on Rousseau's *Emile*. Published in French in 1762, it was translated into English in the same year; two other translations appeared in the following year. 'Few books have had a greater immediate effect on English educational thought'.[6] Rousseau's protests against the values of the civilization of the Enlightenment, and his ideas about 'natural man', reinforced some of the doctrines of the 'benevolent' philosophers, Shaftesbury and Hutcheson. These doctrines, in a somewhat garbled form, were by this time very popular in England among sentimental readers and writers. In this growing circle the 'sensibility' of Rousseau's *Emile*, as of his other works, aroused a spontaneous response. In other circles, however, 'the publication of *Emile* aroused an intense storm of antagonism'.[7]

These two pedagogical books, Rousseau's *Emile* and

Chesterfield's *Letters*, give the most single-minded exposition of the two currently most attractive ideals of life, and of the education that is consequently to be regarded as the best preparation for a happy and fulfilled life. In their clash of values these two books present the eternal conflict between realism and idealism, sophistication and simplicity, civilization and nature, cleverness and goodness, intellect and emotion.

The two writers reveal a fundamental difference of opinion on almost every point. One denounces worldly success, the other exalts it. One recommends faith in mankind, the other insists on doubt and cynicism. For one the test of a refined spirit is the ability to display sensibility and to shed tears, for the other it is the ability to talk wittily and to remain imperturbable. One thinks the purpose of education is to make the pupil happy and affectionate; for the other, it is to make his pupil '*un galant homme, un homme de cours*, a man of business and pleasure, *est mé des hommes, recherché des femmes, aimé de tout le monde*' (*Letters*, 27 May 1753).

Rousseau preached the natural, simple life, and warned the man in pursuit of sophistication, success and glory that he was but making ready to 'devour his gold on a dung-hill'; that he would 'never know what it is to live' (bk. iv). Chesterfield dismissed such talk as nonsense:

> ... plainness and solidity unadorned ... will do in nothing: mankind has been long out of a state of nature, and the golden age of native simplicity will never return. (*Letters*, 20 Nov 1753)

Chesterfield repeatedly proclaimed his love for 'capital cities', and believed that the final test of a gentleman's education was his ability to make a figure in Parisian society. After a brief visit to Paris to make Emile develop a distaste for its culture, Rousseau snatched him away from it, bidding it the famous farewell:

> Then farewell Paris, far-famed Paris, with all your noise and smoke and dirt, where the women have ceased to believe in honour and the men in virtue. We are in search

of love, happiness, innocence; the further we go from Paris the better. (bk. iv)

Rousseau adopted the most extreme and artificial methods in order to preserve his pupil's innocence, even disapproving of parents cautioning their children against the wiles of the world. On the other hand Chesterfield, in letter after letter, put before his pupil a cynical analysis of the actions and motives of men. From his earliest years he sought to make his son wise in the ways of the world, and constantly endeavoured to teach him how to exploit men and play upon their passions. He repeated this process with his godson, to whom he wrote a series of letters upon 'the *duty*, the *utility* and the *means* of pleasing' (to godson, 31 Oct 1765). We find the boy being initiated into the art of flattering women when only ten : 'Make the dose strong, it will be greedily swallowed' (to godson, 4 Dec 1765).

The snare from which Rousseau most sought to protect his pupil was the wiles of wanton women. Chesterfield tried to push his son into their arms before he was fifteen, for according to him, philandering with women was an indispensable means of acquiring polish and refinement.

Rousseau taught that the 'laws of politeness' were 'to be found in a kindly heart' (bk. iv); according to Chesterfield :

> Manner is all, in everything ... All your Greek will never advance you from Secretary to Envoy, or from Envoy to Ambassador; but your address, your air, if good, very probably may. Marcel [the Parisian dancing-master] can be of much more use to you than Aristotle. (*Letters*, 18 March 1751)

Rousseau announced that his aim was to make his pupil acquire a mastery over his passions, and yet remain frank and ingenuous; Chesterfield told Philip that a young man 'should have an apparent frankness and openness, but with inward caution and closeness' (*Letters*, 24 May 1750). Mandeville gives an honest résumé of this prevalent code of manners : 'Virtue bids us subdue, but Good Breeding only requires we should hide our Appetites' (Remark C). Confounded by this dissimulation Saint-Preux, the hero of *La Nouvelle Heloise,* exclaims: 'Jusques ici j'ai vu beaucoup de masques, quand verrai-je des visages d'hommes?' (II, xiv)

Of course the fashioning of the gentleman had branched off into two diametrically opposite directions long before the publication of the *Letters* and *Emile.* In many ways Chesterfield belonged to the courtly Renaissance tradition which equated the ideal gentleman with the perfect courtier. This tradition, as first developed by Italian courtesy writers like Castiglione, was too exclusive and rarefied for an expanding society with a rapidly prospering commercial and professional class. To those who cannot practise such a code, it seems mere affectation and foppery; as Chesterfield knew well, 'English bucks' would describe his manners as 'outlandish, finical airs' (*Letters,* 27 May 1752). Moreover, the courtly ideal had come to be associated with the code of prudent, suave conduct, of clever dissimulation, which was first framed by Machiavelli, later by Bacon and la Rochefoucauld, and lastly and perhaps most brilliantly, by Chesterfield. Machiavelli had advised the Prince:

> It is necessary for a prince wishing to hold his own to know how to do wrong... those princes who have done great things have held good faith of little account, and have known how to circumvent the intellect of men by craft... it is necessary... to understand how to avail himself of the beast in the man... but it is necessary to know well how to disguise this characteristic...[8]

Even during Renaissance times, in spite of the popularity of Hoby's translation of Castiglione's *Il Cortegiano,* the courtier ideal never took root in England. Sir Thomas Elyot and Roger Ascham, who wrote the most characteristic advice books of the time for the governing class, have a far more sober and realistic outlook than Castiglione. During Puritan times the courtly ideal received a crippling blow from courtesy writers like Richard Brathwait, for whom courtesy and gentility betokened morality at its strictest. But perhaps the courtiers of Charles II gave it an even more severe blow by confounding courtly grace, charm and urbanity with dissipation, sexual excesses and complete irresponsibility. A shocking coarseness of behaviour now often came to be associated with the 'fine gentleman', as he had come to be called.

Writing in the opening decades of the eighteenth century, the *Spectator* essayists were scornfully indignant about the foppery and profligacy of the Restoration gentleman. The tone of society no longer encouraged the notion, so prevalent in the previous decades, that a gentleman may do anything so long as 'it be done with an air' (no. 6). With persistence and feeling the Queen Anne essayists pointed out the difference between 'this fine thing called fine breeding' and 'that plain thing called good breeding' (no. 66).

During the eighteenth century these two aspects of behaviour came to be distinguished under the heads 'ceremony' and 'civility'. It was the 'sagacious Locke', who first called attention to the difference in the final decades of the preceding century, and throughout the next hundred years writers continued to stress the difference. The word 'civility' came to be associated with the kind of behaviour which may be expected of a cultured individual who has common sense, and treats his fellowmen with consideration. On the other hand, 'ceremony' stood for the art of consciously studied forms and formalities.

The manners of even the professional class of the time would appear extremely formal and studied to us; as for the upper class, it had developed the practice of manners and the modes of dressing into an elaborate art. Ceremonious manners reached the zenith of sophistication at the court of Louis XIV. Fixed formalities and subtle distinctions of courtesy were prescribed for every occasion and every company; carefully graded angles were established for bending of knees and inclination of bows to people of different ranks.

Nor was elaborate etiquette confined to a few men like Chesterfield who lived with his memories of Le Roi Soleil. A century later in England in the court of even 'Farmer George', utterly dowdy and domestic though it was in comparison with Versailles, etiquette was still rigorously formal, and imposed an intolerable strain on people who were frequently required to meet royal personages. The diaries of Fanny Burney furnish revealing and delightfully readable accounts of the tyranny of court etiquette which within a few years quite destroyed her constitution, when she served Queen Charlotte as

Mistress of the Robes. To sit down in the royal presence was out of the question; to eat was unthinkable. Ladies of rank stood bolt upright even for six or seven hours at a stretch, and would not put a morsel in their mouths though they felt faint with hunger. To turn one's back to royalty was utterly *hors d'usage*. Fanny Burney's *Diary and Letters* show how when bowing out of their majesties' presence, those accomplished in court ceremony walked backwards down long halls and stately winding staircases as gracefully as when walking forwards; but novices unused to 'the true court retrograde motion' tottered and stumbled and covered themselves with embarrassment.

Nevertheless, now for a century in England there had been a new mood which showed a distaste for the courtly, sophisticated attitude to culture and good breeding. Writers of the period repeatedly try to define 'true' politeness or 'civility', and oppose it—some contemptuously, some with despair—to 'ceremony' and the superficies of good form : a significant reflection of the trend which leads away from the admiration for the successful man of the world, the polished courtier, and results in the idealization of the simple, honest man, living a virtuous and benevolent life on his estate in the countryside. Of course we must take into account the fact that most of the comments on gentlemanly behaviour and most of the technical treatises on conduct during this century are written by the professional writer, lower gentry or middle class by origin; though, even with regard to this point, it must be remembered that Fielding traced his descent from an earl, and that Addison, Swift and Pope often proudly asserted that they moved in the very highest aristocratic circles.

Unlike writers like Castiglione, the theorists on conduct are now not writing for those born and bred in court circles. Gentlemanship is no longer the preserve of the courtly few; it must now come down, if not quite to the market-place, at least to the first-generation students of the art—sons of merchants, and of nabobs returning from India and the plantations of the Indies, who are establishing a new gentility of wealth. Moreover, the old country gentleman of the Squire Western type, the illiterate, uncouth figure ridiculed in Restoration comedy, is now fast becoming a thing of the past. With improved means of communication, there is more contact with London; books and fashions, and with them new ideas of sophistication, travel easily even to the remote country mansion; the occasional 'season' in London or Bath, or the other fashionable watering-places nearer the country-seat, leaves behind a permanent hankering after elegance and sophistication. As the century advances most of the young country squires have had a taste of the sophistication and artistic beauty of the European capitals, and have picked up at least a smattering of culture. Though Swift, in 'Of the Education of Ladies', put the number of educated men among the gentry at only one in thirty, and Defoe at scarcely more, and though Fielding's and Richardson's novels give unforgettably satirical pictures of illiteracy among the gentry, the research of modern scholars[9] has shown that by the time Fielding and Goldsmith immortalized them, the Western-Tony Lumpkin type of squire was a thing of the past.

In the Renaissance tradition of courtly behaviour good breeding was, as it indeed is, when the subject is not clouded by a controversial atmosphere, something amoral. Unfortunately the theorists of the Chesterfield-Bacon-Machiavelli school came to regard good breeding as a useful cloak for the absence of good-nature, in the eighteenth century sense of benevolence and humanity. Rousseau was not indulging in one of his characteristic exaggerations when he wrote: 'The worst effect of artificial politeness is that it teaches us how to dispense with the virtues it imitates' (*Emile*, iv).

On this matter of natural *versus* artificial good breeding it is Swift who speaks out most vehemently. In two fairly long treatises and five essays[10] on the subject of good breeding and the 'modern education' which genteel parents thought best suited for the young gentleman, he writes contemptuously of 'the impertinences of ceremonial behaviour'. In 'Hints on good Manners' he states: 'good sense is the principal foundation of good manners . . . a tolerable degree of reason will instruct us in every part of good manners, without other assistance.'

In the *Rambler* essays Johnson often makes the same points as Swift. In no. 147 he describes the visit of a sophisticated London gentleman to his country-bred nephew. The uncle is so skilled in 'all the stratagems of endearment' that 'he had the power of obliging those whom he did not benefit'. The nephew repines 'at the inelegance of my own manners . . . and at the inefficacy of rustic benevolence, which gained no friends but by real service'.

However though writers like Steele, Swift and Johnson spoke sarcastically of 'ceremony' and the theorists had begun to attack the exaggerated emphasis on artificial good breeding, an importance which seems quite disproportionate to our plebian times continued to be attached to ceremonious behaviour and to the accompanying arts of dancing and fencing, which were supposed to give a graceful bearing and self-assurance. Even Goldsmith, who had no pretensions to belonging to the upper class and who wrote the two most celebrated idylls of village life in English literature, *The Vicar of Wakefield* and *The Deserted Village*, asserts: 'no Country was ever yet polite, that was not first ceremonious' (*The Life of Beau Nash, Works*, III, 307). Edmund Burke, the high-principled idealist, was so dazzled by the polished veneer which disguised the corruption of the French aristocracy, that when he wished to plead their cause with all his fervour and sincerity, he selected for emphasis the beauty and grace of their queen, and the polished manners of her court, where 'vice lost half its evil by losing all its grossness' (*Reflections*, p.86).

It was in this atmosphere in which the conflicting claims of simplicity and sophistication, idealism and realism, emotion and intellect were being heatedly debated, that the questions related to education and good breeding, which were exercising the minds of parents and educationists, were reflected upon by one or the other of the novelists. The chief points of controversy at this time were the nursing of the child by the mother, physical and moral discipline during childhood, the right attitude towards punishments and rewards, the merits of a school education as against education at home by a tutor, the tutor's qualifications, the desirability of residing at a university for a few years, the necessity and nature of the 'grand tour', the academic subjects and social accomplishments to be taught to a young gentleman and, most tricky of all, and underlying all of these, the just proportion of *bon ton* and polish requisite to avoid the two opposite dangers of turning out a coxcomb or a 'booby squire'.

At least as early as Antonio de Guevara's *Diall of Princes* (1529) and Montaigne's *Essays* (1580-8) it had been customary to begin educational treatises by discussing the problems of mothers nursing their babies, and of children being constricted in swaddling clothes. In swaddling clothes, Rousseau saw the symbol of the life of 'civilized man' who 'is born and dies a slave...imprisoned by our institutions' (*Emile*, bk. i). To mothers putting their babies out to nurse, Rousseau traced the original sin in the life of man, born innocent: 'Every evil follows in the train of this first sin; the whole moral order is disturbed' (bk. i). Incredible as it seems to us, many wealthy parents sent away their infant children to live in the squalid homes of women who nursed them alongside their own babies. Henry Brooke shows his young hero, the son of the Earl of Moreland, being brought up in a peasant's cottage. Smollett deplores the fact that 'people of the highest distinction put their children out to nurse into farmhouses and cabins' (*PP*, II, xcviii).

Richardson's domestic and sentimental instincts are outraged by the fashionable disowning of the mother's responsibility of nursing her babies. The nursing of her baby is the only issue in her married life on which Pamela feels she has a right to oppose Mr. B.'s wishes. The conflict starts months before the birth of her first baby; ultimately Pamela is constrained to engage 'a good sort of woman, that is to be my poor *baby's mother*' (II, xiv-xlvii). In *Grandison*, the flighty but amiable Charlotte Grandison's reformation after marriage is signalized in a quaintly sentimental scene in which she is discovered nursing her baby by her husband. A quaint illustration in the 1783 edition of the novel depicts the incident.

Other current controversies about the upbringing of the child during infancy are also reflected in Richardson. Pamela finds herself in entire agreement with the warning given by Locke against constricting clothes for the baby, and with his advice on fresh air and plain diet. She is also in general agreement with Locke about inuring children to hardship by, among other methods, keeping the head and feet cold; but her mother's heart rebels a little against Locke's recommendation that the infant's shoes should be 'so thin' as to 'leak and *let in Water*' (*Thoughts*, sec. 7). She feels she ought to report this to Mr. B., giving reasons why Billy, who is one and a half, has not yet been 'wet-shod' (II, xc).

In a delightfully farcical scene in *Peregrine Pickle*, we see these problems from a comic angle. Peregrine's termagant mother, in her desire to defy her sister-in-law on every point, orders 'that the bandages with which the infant had been so neatly rolled up like an Egyptian mummy, should be loosened and laid aside'; and herself plunges the infant 'headlong every morning into a tub full of cold water'. The boy, we are told, 'seemed to acquire fresh vigour from every plunge, as if he had been resolved to discredit the wisdom and foresight of his aunt' (I, vi). But Locke's advice on inuring children to hardship was dictated not so much by his training as a physician as by his ideas as a moralist who believed that the body must be submitted to a discipline such as may enable it at all times to 'obey and execute the Orders of the *Mind*' (sec. 31). Since a gentleman's character depends on his ability to 'submit his Appetite to Reason' (sec. 200), a child must be taught spartan self-denial.

The question that eighteenth century educationists and parents found perhaps most difficult to decide was that of a home *versus* a school education. Arguments on both sides seemed equally strong, and the decision continued to vex parents till the end of the century. Locke clearly states the arguments on both sides, while himself leaning heavily on the side of education at home, claiming for it superiority in teaching virtue and good breeding. Locke's distaste for the learning, the morals and the manners acquired at school, in 'a mix'd Herd of unruly Boys', was well-known to all who had any comments to offer on education; but they were all also only too conscious of the lead in worldly knowledge, circumspection and assurance of manner that school education gave, and which Locke had condemned them for choosing. Periodical writers frequently merely summed up the arguments on both sides, showing a hesitating preference for one or the other. However *The Spectator's* educational expert, Budgell, found Locke unrealistic (no. 313). Swift vehemently favoured school education; Goldsmith also, though he deplored the poor quality of schoolmasters and ushers, emphatically declared himself on the side of school education: 'It is not from masters, but from their equals, youth learn a knowledge of the world' (*The Bee*, 10 Nov 1759). Lord Chesterfield, sent his son to Westminster for three years though he described it as 'undoubtedly the seat of illiberal manners and brutal behaviour' (*Letters*, 16 Dec 1749).

Those who took part in the tirade against public schools condemned the brutal beatings, the hateful fag system, the bullying, the antiquated curriculum, the mechanical methods of cramming Greek and Latin, the huddling together of boys of different abilities as well as different social status, and the fawning, flattery and false friendship which the poorer boys offered and the rich boys received.[11]

In both *Joseph Andrews* and *Tom Jones*, Fielding is ironical about the fear expressed by parents about the corrupting influence of public and grammar schools, and referring to fond mothers who fear the hardships and discipline of school life. He is sceptical about the value of home education; about the brutal and dissolute squire whom Joseph Andrews and Parson Adams encounter on their way, he says:

> He had been educated (if we may use the expression) in the country, and at his own home, under the care of his mother, and a tutor who had orders never to correct him nor to compel him to learn more than he liked, which it seems was very little. (III, vii)

Nor does Fielding give a much more inviting view of the small private school, which many of the gentry chose in preference to the public schools and the big grammar schools. The school that Partridge runs in Allworthy's village, is in 'no danger of becoming formidable to the learned seminaries of Eton or Westminster'. Partridge adds to his office of school-master those of clerk and barber; learning is 'the least of his commendations' (II, iii). And much as he loves Parson Adams, Fielding is far from suggesting that a school run by so clumsy, uncouth, forgetful and naive a master, is the ideal training ground for young gentlemen.

From Smollett's *Roderick Random* we get our only account of Scottish education. Compared to the English village school, the Scottish parish schools, on the whole, gave a better education, and were usually more democratic in composition. However the description of the village school to which Roderick is sent is hardly likely to tempt parents. Managed by one brutal, tyrannical master, with the help of one kindly usher, it is apparently a fairly large school, since Roderick's own 'faction' consists of 'thirty boys most of them of my own age' (about twelve). His grand-father, the judge, has 'been dictator time out of mind' of the school, but Roderick is treated with barbarous injustice by the master, who knows that he is out of favour with the judge and the judge's heir. The heir himself is not sent to school or university, but is educated at home by a tutor, who acts also as the parish clerk. At eighteen, the heir cares for nothing but fox-hunting, and, indeed, is 'qualified for nothing else' (I, ii). This bears out the attacks which we find in Defoe, Swift and other writers of the century, on the practice of keeping the eldest sons at home, and the consequent lack of discipline in their upbringing.

Peregrine Pickle takes us into four different schools—two private village schools, one preparatory school near London and finally Winchester. At four, Perry is sent to a day-school kept by a woman. Here he makes little progress except in mischief, 'because the school-mistress would not run the risk of disobliging a lady of fortune' like his mother. So he is sent to the school of a less obliging pedagogue who flogs him regularly, twice a day. Luckily when he has just turned six, his mother decides to send him to a boarding school not far from London. This is one of those preparatory schools which equipped the children of the wealthy to enter the public schools. Here the principal master is 'an old illiterate German quack', but the usher, who is paid the paltry sum of thirty pounds a year, is 'a man of learning, probity and good sense', who is also fortunately skilful in the art of 'well-timed praise and artful comparison'.

Perry's last school is Winchester, which he enters 'on a very genteel footing', accompanied by a footman and a private governor, as was customary with rich young gentlemen at public schools. But Perry's governor, Mr. Jacob Jolter, because of his 'violent prejudices, ridiculous vanity, awkward solemnity, and ignorance of mankind', soon becomes an object of ridicule to Perry and his friends. He is unable to exercise any control over his pupil, so that during the two years spent at Winchester, Perry's 'behaviour was no other than a series of license and effrontery'.

Where Fielding and Smollett draw vivid pictures of education at home and school, Richardson presents us with an exhaustive discussion on the problem of home *versus* school education. Quoting at length from Locke's treatise on education, Pamela supplies corrections, improvements and new suggestions (II, xcii-xciv). The most difficult problem, she finds, is the tutor. As Locke points out, good tutors are not easy to find; though in Pamela's opinion this is not so much because of the 'ordinary salaries' about which Locke had complained, as because the tutor's post has been so downgraded that these 'useful men' are 'frequently put upon a foot with the upper-most servants'. To avoid the disadvantages of both home and school education, Pamela suggests a middle way out—a small private school run by a master who should be so well rewarded for the care of a *'few* young gentlemen', that he will be satisfied with only a few —'from five to eight at most'. To help him this master can appoint 'assistants in the different branches of science and education' who 'will be persons of approved prudence'. However, for her own Billy, Pamela has no hesitation in giving preference to a home education, considering what an admirable home Mr. B. and she can provide.

This topic of the tutor's qualifications, repeatedly and tediously debated in the contemporary educational treatises, is treated with impish ridicule in *Tristram Shandy*. Sterne is at his eccentric best when he caricatures the worries of educationists about what a tutor should and should not be :

'The governor,' said Mr. Shandy, 'I make choice of shall neither lisp, or squint, or wink, or talk loud, or look fierce, or foolish;—or bite his lips, or grind his teeth, or speak through his nose. . . .He shall neither walk fast,—or slow, or fold his arms,—for that is laziness;—or hang them down, —for that is folly; or hide them in his pocket, for that is nonsense.' (VI, v)

Sterne's own preferences are made quite clear in a conversation between Walter, Yorick and Toby. Walter is all for learning, intelligence, wisdom and prudence. But the other two see things differently :

'And why not humble, and moderate, and gentle-tempered, and good ?' said Yorick—'And why not, cried my uncle Toby, 'free, and generous, and bountiful, and brave?' (VI, v)

Among the disadvantages of a home education that Locke had pointed out was that, lacking fellow-students, the home-educated child lacked all incentive for emulation. Pamela's suggestion for overcoming this difficulty is to take into the family, 'the child of some honest neighbour of but middling circumstances', who would serve the embryo gentleman as an incentive to effort. It is to be expected that Rousseau would write indignantly about employing the instinct of emulation as an incentive to effort. Rousseau prohibits all competition with other children, even in running races. He would far rather a child did not learn anything, than that he should learn it through hatred, jealousy and self-conceit (bk. III).

Under the influence of Rousseau, Brooke, Mackenzie and Thomas Day protested vehemently against educational methods which thus inculcated envy and hatred. They consider both the conventional home and the conventional school quite undesirable as places for educating a child. In *The Fool of Quality* and *Sandford and Merton*, as in *Emile*, the child is removed from all parental influence. Like Rousseau, these writers believe in the value of experience, not of precepts. Like him, they hold that learning should not be imposed upon children, but that they should be made to feel the need for it by subtle contrivances. As carefully as Rousseau, they try to preserve children from 'the falsehood of politeness' and, instead, try to make them realize that 'true good breeding is the sister of philanthropy' (*Man of the World*, I, vi).

In spite of the close resemblances between Rousseau and these English writers, important differences in attitude and approach give the novels of Mackenzie and Brooke a very different tone from Rousseau's *Emile*. Rousseau writes with the bold defiance of a conscious revolutionary, challenging every existing theory and practice; Mackenzie and Brooke, who find Rousseau's view of human nature as well as some of his theories about education quite appealing, baulk at the idea of cutting completely loose from tried methods and the traditional curriculum. They also lay much stronger emphasis than Rousseau on the cultivation of the feelings; in sentiment, pity and tears, they recognize the most effective teachers. Consequently what they prescribe is not the 'natural' education as given by Rousseau through the famous 'negative' methods, but the education of the heart, which must be developed to overflow with feeling.

Indeed Rousseau also puts great stress on 'the enthusiasm of an overflowing heart' (*Emile*, bk. iv) as the only means of teaching man to identify himself with his fellow-men. His *Nouvelle Héloise* is of course an impassioned exposition of the cult of sensibility; his educational treatise also exalts feeling. Nevertheless Rousseau positively forbids any attempt to instil feeling till the pupil reaches a carefully postponed adolescence at eighteen. Nor is the pupil to be permitted to establish any relationship with his fellow-men till that age. Till eighteen Emile is brought up as a completely amoral being: 'Speak to him of duty or obedience; he will not know what you are talking about' (bk. ii). 'There is the same insensibility in his heart as in his manners' (bk. iv).

This advice is ignored by both novelists. In Brooke, in particular, the education of the emotions, through the emotions, gets overwhelming emphasis from the beginning. Soon after he first sees his nephew Harry aged six, Henry Fenton encourages him to shed copious tears over the plight of the beggar boy, Ned, and takes the waif into his house as Harry's companion. Harry is constantly confronted by scenes of woe, and is perpetually to be found sitting, his face 'bathed in tears', listening to stories told by the insulted and injured. Brooke narrates these affecting stories with the most unabashed sentimentality and lack of concern for realism. When he is six, Harry is given a whole room full of clothes to distribute to the needy. He is about nine when he is given fifteen hundred pounds and sent with his tutor to London 'to take lodging near the Fleet-prison'. He is expected to relieve the miseries of the inmates of the prison and release those who, in his judgment, deserve to be rescued, by paying their creditors (ch. XII-XV). Rousseau advocates the teaching of benevolence, even at a later stage, in quite a different fashion :

> Is Emile aware that he is rich?. . .he has no need of riches, he can do good without their aid. The good he does comes from his heart, not his purse. He gives the wretched his time, his care, his affection, himself . . .(bk. V)

Rousseau's ability to work out a consistent theory, idealistic though it might be, is not shared by Henry Brooke. The ideals that Brooke cherishes are scattered away in sentimental fantasies. Rousseau is firm about his ambitions for Emile :

> God grant he may not be unlucky enough to shine in society; the qualities which make a good impression at the first glance are not his. . . His path is narrow and clearly defined. . .he will neither distinguish himself, nor will he lose his way. (bk. IV)

Brooke shows nothing of this sobr.ety. Though in his early years, because of his truthfulness and lack of affectation, the children of the gentry give the title of 'fool' to Harry, when he goes into society in adolescence, he takes the whole town by storm.

The culminating, and perhaps the most carefully planned, stage in Emile's education is the selection of a fitting mate for him. With the utmost care, and by skilful stratagems, Emile is led to the girl his tutor has set his heart on, because she has received the kind of education which Rousseau recommends for the female sex, and which he describes in detail. In *The Fool of Quality*, the culminating point of fantasy and sentimentality is reached in the description of Harry's marriage to the daughter of his uncle's long-lost daughter. His uncle's daughter, when a baby, had fallen into a river and was thought drowned. But she had drifted down the water to the land of a Moroccan prince, fortunately a pious Christian, who married her. Her daughter has been brought up to wear a veil according to the custom of her father's country. Yet this Moroccan granddaughter is not only the best-hearted and most beautiful, but also the liveliest creature on earth.

The education in sensibility of the heroes of Henry

Mackenzie's novels does not begin as early as that of 'the fool', but the miseries and scenes of woe which educate their hearts, and train their eyes constantly to shed floods of tears, are described with scarcely more restraint.

If Brooke and Mackenzie thus differ from Rousseau in their methods of educating the heart, they have little use also for many other characteristic suggestions made by him; for example they do not pay much attention to his elaborate discourses on teaching a 'trade'. Branding every idler as a thief, Rousseau enjoins: 'Stoop to the position of a working man, to rise above your own' (bk. iii). Emile and his tutor both work as apprentices to a carpenter. Many echoes of this are heard in the radical Thomas Day, but we hear hardly any in Brooke and Mackenzie.

In the education of the Annesly children, Mackenzie accepts Rousseau's advice about teaching a trade but adapts it to his own requirement of 'instilling sentiments'. Little Billy Annesley is allotted a part of his father's garden as his own property; he works there on his own, and his father purchases the produce. 'With part of the purchase money Billy was to lay in the stores necessary for his future industry, and the overplus he had the liberty of bestowing on charitable uses in the village.' The same scheme is followed in the case of Billy's sister and her needlework: " 'For it is necessary', said Annesly, 'to give an idea of property, but let it not be separated from the idea of beneficence' " (I, iv).

It is surprising that Brooke, who invents a long and witty dialogue to emphasise the complete uselessness of the conventional education given to gentlemen does not follow Rousseau's advice about teaching a trade. But in describing the futile attempts made by Mr. Clement, educated at Westminster and Cambridge, to earn even a few shillings, Brooke's irony is at its sharpest. Here (ch. VII) we get a vivid realization of the plight of the man whose gentleman's education has rendered him unfit for any gainful occupation.

Another piece of advice given by Rousseau which leaves no significant impression on either Brooke or Mackenzie is his recommendation about a close study of the laws and phenomena of nature. It is, however, taken up by Thomas Day with great enthusiasm. One of the chief purposes of the numerous stories in *Sandford and Merton* is to demonstrate the value of

FASHIONING THE GENTLEMAN

practical and scientific knowledge, which makes the man who possesses it powerful and independent, giving him superiority over his fellow-men. It must be remembered that till the end of the century and later, the public and grammar schools, where the sons of gentlemen were educated, concentrated almost exclusively on the study of Latin and Greek, and that even these were taught by the most mechanical and unimaginative methods. If a young gentleman was educated at home, he was often taught French; men like Chesterfield insisted also on Italian and German, and on speaking and writing English correctly and elegantly. Many gentlemen insisted that their sons should have a smattering of law. But the schools refused to teach either modern languages or modern history; even more deplorable, in an age when science was beginning to make rapid progress, was the complete neglect of the study of the natural sciences.

However while the gentleman concentrated on learning the classics by rote, the new 'academies' popular among the dissenters had modernised the curriculum. In these schools the pedantry of classical learning gave place to an eager interest in science, in modern subjects and practical knowledge. Men like Defoe, who were denied the gentleman's education, stressed that 'the knowledge of things not words make a scholar' (*Compleat Gentleman*, pp. 212-5). Similarly the outsider Richardson spoke out against the pedantry of the conventional education of the gentleman (*Grandison*, I, xii-xiii).

The various fashionable accomplishments to which society parents gave a pre-eminent place are not scorned by Mackenzie and Brooke, as they are by Rousseau. The Annesly children learn dancing every week, although they are the children of a poor curate who has decided to settle far away from the corruption of civilization in a remote village even at the cost of forfeiting a handsome legacy. Brooke's Harry Clinton is provided with 'a dancing master' when he is seven and is 'instructed in all the arts and elegancies of horsemanship' (ch. ix).

Rousseau poured scorn on dancing (bk. ii); however even sober judges of good-breeding, like Budgell, *The Spectator's* education expert, rated the 'science' very high (no. 67), and Locke pointed out : 'For tho' this consists only in outward Gracefulness of Motion, yet, I know not how, it gives Children manly Thoughts and Carriage, more than any thing' (sec. 67). The linking of dancing with 'manly thoughts' would not sound surprising to the reader who recollects that Sir Thomas Elyot devoted several chapters of *The Governour* to an elaborate philosophical interpretation of the various turns and figures in dancing (bk. i, secs. 21-5). For the purpose of learning dancing was not so much to learn how to dance, as to acquire a 'graceful carriage'; to learn how to 'make a leg', to carry the head and the hands in the most elegant position, to walk with toes out, and to receive people in different conditions of life with different gradations of deference or hauteur; even Fielding declared that he had 'a very high regard' for the profession of dancing master (*Amelia*, V, ii). Richardson also considered the art sufficiently important to make his ideal gentleman, Sir Charles Grandison, 'one of the first dancers in England' (IV, xii).

As for the other indispensable part of fashionable education, 'riding the Great Horse', Rousseau has this to say more than a century before Thorstein Veblen postulated a similar theory in *The Theory of the Leisure Class*:

> An exclusive education, which merely tends to keep those who have received it apart from the mass of mankind, always selects such teaching as is costly rather than cheap, even when the latter is of more use. Thus all carefully educated young men learn how to ride, because it is costly, but scarcely any of them learn to swim, as it costs nothing, and an artisan can swim as well as anyone. Yet without passing through the riding school, the traveller ... learns to ride well enough for practical purposes; but in the water if you cannot swim you will drown, and we cannot swim unless we are taught. (*Emile*, bk. ii)

About fencing, another accomplishment regarded as indispensable, even Locke is not enthusiastic; he is inclined to think that wrestling is more useful. Nevertheless he does not feel confident about prohibiting fencing and riding the Great Horse since they are 'so generally looked upon as necessary qualifications in the breeding of a gentleman' (sec. 199).

If dancing, riding and fencing were regarded as indispensable, skill in music or poetry was frowned upon by parents and teachers of gentlemen. Most readers would not be surprised when they hear the worldly Chesterfield heaving a sigh of relief when he finds that his son does not have a gift for poetry (*Letters*, 24 Nov 1749); but Locke's views on the subject are far more philistine and worldly than Chesterfield's. No gentleman, says Locke, would like his son to be a poet; 'for it is very seldom seen, that any one discovers Mines of Gold or Silver in *Parnassus*. 'Tis a pleasant air, but a barren Soil' (sec. 174). Locke and Chesterfield were convinced that music, also was a dangerous accomplishment for a gentleman and forced him into 'odd Company' (*Thoughts*, sec. 19). However it must be remembered that the court of Charles II boasted of 'the mob of gentlemen who wrote with ease', led by the most dazzling aristocrats of the time, Rochester, Sedley, Buckingham and Dorset.

This antagonism to the arts is materially different from the tone and temper of the Elizabethans and their immediate followers, and of the courtesy books like Castiglione's *The Courtier*, on which they formed themselves. Castiglione praises music as 'a custom enclyning to virtue' (pp. 89-90); Milton in his tractate, *Of Education*, gives it an important place in his academy; even Henry Peacham, whose temper is much more utilitarian than Castiglione's, gives both music and poetry an honourable place in the education of 'the compleat gentleman'.

Yet Chesterfield, Locke and their contemporaries were in fact reverting to an older position. Sir Thomas Elyot, writing in 1531 on the education of 'the Governour' advised the tutor to 'commende the perfect understanding of musike' to the gentleman pupil, but at the same time pointed out the necessity of warning the pupil that 'a gentilman plainge or singing in a commune audience, appaireth his estimation : the people forgettinge reverence, when they beholde him in the similitude of a common servant or minstrell' (bk. i, sec. 7).

As usual some idea about the century's attitude to these two controversial accomplishments can be obtained from Richardson, who carefully considers every aspect of the gentleman's behaviour and education. Sir Charles Grandison plays the violin and the harpsichord. Mr. B. plays the violin and his brother-in-law, Lord Davers, the violincello. They are shown entertaining the family with their skill in a happy domestic scene (II, cii). Though they are typical products of the fashionable education which is so strongly condemned by him, Richardson seems to approve of a skill which equips the gentleman to manifest such attachment to the domestic circle, and keeps him away from the temptations of masquerades and gaming tables.

In his opinion of poetry as an accomplishment for the gentleman, Richardson does not differ much from Locke and Chesterfield. Mr. B., who composes verses and sings them, asserts that a 'tutor should have a taste for poetry' but that poetry should not be a 'predominant passion' with the tutor, 'for we see very few poets, whose warm imaginations do not run away with their judgments' (II, xciii). An incident in *Grandison* places poetry in an even more dubious light. Though 'Sir Charles is an admirer of good poetry', he feels it is wise not to encourage young gentlemen and ladies to write verse, for 'the titles of Wit and Poetess have been disgraced too often by Sappho's and Corinna's ancient and modern' (II, xxiii).

Not only music and poetry, but even 'learning', could be dangerous for the gentleman. Chesterfield, who cannot be accused of sharing the shallow outlook of the ignorant town fop or the uncouth country squire, frequently warns his son against taking too deep, or too professional, an interest in learning; he cautions him against too great a fondness for the company of 'men of learning' which, 'though greatly to be valued and respected, is not meant by the words *good company* : they cannot have the easy manners and *tournure* of the world, as they do not live in it' (12 Oct 1748). Not only Chesterfield, the 'man of fashion', but even Locke, the philosopher and scholar, gives similar warnings against absorption in scholarly pursuits, since the purpose of a gentleman's education is to fit him for the world and not for the university (sec. 94).

This antagonism between learning and the gentlemanly accomplishments was not by any means a new attitude. As Ruth Kelso points out,[12] from the Middle Ages two different types of education had been associated with the knight and the scholar. The former, a practical man of affairs, scorned the latter's absorption in books. During the Renaissance the cleavage still existed; even Castiglione, who believes 'that to be the true glory, that is stored up in the holy treasure of letters', insists that the courtier, though he should be a scholar, should 'remove all smell of the lamp and display his accomplishments as natural and not acquired' (pp. 82-4).

The warnings given by Locke and Chesterfield against too deep an absorption in learning seem surprising, when we set them against the picture which we get of the gentleman from Restoration and eighteenth century literature in which one of the commonest subjects of satire is the crass ignorance of the contemporary gentleman. Representative of such satire is the specimen which Fielding gives in *Joseph Andrews* of the illiterate spelling of 'one of his majesty's justasses of the piece for Zumersetshire' (IV, v), and the delightful one given by Richardson in *Pamela* of Mr. H.'s epistolary style (II, c).

The distinction that Locke and Chesterfield make between a scholar and a gentleman, is a distinction that obviously found much favour among ignorant gentlemen. Addison gives an amusing anecdote about Will Honeycomb trying to impress the Spectator and his friends by displaying two or three letters written 'in his youth to a coquette lady'. Twitted about his mistakes in spelling, Will 'said that he spelt like a gentleman, and not like a scholar' (no. 105).

The conflicting claims of the scholar and the gentleman, of learning and the Graces, asserted themselves most strongly when the young gentleman reached adolescence. Now the difficult question of whether to send him to a university or on the grand tour had to be decided. However anti-'ceremony' the trend among theorists and educationists, and however strong the tendency to deprecate French sophistication since the time Addison spoke of France as 'this ludicrous nation' (*Spectator*, no. 45), as the century advanced, an increasing number of young gentlemen took the tour, a large number of them bypassing the universities, or spending only a few terms at them.

Many parents of the gentry class had come to look upon the universities with distrust. The *beau monde* of course preferred the polish and poise given by the 'fashionable exercises' offered by the finishing academies in Paris to the load of Latin and learning to be imbibed at Oxford and Cambridge from the dowdy, cloistered ecclesiastics, generally recruited from the poorer class of student. Most high society parents would be of the opinion of Leonora's aunt in *Joseph Andrews*, who asks her niece with surprise, 'can you prefer a sneaking fellow who hath been bred at the university, to a fine gentleman just come from his travels?' (II, iv). It is certain that the grand tour was fast becoming obligatory for anyone with pretensions to entry into the higher circles, and only the wealthiest could afford both university and tour, even if they reserved this luxury only for the eldest son.

Enlightened parents were put off by the antiquated courses and the shocking indifference to learning now prevailing at both universities. Chesterfield, who belonged to the *beau monde*, and to the class of enlightened people, described Cambridge, where he was educated in the early years of the century, as an 'illiberal seminary' (28 Feb 1751) and sent his son straight from Winchester to the Continent. Horace Walpole, who was a dilettante but undoubtedly a man of lively intellect, dismissed Oxford as 'that nursery of nonsense and bigotry' (30 May 1751).

The less sophisticated among the gentry feared the two universities as haunts of vice. When the celebrated Coke of Holkham was seventeen, and his father was hesitating between Oxford and Cambridge, his great-aunt, Lady Leicester, wrote saying that if the boy would give up 'these schools of vice, the universities' and travel instead, she would allow him £500 a year.[13] The offer was of course promptly accepted.

Till modern research[14] corrected some of the highly adverse and picturesquely lurid opinions about the Oxford and Cambridge of those days, it was supposed that they had fallen into a completely moribund condition. The extremely damaging descriptions given by Gibbon and Adam Smith helped to create an even more unfavourable idea of the state of the universities than they deserved. Forty years after leaving Magdalen, which he had entered in 1752 before he was fifteen, and where he had stayed only fourteen months, Gibbon wrote of Oxford with utter scorn :

> The greater part of the public professors have for these many years given up altogether the pretence of teaching... the obvious methods of public exercises and examinations were totally unknown. (*Autobiography*, pp. 40-5, 81)

Adam Smith, who was at Oxford for over six years, spoke with similar scorn, of the two universities as 'sanctuaries in which exploded systems and obsolete prejudices found shelter and protection after they had been hunted out of every other corner of the world' (*The Wealth of Nations*, bk. v, ch. 1).

The eighteenth century is certainly the least distinguished period in the long history of both Oxford and Cambridge, the two decades from 1760 to 1780 marking the lowest ebb of their reputation. By the beginning of the century the old system of disputations and exercises for degrees had been reduced to a complete mockery; often the undergraduate merely crammed a few sentences from a crib the day before; and the tutors hardly listened when he appeared before them. A more serious drawback than the absence of a proper examination system was the arid, outmoded curriculum at a time when scientific studies were making rapid progress. The dissenting academies (at the two older universities students had to subscribe to the Thirty-nine Articles) and the Scottish universities proved far more adaptable in this respect.

The extraordinary lack of discipline at both the older universities contributed further to their decay. The descriptions in *Peregrine Pickle* of Perry's life at Oxford would be dismissed as the exaggerations of a novelist, if numerous accounts of riotous brawls in the colleges and violent rampages in the town had not come down to us from those times. We read of pitched battles in the streets of Oxford and Cambridge between town and gown :

> Breaking of lamps and windows. . .fighting and mobbing in the town and neighbouring villages; in the day time breaking down fences and riding over corn fields, then eating, drinking, and becoming intoxicated at taverns or ale-houses, and lastly in the night frequenting houses of ill-fame, resisting the lawful authorities; and often putting peaceable inhabitants of the town in great alarm.[15]

It was mainly the rich Gentlemen Commoners and Noblemen who specialized in such dissolute and violent conduct; the impoverished Sizars and the majority of the Pensioners had to apply themselves to their studies if they were to make their way in the world, and could not afford to indulge in such luxuries.

Three of the most distinguished writers of the time did not

hold contemporary Oxford and Cambridge in contempt. Swift, Johnson and Fielding much preferred university education to the foppery of the grand tour, though Fielding informs us that his model gentleman, Allworthy, had never been to a university (IV, xi). Smollett's Matthew Bramble and his circle are all Oxford men. However Henry Brooke does not care to send the ideal gentleman whose education he plans to a university. Mackenzie's new-educationist-cum-clergyman, Mr. Annesly, sends his son with the greatest reluctance to the university, and within a few months the really fine and sensitive lad is corrupted.

To the modern reader what seems most reprehensible about the universities of the time is the system of clear-cut class distinctions, the official grant of privileges to some students and the imposition of servitude on others. At both universities, the students were separated into four classes, according to their social status, and the fees they could afford to pay—the highest class was designated Noblemen, the second, Gentlemen Commoners at Oxford and Fellow Commoners at Cambridge, the third, Commoners at Oxford and Pensioners at Cambridge, and the last, Servitors at Oxford and Sizars at Cambridge. The first two classes wore richer gowns and enjoyed the privilege of sitting at the high table where they enjoyed much better food and wine. The Servitors and Sizars ate later, and got the leavings from the gentlemen's tables.

However, the privileges of dressing and eating better, seem quite innocuous beside the fact that financial status was taken into account for granting strictly academic privileges also. Noblemen were allowed to proceed to a degree without undergoing the statutory tests and without residing at the unversity for the prescribed number of terms. Gentlemen and Fellow Commoners were usually exempted from attendance at lectures and from performing most of the college exercises imposed on undergraduates of lower rank.

Not all sons of gentlemen could afford to go up as Gentlemen Commoners; about fifty per cent entered as Pensioners or Commoners. At least half the sons of the clergy were compelled to go up as Sizars and Servitors, most of the students in this rank being sons of clergymen, though some came from the even more humble homes of small farmers, artisans and petty tradesmen. The middle class was on the whole not interested in university education.

The Sizars and Servitors were at the beck and call of the richer students; in the morning they went up and down the cold staircases knocking at the doors of the gentlemen; they did menial tasks for them, acted as valets, waited at table and earned a few shillings. The sensitive Oliver Goldsmith who was compelled to go up as Sizar to Trinity College, Dublin, in 1745, felt humiliated by the menial tasks imposed upon him, and recorded his protest in *The Present State of Polite Learning*: 'It implies a contradiction, for men to be at once learning the *liberal* arts, and at the same time treated as *slaves*, at once studying freedom, and practising servitude'.[16]

After a few terms at these decadent, 'illiberal seminaries', and often bypassing them altogether, most sons of gentry and noblemen escaped to Europe to take the grand tour, the hallmark of the education of the gentleman. The Englishman, placed on the northern fringes of Europe, regarded France and Italy as the home of culture—Italy as the storehouse of the masterpieces of ancient art, and France as the teacher of elegance and sophisticated, graceful living. English manners were as yet comparatively barbaric, and England was not thought to possess any treasures of ancient art or architecture in which Englishmen could take pride. Because of the popularity of the tour, by the end of the century, the country houses of England could display some of the finest examples of European art, ancient and contemporary, though, since the gullible collector and the shark that feeds on him are always a part of the art-collecting scene, quite a few fake pieces were also carted into the country. Similarly, the study of European architecture by the grand tourist had by the end of the century inspired some of the most beautiful buildings in the history of English domestic architecture, and, inevitably, had led to several vulgar imitations as well.

When the century opened, England still had little to offer to those who would consider themselves civilized and sophisticated, especially as the Augustan eye had quite lost the ability to appreciate the beauty of the native Gothic architecture. Consequently, when their sons reached adolescence, parents felt that they ought to be shipped off to Europe to 'finish' their education. As Fielding quipped in *The Fathers* education had to be given a 'finish', it mattered not if no education had been received before this finishing process started. Latin and learning were all very well, but, as Chesterfield put it, a young gentleman must acquire the *tournure* of the man of fashion, 'la douceur et les graces', by picking up 'tous ces petits riens' without which all the sound wisdom and solid learning in the world would take him nowhere (16 May and 1 March 1751).

Since it was considered impossible to pick up this *tournure* in England, every year, especially after 1720, larger and larger numbers of young aristocrats, and sons of country squires and even sons of prosperous merchants began to embark for Europe. In *Tristram Shandy* Sterne quizzically described the Englishman's passion for the tour as the fulfilment of the curse, 'make them like unto a wheel', 'which David prophetically foresaw would haunt the children of men in the latter days' (VII, xiii). The fastidious Chesterfield, who was revolted by the manners of the English, remarked that the French rightly looked upon the invasion of their country by swarms of Englishmen as 'a second incursion of the Goths and Vandals' (*The World*, no. 18).

All through the century essayists and educational theorists inveigh against the superficial culture, the hypocritical manners and the degenerate morals of the Frenchified young man corrupted by his stay on the Continent. Addison, the 'Arbiter elegantiarum' of the century, spoke of France as a 'country which has infected all the nations of Europe with its levity' (*Spectator*, no. 435); Steele censured the French as 'a people who are taught to do anything, so it be done with an assurance' (*Spectator*, no. 104). Pope pilloried the empty-headed tourist in one contemptuous line—'Europe he saw, and Europe saw him too' (*The Dunciad*, iv, 294). In *Joseph Andrews* Fielding satirized the tour-returned young gentleman in the sketches of the foppish, hypocritical, treacherous beau, Bellarmine (II, iv), and the ill-bred country squire, who has 'returned home well furnished with French clothes, phrases and servants, and a hearty contempt for his own country' (III, vii). Adam Smith, who resigned his professorship at Glasgow to become a travelling tutor to an adolescent duke, showed no faith at all in the educational value of the tour, even though his duke had proved a studious and well-behaved pupil. For the periodical essayist at the end of the century the tour still remained a favourite subject for attack.

In spite of the many dangers that writers saw in this fashionable mode of education, they felt obliged to refer to the merits of the system. Though he often criticised French influence on English manners, Steele was quite emphatic that the ideal gentleman must travel, both in order to 'fashion and polish himself', as well as in order to 'get clear of national prejudices, of which every country has its share' (*Guardian*, no. 34). Similarly, Sterne questioned the value of travelling; but even from the pulpit he stressed that the tour helped the traveller 'to acquire an urbanity and confidence of behaviour and fit the mind more easily for conversation and discourse' ('The Prodigal Son', *Sermons*, I, 330). Characteristically, he also pointed out that travel 'taught us mutual toleration; and mutual toleration . . . taught us mutual love' (*SJ*, 'The Rose—Paris').

Many theorists, attempting to weigh the advantages and disadvantages of the tour, concentrated on suggesting reforms and improvements in its planning. Among the most frequent and important of these suggestions was that the tour should be undertaken only after the young gentleman had seen his own country, studied its institutions, and developed a respect and love for them. Richardson shows that the sagacious Pamela has resolved that before going abroad she and her sons would travel at home and 'enlarge' their 'notions of the wealth and power of the kingdom, in which God's goodness has given [them] so considerable a stake' (II, xcii). Sterne gives a quick satirical side-glance at the subject:

> Now hang it! quoth I, as I looked towards the French coast—a man should know something of his own country too, before he goes abroad—and I never gave a peep into Rochester church, or took notice of the dock at Chattham. (*TS*, VII, ii)

Another aspect of the tour which was frequently criticised was the age at which it was undertaken. Theorists found it deplorable that boys of fifteen or sixteen should be let loose in the dissipated capitals of Europe. Locke recommended that they should be sent either several years earlier or several years later (secs. 212-6), reasoning that if the purpose of the tour was to learn languages, the usual age was far too late. On the other hand, if the purpose was to acquire wisdom, prudence and good breeding by mixing with people, the tour ought to be postponed to a later period when the young gentleman was mature enough to govern himself, and could go without a governor.

In spite of the recommendations of the treatise writers and moralists, the upper class parent found the adolescent years the most convenient for the tour. Since he left home at such an early age, the young gentleman had to be provided with a tutor, who was expected to keep him at his studies for at least some part of the day, and guard his morals during the rest of the day, while he, it was hoped, was acquiring polished manners in sophisticated company. The young bucks usually gave a tough time to these travelling governors, or 'dry nurses' as they called them. Generally selected from the cloisters of Oxford and Cambridge, or from country parsonages, and often employed on salaries not much higher than those of valets, many tutors were uncouth pedants quite unfit to accompany pupils who were expected to move in fashionable company, and naturally quite powerless to control wealthy, high-born adolescents who were determined to have a good time.

The general opinion of these governors in the public mind is reflected in Smollett's strictures on Perry's tutor, Jolter. Jolter's is the only full-length portrait of a travelling governor in the literature of the period. Besides involving Jolter in a series of ridiculous situations, Smollett devotes a whole page to passing strictures on the unsuitability of such tutors, stressing that Jolter is neither a caricature, nor an extreme example (I, xxxix). In addition to the travelling governor, the sons even of gentlemen of moderate means, had to be provided with at least one servant; the sons of noblemen and the richer gentry were of course given more.

After landing in France, the young gentlemen set about the task of furnishing themselves with French clothes. At least two or three suits in the latest Parisian fashion were *de rigueur*; till Perry is able to get French clothes, he is obliged to confine himself to the company of the English at the famous 'English coffee house', which unfashionable haunt of the English grand tourist Chesterfield's Philip was given very strict injunctions never to go near.

Three years in Europe, to be spent on such a scale, made the tour a formidably expensive proposition. The exceptionally grand, grand tour of the Duke of Kingston cost well over £40,000; the average nobleman spent about £3,000 on the continental education of at least his eldest son and heir, more than £30,000 at today's rate. Younger sons were given a much less lavish tour. The Earl of Nottingham who spent over £3,000 on the tour of his heir, spent only £415 on the two-year tour of his second son. Smollett who wants to show that the Commodore does not stint money in giving Perry a gentleman's education, makes him settle an annuity of £800 on him (I, xxx).

The grand tour itinerary always included France and Italy; most young gentlemen spent a few months also in the Low Countries, Germany and Austria. It was customary for the uncouth novice to settle at first for some months in one of the French provincial towns, to undergo the process for which Chesterfield used (to Mme. de Monconseil, 5 Juin 1764) the verb *décrotter* (from *décrottoir* a 'door-scraper'), before being introduced into the elegant salons of Paris where he was to have the 'last fine varnish' (to son, 22 Sept 1752) applied to him.

The letters which Chesterfield wrote to his son during the years when he was being fashioned in Europe into a great gentleman give a vivid idea of the arts and accomplishments the grand tourist was expected to master. Every action, every gesture, is required to be carefully studied. Further it has to pass beyond a careworn, studied, rigid look, and is to be performed with a natural ease : 'A twist or stiffness in the wrist will make any man in Europe look awkward' (21 Jan 1751). Everything, as he later wrote to his godson, must be done 'in minuet time', with an unhurried, easy grace (12 Dec 1765).

A well-bred gentleman must shun singularity in all things, and even conform to 'the thousand foolish customs of the world'; he must avoid the bad habits of his companions by stratagem, not by open refusal, which is a tacit reproach to the company he is in (no date; ? July 1752). Both Richardson and Fanny Burney stress this kind of *bienséance* in the characterization of their heroes and heroines.

The most gnawing worry for a parent who had an adolescent son abroad was that the young gentleman would fall into the trap of women, and would return home debauched, to be plagued by venereal disease for the best part of his life. Nevertheless, the acquiring of some sexual experience was a recognized part of the curriculum of the grand tour. In the opinion of men like Chesterfield, an indispensable stage in the process of polishing a gentleman was an *arrangement* with a sophisticated society woman in one of the European capitals. Even during the eighteenth century, when Chesterfield's letters were first published, many readers claimed to be scandalized by his insistence on involving a boy in 'transient passions' in order to make him acquire *du brillant*; others defended the *Letters* on the ground that fashionable liaisons would preserve a young man from 'vulgar and infamous debauchery'.[17] Of course, few parents actively recommended such affairs to a son; but most accepted them as a matter of course, and thought it safest that young gentlemen should sow their wild oats on foreign soil, and in the arms of safely married Italian countesses and French baronesses, rather than in England in the company of low-class women who might entangle them in marriage. Even Dr. Johnson did not hesitate to assert: '... it is better this should be done abroad, as, on his return, he can break off such connexions and begin at home a new man.'[18]

However while parents flattered themselves that their sons were being schooled by sophisticated women, the average English grand tourist had to be satisfied with far less elegant mistresses. Chesterfield speaks contemptuously of the 'British Yahoo' being able to manage affairs only with 'Irish Laundresses' (30 April 1750); Smollett shows how the arrogant Perry, though he was considered dashingly handsome and brilliant in England, made absolutely no headway with the fashionable European women. If the society women allowed him into their circle at all, it was only to fleece him by cheating him at cards, with the result that Perry's 'very amorous complexion'

(II, lxxxv) had to find an outlet in visiting brothels, picking up casual adventures with all sorts of women, and appointing a 'fille de joie at twenty louis per month' (I, xxxix).

Thus fully fashioned by the grand tour, the young man returned home a 'finished gentleman'. He is so often and so contemptuously satirized in the literature of the period that one cannot but conclude that a fair number of grand tourists must have returned home the 'yahoos' Chesterfield called them, and the yahoo Smollett's Peregrine seems to the reader, though not always to Smollett. However, having enjoyed a privilege denied to all but a few, the young cubs themselves, and probably their proud parents, felt they were far superior to the hempen homespuns who could not afford the luxury of the Continental spree. After his rampage on the Continent, Peregrine 'thought he was now sufficiently qualified for eclipsing most of his contemporaries in England . . . His heart dilated with the proud recollection of his own improvement since he left his native soil' (I, xlii-lxvi). But the reader finds that Perry has done little except indulge in low amours and ruffianly adventures, though 'a noted academy' which he enters 'in order to finish his exercises' is mentioned in passing (I, xxxix).

However, as the century advanced, the cultural and civilizing influence of the tour did manage to make itself felt on English life. It certainly extended the horizon of the educated classes, making them noticeably less insular, till they came to regard the culture of Europe as their heritage. The English governing class of the time breathed a cosmopolitan atmosphere, spontaneously imbibing the philosophical ideas and political theories, the languages and literatures of the European countries. The visual arts of Italy and the elegance, politeness and urbanity of French society established a new 'rule of taste'[19] in England. In theory at least, it was now widely accepted that a gentleman is a man of culture and good taste, intelligent, widely travelled, free from prejudices, a 'citizen of the world'.

4 The Woman's Gentleman
or
The Anatomy of the Rake

SAMUEL RICHARDSON

So please your majesty, my master hath been an honourable gentleman: tricks he hath had in him, which gentlemen have ... He did love her, sir, as a gentleman loves a woman. —*All's Well That Ends Well.*

It is curious that of all the novelists of the century, the one who had the most sensitive insight into the mental processes of feminine characters, and was endowed with the most outstanding gift for dramatising emotional conflicts, should deliberately undertake the task of framing rules and devising warnings in order to teach the gentleman how to conduct himself. But in Richardson the desire to teach and reform was at least as compelling a force as the desire to create. Repeatedly, and with pride, he stated that he wrote only in order to preach, and made it clear that he had condescended to put his views in the form of novels only in order to make sure that a frivolous public, greatly in need of instruction, would be lured into reading what he had to say.

If we disregard Richardson's subtle perception of the motives of human conduct, which gives him an outstanding stature as a psychological and moral novelist, and consider him only as a didactic writer, we will find him not very different from the writers of the numerous run-of-the mill conduct and courtesy books popular in his day. His is the representative voice of a large section of the middle and upper-middle ranks of contemporary society. Except that he gives more emphasis to sexual morality and to the menace to women of attractive libertines who destroy their lives, Richardson's exposition of moral principles and his recommendations about the day-to-day behaviour of the gentleman are very like the principles set forth in a much-read treatise like Thomas Gisborne's *An Enquiry into the Duties of Men in the Higher and Middle Classes of Society in Great Britain* which appeared towards the end of the century. The principles had been formulated at the beginning of the century by Addison and Steele with wit and graceful urbanity in their essays and plays. Like Addison and Steele, Richardson attempts, on the one hand, to debrutalize and christianize the fundamentally coarse and inhuman, though seemingly elegant and civilized, conception of the 'fine gentleman' prevalent among the courtiers of Charles II and their eighteenth century heirs; and, on the other hand to make the rigid, morose, Puritan ideal of the virtuous life more human, civilized and urbane.

If Richardson's ideas are not very original or exciting, the popular charge against him fo moral insensibility is unwarranted. Even Pamela is not as much of a Shamela as has been made out. Lady Mary Wortley Montagu's witticism, 'Richardson is as ignorant in morality as he is in anatomy',[1] is amusing, but unjust. Undeniably, in many places, Richardson shows a narrowness and lack of taste quite unparalleled in a writer of his stature. On a number of occasions he seems quite unable to perceive the vulgarity of certain actions of his admired characters or of his own assertions; the solemn, judicial pose he adopts to make weighty pronouncements on every trifle can be both ridiculous and exasperating; many issues which he considers of momentous importance, most people do not think worth a minute's consideration; his dogmatism, his prolixity, and the tacit assumption behind the interminable length of his novels of the tremendous importance of his own ideas, can be extremely irritating. Quite apart from these limitations, the envious contempt he expressed in his letters for some of his great contemporaries is damaging to his own reputation. Consequently, there are times when any reader of Richardson will sympathise with the feeling Coleridge expressed in a somewhat vicious mood :

> I confess that it has cost, and still costs my philosophy some exertion not to be vexed that I must admire, aye, greatly admire, Richardson. His mind is so very vile, a mind so

oozy, so hypocritical, praise-mad, canting, envious, concupiscent.[2]

But 'greatly admire' him one must, even in this matter of moral values, for Richardson, in spite of all his pomposity, and all his subservience to accepted ideas, shows in his best moments a moral perception and creative power that give him a high claim on our admiration. Ungrudging admiration must be given to him for his imaginative realization of the need of the individual to carve out his own destiny in defiance of convention; for his sensitive understanding of motivation and emotion; for his deep feeling for the harassed individual caught in the tangle of circumstances and his ability to express this feeling with a genuine pathos that brings with it a sharp awareness of the moral issues of life.

Not without value, one need not be afraid to say, is even his emphasis on humdrum, old-fashioned virtues: on restraint, self-control and the performance of one's duty, in an age when too many have come to feel, like his selfish Lovelace, that 'happiness consists in being pleased with what we do' (III, cxix), and who have no moral resource to fall back on when happiness evades them.

However, whether one admires Richardson or not, his persistent inquiry in all his three novels concerning the motives and principles that determine the conduct and behaviour of the ideal gentleman and lady, and of their opposites, the frivolous, unregenerate profligates, furnishes a detailed picture of his views about the actual and ideal gentleman and lady.

Richardson's idea of the gentleman is projected in his first two novels in portraits of two libertines, Mr. B. and Robert Lovelace, and in his last novel in the portrait of a perfect gentleman, Sir Charles Grandison. It is this last gentleman who has aroused the most ridicule, for the average modern reader's reaction to perfect characters in fiction is much like Jane Austen's, who wrote: 'Pictures of perfection as you know make me sick and wicked' (To Fanny Knight, 23 March 1817). But this was by no means the universal opinion in the eighteenth century. Readers and critics quite frequently advised novelists to 'confine themselves to the study of characters worthy of imitation' (*The Adviser,* no. 14). Even Fielding, who prided himself on his realism, did not refrain from presenting an 'all-worthy' character; in fact, Sir Charles is a much more vivid and sympathetic character than Squire Allworthy, though in several parts of the novel he becomes unintentionally funny, as Allworthy never does. The ridiculous effects are partly due to the great solemnity of the presentation, and partly to the epistolary technique. The use of this technique often makes it necessary that the perfect character should write a report on his own perfect activities; this makes him sound complacent and priggish; at other times, it compels the writer to make a cluster of admiring girls keep scribbling to each other to applaud the hero's every movement. Seeing how quick he is to perceive every flutter of their loving hearts, they stand together and whisper, an appreciative tremor passing through them : 'Had he been a wicked man, he would have been a very wicked one!' (II, vii). Even this side of Grandison did not seem as funny to contemporary readers as it does to us. Indeed, the only complaint which some of them could find against him was that it would 'give the women an idea of perfection in a man which they never had before, the consequence of which niceness will be a single life for ninety-nine out of a hundred'.[3]

Richardson, however, was convinced that ninety-nine out of a hundred were giddy, credulous, naive girls who fell for exterior glamour, and scarcely one was a wise, far-seeing person who looked for the solid virtues. It is largely as a protector and mentor of women that Richardson fashions his ideal gentleman, and condemns the 'gentlemen of free lives', as he calls them in the Preface to *Clarissa*. Almost everything he writes is inspired by his judgment of women's needs and desires, his very strong feeling about what they ought to desire, and the many dangers that he sees in the way of their happiness. Richardson's ideal gentleman is, before all things, an ideal husband; the gentleman he condemns is the one who traps women in his nefarious designs and makes them miserable. Consequently, he wages a persistent battle against 'that endangering species of triumphant rakes called Women's Men'.[4] One of his principal motives in writing *Clarissa*, was 'to explode that pernicious Notion, that a Reformed Rake . . . makes the best husband' (*Letters*, 29 Oct 1746).

The notion had been in the air for a long time. Some of the

most fashionable and witty public figures of the Restoration and the following period, the Count de Grammont and the Earl of Wharton (often regarded as the models for Richardson's Lovelace), Rochester, Sedley and King Charles II himself, had helped to invest vice with glamour. Society had come to regard the selfish, brutal pursuit of women as a normal pastime, and the dramatists made the unprincipled libertine the hero of their comedies, allowing him all the advantages of the dazzling wit and elegant culture of their style. However, not only Puritan fanatics like Jeremy Collier, but the more urbane writers of *The Spectator* frequently lamented the inversion of values in this society in which the man of true worth and refined sensibilities was scorned as 'ignorant of the world', while the 'man of fashion' who spent his time wenching, drinking and gambling became a favourite with all the women.

The campaign waged by the moralists killed the perverse, but brilliant comedy of the Restoration; but it did not destroy the image of the amiable and irresistible rake. In fact, the final scenes of the 'sentimental' comedy, which took the place of the cynical, amoral comedy of the previous period, often showed penitent rakes falling into the arms of happy heroines whose beauty and love had brought about a complete change of heart in them. Such comedies fostered the notion that the dashing libertine, having conquered many hearts, will at last settle down at the feet of a victorious wife, still exciting, but for the future ever faithful.

Richardson seems to have been firmly convinced that women, 'unthinking, eye-governed creatures' (*Clarissa*, IV, vi) that they normally are, are perpetually in danger of being captured by these seductive 'gentlemen of pleasure'. Both the good and the bad qualities in woman's nature conspire to draw her to her destruction. Her vanity goads her to prove that her beauty and love can conquer the gay trifler who has trampled upon the affections of every other woman, and her tenderness and sensibility urge her to protect and redeem the rash, unthinking man of sin. Even the dutiful and virtuous Clarissa, his 'darling girl', as Richardson called her (*Letters*, 26 Oct 1748) in spite of all her fine judgment and circumspection, falls into this double trap.

Consequently Richardson was determined to impress upon

his feminine readers that behind the 'Form or Figure, an Air of Generosity, and Fire and Flight' of a Lovelace (*Letters*, 14 Dec 1748), there was selfishness, cruelty, utter disregard for all moral scruples and a sinister psychological make-up. The dazzling exterior of these sensualists blinded women to the revolting squalor of their lives. They must be made to see it. With this intention he spends all the resources of his art to paint the lurid, but unforgettable, scene of the death of Mrs. Sinclair, who keeps 'a genteel house of the sort'.

Richardson's most impressive contribution to this battle against the rake is the brilliant figure of Robert Lovelace, Clarissa's ravisher. It speaks much for Richardson's dramatic imagination that, though he tenaciously clings to his didactic purpose, Lovelace does not turn out to be a repulsive monster, but, like Milton's Satan, tempter of Eve, is quite often a seductive and compelling voice of freedom and rebellion Like the greatest dramatists, Richardson had the 'negative capability' of forgetting himself and becoming the person he was portraying. It is surprising how this timid and pious printer, suffering from a nervous ailment which made him so averse to company that he supervised his workmen through a peep-hole, could achieve the swagger, irreverence and wit of the letters that Lovelace wrote to his friend, Belford. In spite of his moral zeal, Richardson permits Lovelace to give expression to ideas and attitudes which he himself detested—scepticism, cynical jests levelled at virtue, impatience with restraint, advocacy of pleasure as the purpose of life. As a result, Richardson succeeds in portraying one of the most attractive and intelligent villains in fiction, without allowing him to become lovable, without failing to reveal him as a complete egoist and a thorough cad, capable of movingly dramatising his own distress when he fails to get his point, but incapable of realizing anyone else's distress, or experiencing any genuine love, sympathy or remorse.

The characterization of Lovelace has been condemned by some as unrealistic and ineffective. Professor David Daiches dismisses him as 'a mild and timid man's picture of the ideal rake, of Satan as gentleman.'[5] The characterization has also been highly praised for a variety of reasons;[6] Richardson himself would have found the grave and moral tribute which Dr.

Johnson paid him the most gratifying, for it credits him with achieving exactly what he set out to achieve:

> It was in the power of Richardson alone to teach us at once esteem and detestation; to make virtuous resentment overpower all the benevolence which wit, elegance, and courage naturally excite; and to lose at last the hero in the villain.[7]

Would that the women had possessed Johnson's sobriety and critical discernment! Richardson's success with the attractive side of Lovelace's character made the 'unthinking creatures' succumb to the seductive charm of the gentleman; there were some who even sided with Lovelace, and accused Clarissa of prudery, of being a 'frost-piece', as Richardson had made Lovelace call her (I, cxxi). To rectify this, in the second edition of the novel in 1749, and once again in the third in 1751, Richardson made several additions to the text to emphasise the blacker, more vicious side of Lovelace's character. He also inserted several footnotes and an exhaustive index, with all the moral lessons forced on the attention by italics, in order to drive the message home. Yet from the first there had been enough of the ugly and frightening in the character to warn off any woman of sense. For Richardson had a definite concept of the moral and psychological make-up of the gentleman who becomes a rake; it inspires his presentation of Lovelace, as well as of the rakes in his other novels (men like Sir Hargrave Pollexfen and his cronies in *Grandison*, and to a large extent, Mr. B. who, however, is reclaimed by Pamela).

Richardson saw cruelty and selfishness as the governing instincts in the character of a rake. Cruelty is an important motive in Lovelace's otherwise motiveless, unaccountable harassment of Clarissa, which, he knows, is quite against his own interests:

> When a boy, if a dog ran away from me through fear, I generally looked about for a stone, or a stick; and if neither offered to my hand, I skimmed my hat after him to make him afraid of something. What signifies power, if we do not exert it?... We begin, when boys, with birds, and, when

grown up, go on to women; and both, perhaps, in turn, experience our sportive cruelty. (II, xcii, lxxi)

Not only the brutal rape, but Lovelace's continuous efforts to violate Clarissa's dignity, womanly delicacy and pride, by trying to put her in the humiliating position of pleading with him for marriage, emanate from Richardson's realization that 'there is more of the savage in human nature than we are commonly aware of' (II, lxxi), and that this savage plays havoc with human lives, unless it is kept under control by an active moral and religious discipline, such as was not too frequently practised in the England of his times, where 'self-denial and mortification [had been] blotted out of the catalogue of Christian virtues' (*Clarissa*, Postscript).

Closely allied to cruelty in Richardson's concept of the rake, are selfishness and insensitivity. The rake is quite incapable of understanding the needs, wishes or predicament of other people. In spite of his undoubted intelligence, wide reading and experience of the world, Lovelace has no understanding at all of the impulses and principles that govern the life of a woman like Clarissa. For the rake desensitizes himself. Such a man has no respect for the sanctions which bind man to man, and which form the basis of civilized society. Lovelace, therefore, in spite of all his polish and learning, is called the 'Savage man' (*Letters*, 26 Oct 1748).

Richardson almost invariably traces the arrogance and ungovernable passions of his self-willed, aristocratic rakes to their deplorable upbringing. Pampered and indulged from childhood, they never learn to control their desires, respect the rights of others and submit to the claims of duty. If they marry, they prove tyrannical and unfaithful husbands. Like Sir Charles's father, and like Mr. B. 'till Lights superior to those of mere Morality broke in upon him' (*Letters*, 21 Jan 1748/9), they expect implicit obedience and slavish submission from their wives. As her cousin Morden tells Clarissa, such a man will hardly ever reform but by miracle, or by incapacity (II, lxxiv).

This detailed analysis of Richardson's conception of the psychology of the rake must not be allowed to create the impression that Richardson sets about his didactic purpose with ponderous seriousness. Lovelace's cruelty, selfishness and perfidy are brought home to the reader in brilliantly entertaining reports given by him of his own behaviour, and in scenes of moving pathos and tense psychological conflict between him and Clarissa.

The irony was that, in spite of all the care which Richardson had taken to expose the repulsive side of the seemingly attractive rake, as the last parts of the novel were being published, he was assailed by readers clamouring for 'a fortunate ending', with Lovelace marrying Clarissa and both living happily ever after. The sentimental appealed to his pity and humanity, the 'critical' demanded what they termed 'poetic justice' on Clarissa's behalf (*Clarissa*, Postscript). Even Fielding,[8] who had derided the complacent philosophy of Richardson's first novel, and had exposed his heroine Pamela's unwillingness to give herself to Mr. B. as a 'sham', because she believed she could do so only after a legal and religious ceremony, wrote to the author to spare his readers a tragic catastrophe.[8] Marriage to their minds was sufficient compensation for the 'premeditated and perfidious barbarity' (III, cxxxi) with which Lovelace had treated Clarissa. Though he knew it would work against the commercial success of his novel,[9] Richardson remained adamant to these pleas.

The question of the historical reality of the gentleman-rake, who was an extremely common figure in the fiction of the eighteenth century, has often been raised. Not only the writers of cheap romances for the circulating libraries, but writers of more respectable reputation, like Mackenzie and Mrs. Inchbald and, not least of all, Fielding, show the rake playing a prominent part in the social scene. Readers who like Freudian explanations may refer to an article entitled *The Rococo Seducer*,[10] which attempts to explain the psychological motivation for the behaviour of the eighteenth-century rake. Most of the arguments of the article are summed up below :

> . . .An Enlightenment individualist asserting the Ego's right to pleasure against God, honour and society. . .
> The right to pursue one's own pleasure had been won by eighteenth century man only by the act of murdering God and the lesser fathers : the unconscious knows that the punishment for this is castration; and the libertine, in

order to ward off the punishment, must continually assert his virility in order to prove that the punishment has not yet fallen on him.

If the perverse gentleman-rake was as common as the fiction of the century would have us believe, who could a lady choose for a husband? According to Pamela's friend, the intelligent and sensible Polly, daughter of Sir Simon Darnford, sexual licence was 'a fault so wickedly common among men that when a woman resolves never to marry, till a quite virtuous man addresses her, it is, in other words, resolving to die single' (II, lxxxiv).

However, according to Richardson, such a feeling arose because even women like Polly, and like the two other highly intelligent girls in the two other novels, Anna Howe and Charlotte Grandison, were too immature to think of any one as a husband, except a thrilling hero who would take their hearts by storm. With sober realism, Richardson undertook to teach them that 'one man cannot be everything' (*Letters*, 18 Nov 1748). In the characterization of Mr. Hickman in *Clarissa*, and of Lord G. in *Grandison*, he deliberately presented as ideal husbands for the two young women, two completely unexciting gentlemen, stolid, reliable, religious and chaste; possessing, as he allows Anna Howe to say with scorn, 'qualities that mothers would be fond of in a husband for their daughters' (I, xlvi). In the Postscript to *Clarissa*, Richardson gravely tells the reader that in Hickman, he has portrayed a type that 'women are not fond of', purposely depicting him as clumsy, over-ceremonious, plagued by 'preciseness and formality'. Though Richardson allows the gay young girls in their correspondence in the novels themselves, to mock these diffident suitors, who woo their sprightly mistresses with a dog-like devotion that exasperates them or reduces them to giggles, he believed that in their own interest women must learn to realise that it is such modest men only who have true generosity and gentleness and 'a feeling heart' (*Letters*, to Lady Bradsaigh, undated). Richardson sent reproving letters to Lady Bradsaigh and to Susanna Highmore (*Letters*, 4 June 1750) who, feeling that he had made his good man too dull, had pointed out that if a woman is to fall in love with a man, he must have some sprightliness, some self-confidence, should be somewhat less uninspiring in his 'dress and address' than Mr. Hickman.

In spite of his strict views on this subject, Richardson shows a finer imaginative understanding of the plight of the sensitive, intelligent, independent-minded girl placed in the circumstances of eighteenth-century conjugal life than any other writer of the period. The unenviable lot of women 'ensnared, like silly birds into a state of bondage or vile subordination, to be courted as princesses for a few weeks, in order to be treated as slaves for the rest of [their] lives', is vividly pictured in the letters of Clarissa and her friend, Anna Howe (I, xxvii). One remembers how the only advice that the gracious Marquess of Halifax could give to a beloved daughter, in a book that ran through sixteen editions during the course of the century, was that she should not be distressed to find faults in her husband; on the contrary, she should be grateful, 'for a husband without faults is a dangerous Observer.'[11] One also remembers what Lady Mary Wortley Montagu, discussing the future of her granddaughters, wrote to her daughter:

> ... a virgin state. I will not say it is happier; but it is undoubtedly safer than any marriage. In a lottery where there is (at the lowest computation) ten thousand blanks to a prize, it is the most prudent choice, not to venture. (*Letters and Works*, III, 47)

Yet Richardson thought the theory of the subordination of woman to man necessary and just, and stressed that it was 'improper for a woman at *any Age* to be independent' (*Letters*, 2 March 1752). But he also stressed that woman will have no cause to repine, if in her choice of a husband, she is governed by reason and by piety, and lets it fall upon the good man.

For the good man is the opposite of the tyrant and the rake; unlike them, he is governed by reason and conscience. The tyrant and the rake are conquered by their passions; the good man conquers his. As Dr. Bartlett, the mentor of the perfect man, Sir Charles Grandison, says, 'the life of a good man is a continual warfare with his passions' (III, xxii). Not cold or passionless, the good man has learnt by arduous discipline to triumph over temptation and the weaknesses of his own nature. Like Sir Charles who was 'naturally passionate, proud, ambitious' (III, xx), he has schooled himself till he 'is used to do only what he *ought*' (III, xxii). Similarly Clarissa, the good and disciplined woman, is intensely sensitive, yet extremely rational; 'so warm, yet so cool, a friend' (IV, clxviii).

One of the causes of Clarissa's sufferings is that she allowed her reason to be deluded by her feelings for some time. Her tragedy is that her 'frail humanity', which she has in common with others, combined with the quite uncommon sensitiveness and depth of her emotional nature, makes her suffer much more intensely than ordinary human beings, before she succeeds in subduing her feeling for the base man whom it has been her fate to love. Unfortunately, because some readers protested that it was impossible that a girl who was 'violently in love' should be as firm and disciplined as Clarissa, in the Postscript to the novel Richardson refused to concede that Clarissa had ever been in love, and irritably coined a new phrase : 'It was not intended that she should be in love, but in liking only, if that expression may be admitted.'

Nevertheless, during the course of writing the novel, when he was not badgered by critics, Richardson had given an intensely human and tragic picture of a girl trapped by her feeling for a compellingly attractive but utterly worthless man whose protection she was compelled to seek because of her family's ruthless persecution. Richardson's portrayal of Clarissa, though he never presents her as passionately in love, has an imaginative truth and naturalness altogether different from the over-stated remarks about love and 'cupidity' in the Postscript. As Lovelace exercises his gloating vanity and cruelty on her, vexes and teases her beyond endurance and repeatedly affronts her womanly pride by his cunning tactics, her feeling for him makes the realization of his worthlessness all the more bitter to her.

In Richardson's day some readers were impatient with Clarissa for standing too much on female delicacy and punctilio; some modern readers accuse her of a sub-conscious desire to be ravished. Richardson has put both these reactions with dramatic frankness in the mouth of Lovelace whose one purpose is to make her yield to him and, as he frequently proclaims, to discover that there is as much desire for sexual gratification in her as in him.

Critics who talk of Puritanism and hypocrisy with regard to every aspect of Richardson's writing, and compare it to its disadvantage at every step with the frankness of Fielding, may be less confident of their stance if they read Fielding's tribute to Richardson's presentation of Clarissa :

> Such Simplicity, such Manners, such deep penetration into Nature ... With what Indignation do I therefore hear the Criticisms made on this Performance. Clarissa is undutiful; she is too dutiful. She is too cold; she is too fond. She uses her Father, Mother, Uncles, Brother, Sister, Lover, Friend, too ill, too well. In short, there is scarce a Contradiction in Character, which I have not heard assigned from different Reasons to this poor Girl; who is as much the Object of Compassion as she can be, and as good as she should be described. (*Jacobite's Journal*, 2 Jan 1747/8)

Richardson's novels were conceived as a warning not only to the victims of the rake but also to the members of 'the keeping class' (*Clarissa*, II, xci). In both *Clarissa* and *Grandison* he paints a series of lurid pictures tracing the rake's progress from a youth of levity and gay peccadilloes, to violence, crime and repulsive disease; and, finally, to an agonising death in the prime of life; the wretched sinner can 'neither repent nor pray ... can do nothing but despair' (*Clarissa*, IV, lviii).

The principles that should govern the conduct of a man with regard to his passions were, according to Richardson, exactly the same as those which should govern a woman. The double standard of morality, which prescribed one code for women and another, or rather none, for men, and which was almost universally accepted in his day by men, women, clergymen and libertines, made no sense to Richardson. In *Grandison*, he went out of his way to assert that his ideal gentleman, Sir Charles, had no sexual experience before marriage, though he was fully aware that most readers would find this quite ridiculous.

Richardson was not alone in thus going against what may be called public opinion. In 1713 Steele's *Guardian* had ventured to recommend to its readers Chastity as 'the noblest male virtue' (no. 45). Yet it was risky, and Richardson knew it. Colley Cibber had laughed in his face when he had protested because Cibber had shown his hero living with a mistress even though he intended to portray him as 'a good man': 'A male-virgin, said he—ha, ha, ha, hah ! and he laughed me quite out of countenance !' (to Lady Bradsaigh, n.d. probably 1750).

Nevertheless, Richardson persisted in proclaiming his position. For him it was a central question concerning a man's moral integrity, his rationality and his obedience to Christian doctrine. He could never compromise on such a question. However, he condemned victimisation of the guilty, and contempt or prudery in dealing with them or their children. Much space is devoted to showing Sir Charles's 'great behaviour' not only to erring men and women in general, but to the two mistresses of his late father, Mrs. Oldham and Miss O'Brien, and to the two sons of Mrs. Oldham, whose education he supervises. Sir Charles proves his generosity not only by giving money to these people; he treats them, especially the older one, with great courtesy, calls her to meet his two young, unmarried sisters, and rebukes them for their haughty behaviour to her (II, xx-xxii). Diana Spearman has pointed out[12] how differently a writer like Thackeray would have treated a similar situation, though Richardson is generally considered to be much more representative of the Puritan middle class.

When he was writing *Grandison*, Richardson told Lady Bradsaigh (*Letters*, 14 Feb 1754) that one of his 'great views' in portraying his ideal man was 'to shew the vincibility' of the passion between man and woman. Richardson's favourite young correspondent, the vivacious Miss Hester Mulso, after reading the first part of the book, wrote to him that she longed to see Sir Charles swept off his feet by passionate love, his tranquil self-possession ruffled for once. Richardson playfully declined to write 'to the taste of girls from fourteen to twenty-four of age' (*Letters*, 27 July 1751). A great part of the novel is indeed occupied with showing Sir Charles in love, or rather, with showing a number of women in love with Sir Charles— the purpose being to demonstrate the honourable, sensitive, magnanimous way in which Sir Charles can love and, what is perhaps more difficult, can refuse love. The truth, goodness and beauty of his character, his generosity, tenderness and 'politeness', his courage, dash and spirit, his loyalty, patriotism and religion, are all tested in the difficult and delicate predicaments in which love involves him.

The three principal contenders for Sir Charles's love are three magnificently beautiful women, heiresses to magnificent fortunes. Two of them are Italian, the third is English. The Lady Clementina della Porretta, whom Sir Charles tries to teach English by introducing her to the beauties of Milton's poetry (III, xx), is the daughter of a noble Italian family, fanatically proud of its honour. Clementina herself is sensitive and noble, and a devout Catholic. In her struggle between her love and her religion, and oppressed by the tyranny of her family who will not allow her to take the veil and let her vast fortune pass to her cousin, she succumbs to a hysterical malady; for some months her condition becomes so bad, that it is feared she will lose her reason. The manifestations of this malady and the cruel treatment given to the ailing girl by her family, particularly by her jealous cousin, are described with minute particularity, in a long series of 'affecting scenes'. Sir Charles is not left unscathed by Clementina's beauty, virtue and suffering.

The Porrettas, whose youngest son's life Sir Charles has saved in very dangerous circumstances, all love and admire him, but they insist on his becoming a Catholic and living in Italy. This of course is an intolerable demand on a man of Sir Charles's piety and patriotism. However, finding so worthy a woman suffering on account of her love for him, Sir Charles enters into patient negotiations for months on end with the Porrettas, and with Clementina, who cannot bring herself to marry a Protestant. When the negotiations break down and Sir Charles returns to England, Clementina loses her reason. Sir Charles is not a man who will forsake a woman at such a time. He 'considers himself bound by his former declarations to the family and Lady Clementina as free' (IV, xl); but when she recovers, chiefly owing to Sir Charles's tender advice and care, she refuses him from 'motives of the highest generosity and piety'; and pleads with him to marry the English girl who loves him and make her happy (V, xxiv). After months of suspense, during which the English girl has been pining for him, this is not an unwelcome decision to Sir Charles.

The other Italian woman who is passionately in love with Sir Charles is Lady Olivia. Of a violent and imperious temper, she lays her splendid beauty and vast fortunes at Sir Charles's feet; but Sir Charles, who has 'never left mind out of [his] notions of love' (III, xx), cannot return her love. Therefore, with modesty and tender kindness, he persuades her to do without him. Feeling scorned, she swears vengeance against him, yet frantically pursues him all over Italy. When after attempts at murder, suicide and even an attempt to abduct him, she is compelled to resign herself to her fate, she sends him several cabinets full of magnificent treasure. Sir Charles, in turn sends her a 'fraternal letter' of frank but delicately worded admonition (V, xli).

The third of the principal contenders for the prize of Sir Charles's hand—alas! that he 'can make but one woman happy'! (II, xxxiv)—is the English girl, Miss Harriet Byron; intelligent, prudent, wise; kind, generous, frank; beautiful, gracious, accomplished; everything, in fact, that a lady should be. One day, while she is being abducted by the vile rake, Sir Hargrave Pollexfen, Sir Charles with 'true heroism' rescues her, and takes her to his stately house in the country where he lives with his sister. There Harriet falls in love with 'her deliverer'; he also, seeing 'the beauties of her mind' finds she is a woman whom he could love and marry; but he feels in honour bound to wait for the ailing Clementina to recover. Harriet, during these weeks of suspense, thinking 'his affections engaged', gradually 'declines in her health'. When at last Clementina releases him, he marries Harriet. We are given many glimpses of their perfect marriage—a marriage not less blissful than that of Adam and Eve in Paradise, except that Harriet believes that Sir Charles would prove more virtuous than the first erring Adam:

> Do you think, my dear, that had he been the first man, he would have been so complaisant to his Eve as Milton makes Adam ... to taste the forbidden fruit, because he would not be separated from her, in her punishment, though all *posterity* were to suffer by it?—No; it is my opinion, that your brother would have had gallantry enough to his fallen spouse, to have made him extremely regret her lapse; but that he would have done *his own duty,* and left it to the

Almighty, if such had been his pleasure, to have annihilated his first Eve, and given him a second. (V, xxxi)

So much for the invincible conqueror love; his 'vincibility' is soon proved, when he tries to contend with a man who has conquered his passions, and is determined to love 'like a reasonable man'.

Like a reasonable man, and yet not like a heartless, insensitive passionless man. For Richardson's reasonable man is very different from the cold, intellectual, aloof man who moves above the realms of emotion and sorrow and suffering. 'The heart rather than the head' is Sir Charles's criterion for judging men (VI, liv). According to Richardson, man is distinguished from the lower animals not only by his reason and conscience, but by his capacity to feel. In this aspect of his attitude to human personality, Richardson seems very close to the sentimentalists and Romantics who consider that the capacity to feel is the supreme test of character. Richardson's insistence on feeling and his minute analysis of emotional predicaments put him at the head of the new movement that was beginning to gather strength all over Europe—the cult of sensibility and tears. Pathetic, blubbering heroines like Clementina della Porretta and Emily Jervois in *Grandison*, who seem insufferably hysterical to the modern reader, more sternly portrayed sufferers like Clarissa, and of course Sir Charles himself, with his deep, manly, silent suffering, made hearts surge with emotion, and eyes fill with tears, all over France and Italy and England. Even Lady Mary Wortley Montagu, who 'heartily despised him and eagerly read him . . . sob[bed] over his works in a most scandalous manner' (*Letters and Works*, III, 125).

However, nothing could be more repugnant to Richardson than the Romantic writer's deification of emotion, his advocacy of a spontaneous response to passion and feeling, or the Shaftesburian sentimentalist's habit of confusing conscience with impulse and emotion, in the belief that man's nature is *naturally* good. Not the exaltation of passion, but the conquest of passion, is Richardson's subject.

'Sensibilities', when they urge the heart to defy duty or reason, have got to be overcome. Yet they must not be cast out, for 'the tender susceptibilities', when properly directed, 'are the glory of human nature' (V, xxxviii). Behind his cheerful appearance (for cheerfulness he considers a social duty), Sir Charles hides a 'bleeding heart' that suffers silently for his own and humanity's sorrows. Clarissa, too, referring to her hardhearted sister, says:

> Bella has not a *feeling heart*. The highest joy in this life she is not capable of: but then she saves herself many griefs by her impenetrableness. Yet, for ten times the pain that such a sensibility is attended with would I not part with the pleasure it brings with it. (I, xlii)

'The pleasure it brings with it': here are the beginnings of that masochistic tendency to relish suffering, which is so pronounced in Mackenzie and the late eighteenth century sentimental writers. Here, too, is that commendation of tears as a purifying agent, and as a touchstone for ascertaining goodness in character, which is one of the principal tenets of the sentimental school.

In this manner, Richardson insists that both reason and sensibility are the distinguishing characteristics of the perfect gentleman; however, higher than both reason and sensibility is religion. To enable him to battle with his passions, and to endure the vicissitudes of life, man needs a discipline and a support which is more firm and objective than that afforded by even the most well-governed reason and emotions. As Pamela learns, we are not 'absolutely to direct ourselves' (I, Pamela's Journal). In her struggle to extricate herself from her difficulties with Mr. B., Pamela has relied too much on her own understanding, prudence and virtue, and too little on God. Having entangled herself more and more at every stage in her own 'foolish contrivances', she is tempted to commit suicide and thus have her sufferings 'infinitely aggravated. . .in a miserable eternity'. Withheld by 'divine grace' just at the moment she is about to jump into a pond, she begins to realize the necessity of duty and resignation to the Divine Will. Similarly Mr. B., in spite of his resolutions to reform and the virtuous influence of Pamela to help him, is frequently tempted to err. Then at last 'higher Lights' dawn on him.

It is interesting to find that in his last novel Fielding arrived at a similar conclusion. Captain Booth, who is a 'philosopher', not a believer, in spite of all his fine instincts, is able to master his weak will and find happiness only when, during his final bitter experience in prison, he falls upon a collection of Barrow's sermons 'in proof of the Christian religion', and a new realization of the nature of man and his need for religion dawns upon him.

The Christian way of life, and the active and daily practice of Christianity, are given a lot of space in Richardson's novels. But like the authors of *The Spectator*, and like many others who had been revolted by the gloom of the Puritan movement, Richardson is careful to insist that asceticism, moroseness, 'enthusiasm' and zeal are no part of religion. 'Religion is the cheerfulest thing in the world', Richardson wrote to Lady Bradsaigh (*Letters*, n.d.?Dec. 1749).

When, with the aid of his religion, his disciplined reason and his refined sensibilities, the good man has arrived at a decision which he knows is right, he will not swerve from it. Neither the opinion of the world nor the entreaties even of very beloved friends or relations should influence a just decision. Sir Charles's proudest boast is, 'I live not to the world; I live to myself; to the monitor within me' (I, xxxix). By contrast, Lovelace, in spite of all his bravado, is afraid to act without worrying about the 'figure' he will 'make in rakish annals' (II, lxxii).

Though they act only according to the voice of their conscience, neither Clarissa nor Sir Charles despises the opinion of the world; to do so is not only injudicious, it is also bad manners. However, when one is convinced that the world is wrong, one must defy it. To do so requires a courage which few people have. It is such courage that Richardson requires of his heroes; whereas the only code of behaviour that unprincipled men and women ever have, is to live so as to save appearances.

This ideal of conduct is asserted most emphatically in Sir Charles's attitude to duelling. The custom of duelling, so contradictory to reason, sensibility and Christian principles, yet so fashionable that every gentleman felt it compulsory to conform to its outrageous demands for fear of a stigma on his 'honour', could at any moment involve the man of principles in a painful dilemma. Consequently, the custom gives an admirable opportunity to Richardson to demonstrate how his ideal gentleman adheres to his principles in spite of the world's opinion.

Since the middle of the sixteenth century the practice of duelling had occupied an important place in discussions of conduct and ideals. Soon after it became fashionable, most European countries had framed severe laws against it. In real life, challenges, and even encounters, were frequent, but seem to have been seldom attended by fatal consequences, except a few notorious ones like those between Lord Mohun and the Duke of Hamilton, and between Lord Byron and Mr. Chaworth. Boswell's son was killed in a duel with a political opponent in 1822, but of Boswell himself it is reported, that though seven times in his life he was on the point of fighting a duel, he never actually fought one.

The practice of duelling was so closely linked with the idea of honour, that even the most peaceful, reasonable and religious gentlemen sometimes found themselves in a situation in which it was impossible to avoid a challenge. For 'honour', the code by which the gentleman was supposed to guide his life, had its own laws, quite distinct from the laws of the constituted legal system, or the laws of the religion of the countries which these gentlemen inhabited. According to the code of honour, there can be no degradation greater than to endure an injury without retaliating; according to the code of Christ, the test of virtue is the ability to turn the other cheek.

It was taken for granted that honour was an innate instinct in the gentleman; lesser men could not possess it. One reads in Boswell how Johnson snubbed 'a gentleman-farmer who spoke in favour of Mungo Campbell, who shot Alexander, Earl, of Eglintoune':

> The gentleman-farmer said, 'A poor man has as much honour as a rich man; and Campbell had *that* to defend.' Johnson exclaimed, 'A poor man has no honour.' (*Life*, III, 188-9)

Since duelling and despising the rights of all but gentlemen were the only ways in which the idea of honour manifested itself in the conduct of the average gentleman, it is natural that Sir Charles should be 'governed by another set of principles than those of false honour' ('concluding note'), and should do his best to put down the infamous institution of duelling. Sir Charles is himself a most skilful hand at the sword. Since he rushes to the rescue of the weak and unjustly treated, he repeatedly finds challenges flung at him, but he has his own way of dealing with 'these polite invitations to murder'. Though in a crisis he does not refuse to draw his sword in his own defence, it is his policy, as far as possible, to talk his opponent out of his violent and impious intentions. Because of his superb skill with every weapon, in his own mind he is quite clear that in declining to fight 'he consults his conscience rather than his safety'. Since his demeanour is such that even rakes reverence him, and since he can also disarm an opponent with one stroke of the sword and can knock out three or four teeth with one punch, he emerges from every encounter with his courage vindicated, having set an example which proves that 'reputation and conscience are entirely reconcilable'.

Richardson's presentation of the problem is highly romantic, and would hardly be able to stand the test of a real life encounter. As readers pointed out, opponents were unlikely to wait for Sir Charles's 'expostulation'; besides, the average gentleman, being a less skilful duellist than the invulnerable Sir Charles, would not be able to extricate himself with honour from such a situation. Though Richardson tried to defend his presentation of the subject both in the 'concluding note' to the novel and in letters to his friends, he could offer no effective answer to the criticism. According to him, the incidents and arguments in the novel were bound to influence public opinion; consequently they would enable lesser men to take, without feeling cowardly or ridiculous, a stand that so heroic a hero took.

Richardson thus failed to resolve an important point on which he chose to battle with the fashionable code of gentlemanly conduct. His failure was partly due to the fact that the problem itself was difficult, but to a large extent it must be put down to his obstinate insistence that the virtuous man living according to Christian principles, can also be a 'fine gentleman' —fashionable, sophisticated, a gallant courtier, well-versed in the manners of high society, able to be all things to all men. In portraying Sir Charles as the ideal gentleman, Richardson insisted that truth, sincerity, piety and industry are perfectly reconcilable with style, charm, polish and social brilliance; his approach, part utilitarian, part idealistic, would not allow him to concede that the true Christian, can seldom be also a prudent, worldly-wise man, capable of achieving brilliant success in the world.

Consequently, Charles Grandison, the virtuous Christian, is a rich, 'polite', polished, handsome baronet; an irresistible young gallant and a shrewd man of the world; a successful negotiator, a brilliant mediator; a reformer, whose temper is not spoilt by any asperity or censoriousness; a crusader, who can go through life without incurring any serious opposition, contempt or suffering.

The essays of Addison and Steele first presented the idea of the Richardsonian type of perfect gentleman to the public mind:

> ...by a fine gentleman, I mean a man completely qualified as well for the service and good, as for the ornament and delight of society... He is properly a compound of the various good qualities that embellish mankind. (*Guardian*, no. 34)

But it was one thing to advocate the practice of all the virtues and the mastery of all the accomplishments in periodical essays, and quite another thing to project all of them into one perfect character in a novel. Other novelists of the century saw the difficulty of making a good man a man of the world; consequently, they portrayed their good men as saintly eccentrics—lovable and even admirable, but quixotic; simple, unworldly people, stumbling along, falling into traps laid by the smarter ones of the world, suffering their contempt, never achieving any brilliant success. These novelists found that it was best to present such characters with a humorous touch that made it possible both to apreciate and to criticise the eccentric goodness.

Indeed, Richardson too saw the artistic as well as moral problem quite clearly when portraying his two other good men, Hickman and Lord G., both of whom are presented not only as awkward and unfashionable, but as humorous characters, so that the author is able to have the best of both arguments —is able to present goodness as worthy of praise and imitation, and yet is able to preserve his own balance by laughing at the uncouthness and simple-minded innocence of these good people. But when portraying his ideal gentleman, Richardson could not rest satisfied with a quixotic lovableness. Like Chaucer, who bowed to the royal command of a lady and composed the deadly dull *Legend of Good Women* after having presented the moving reality of the wicked woman, Criseyde, Richardson submitted to the demand of his women correspondents that he balance his portraits of good women and of men either wicked or uninteresting, with the portrait of a perfect gentleman; forgetting his own dictum, 'the same man [can] not be everything' (*Clarissa*, Postscript), he undertook to present a man at whom people would gaze in admiration and exclaim : 'Bless me. . . . this man is every thing !' (VI, xxv).

And indeed Sir Charles Grandison 'is everything'; but 'everything' according to the characteristic eighteenth century concept of the ideal gentleman. The earlier heroic, chivalric idea of the gentleman as a dazzling, sophisticated courtier, who would find his highest fulfilment in living as an able, suave politician in the palaces of princes, or in seeking glory and defying death on the battle-field, was replaced by a new ideal of philanthropy, honesty and usefulness. The ideal gentleman now found fulfilment in living on his country estate, 'improving' his land, and helping his neighbours.

Consequently, 'Chevalier Grandison', as the Porretta family, living in a more barbarous, romantic, heroic Italy, insist on calling him, is a 'private' gentleman, a 'domestick man', who is convinced that 'the private station is. . .that of true happiness' (VII, v). When 'gentlemen of prime consideration in the county' coax him to accept a seat in Parliament, and promise him 'their interest against the next election', he rejects the offer. Sir Charles would of course serve his country even by entering Parliament, if duty called, but the political ambition that destroyed personal happiness and personal honesty, and gave the country corrupt, unprincipled legislators and office-seekers, has no place in his scheme of life. Nevertheless, even the 'domestic man' must be a man of public spirit; Sir Charles subscribes fully to the ideal of social responsibility. As a trustee, executor and guardian, he is painstaking, reliable and much sought after (he himself makes his will at seventeen); to the church livings that are in his power to confer, he makes judicious and impartial appointments; he is a learned and devoted justice of the peace, who ungrudgingly spares his time for public welfare and justice. He is perpetually, and most successfully, settling differences between his friends, relations and neighbours. As a public-spirited man, and as a patriot, though he is 'in the noblest sense, a citizen of the world... .he encourages the trades-people, the manufacturers, the servants, of his own country' (VII, iii).

Sir Charles is 'a great planter'; 'he will do any thing that tends to improve the estate; so that, it is the best conditioned estate in the country. His tenants grow into circumstance under him' (VII, viii). He even maintains a sort of health-service; he has appointed 'a skilful apothecary' and a surgeon to attend to his tenants, servants and the poor, and supplies the drugs at his own expense. For his own servants he provides a library—his future wife is struck by the thoughtfulness which provides such an unusual amenity.

Sir Charles's enlightened charities similarly show the 'magnificence' of his spirit. The charity he is 'most intent on promoting in France and in England' is quite extraordinary; it 'is that of giving little fortunes to young maidens in marriage with honest men of their own degree' (III, ii). However, another favourite scheme with Sir Charles, the establishment of 'places for retirement for female penitents' (IV, xvii), was practical enough to be implemented. Magdalen House was founded in 1758 in order, as Richardson put it in his additions to Defoe's *Tour thro' the Whole Island of Great Britain* (1762), to '*reclaim* and *reform* such unhappy wretches as had *not* escaped the snares of vile Men'. Richardson generously supported Magdalen House and was a governor of the institution.

Still another scheme close to Sir Charles's heart was the establishment of a kind of 'nunnery' for Protestants, where single women 'of small or no fortunes' could retire and live an independent life. Women who entered this kind of nunnery would not be obliged to remain in it permanently; at the end of every two or three years they would be given the option to renew their vows. Such an institution would make 'a stand for virtue' in a licentious society, in an age when 'genteel' women who had no 'portions' to enable them to get married, as well as women who possessed handsome fortunes but were not inclined to marry, found it quite impossible to carve out a life of their own. Incidentally, this scheme was the only thing in Richardson that appealed to Lady Mary Wortley Montagu, who said, 'It was a favourite scheme of mine when I was fifteen' (*Letters and Works*, III, 41).

The correspondents who had kept urging Richardson to create 'the compleat gentleman' had certainly made a shrewd estimate of his talents. Responding with a stern didactic fervour, and yet with a sensitive understanding of the diverse moral problems involved in the question, he projected within the framework of a dramatic and psychological narrative all aspects of his century's idea of the perfect man. In the plethora of periodical essays and courtesy books the various attributes of the ideal gentleman are described from the first years of the century to the last. Almost all the novelists, major and minor, repeatedly undertake the duty of enforcing this ideal. The life that all of them advocate as the most admirable, beneficent and happy, is the life of the philanthropic and industrious country gentleman who, with benevolent heart and thoughtful mind, is constantly, as Fielding said of Allworthy, 'meditating in what manner he might render himself most acceptable to his Creator, by doing most good to His creatures' (I, iv).

Unlike Fielding's other characters Allworthy, in whom the ideal is pictured, remains a didactic dummy. Smollett also attempts to present the idea of the gentleman in elaborate detail in long sections of *Humphry Clinker*. But though in these sections of the novel Smollett's writing glows with moral conviction, he allows it to remain unashamedly didactic, and makes no effort to create individual characters or to generate emotional tension. Richardson is the only writer who is able to present all the many facets of the ideal within the framework of a novel of manners, in the central character of a story of psychological tension and moral conflict.

In spite of his firm convictions about presenting ideal characters in novels, Richardson felt some qualms when he embarked on the project :

> ...the fear I have, that a good man must have a tame appearance, must not a little dishearten me...I own that a good woman is my favourite character; and I can do twenty

agreeable things for her, none of which would appear in a striking light in a man...Philanthropy, and humanity, is all that he can properly rise to. (*Letters*, 24 March 1751)

The problem was indeed quite formidable. But Richardson was able to project the two attributes of philanthropy and humanity, combined with the culture and intelligence with which he endowed Sir Charles, in a large variety of incidents to illustrate the ideal code of behaviour in every circumstance in which an English gentleman may be called upon to prove his gentlemanly qualities. That the incidents fit with such ease and naturalness into a story of considerable suspense and emotional power is a tribute to Richardson's inventive genius and his gift for character delineation. It need not be denied that Grandison himself remains a more remote figure than the lively women characters of the novel, or that he becomes quite ridiculous at times; but he is a far more vivid character than Fielding's 'all-worthy' gentleman. So common is the talk of Grandison's ridiculous pompousness among people who have never read the novel that its sprightly scenes of natural and spirited conversation are not even mentioned, except by the few scholars who seek painstakingly to give its just due to Richardson's much maligned reputation. From the realistic and vivacious scenes of the domestic life of the gentry in *Grandison*, Jane Austen learnt how to strengthen the vivacity of dialogue with a moral backbone, and prevent it from degenerating into a mere flippant liveliness. Jane Austen's nephew recorded:

> Her knowledge of Richardson's works was such as no one is likely again to acquire...Every circumstance narrated in *Sir Charles Grandison*, all that was ever said or done in the cedar parlour, was familiar to her; and the wedding days of Lady L. and Lady G. were as well remembered as if they had been living friends.[13]

Richardson's shortcomings are of the kind that every schoolboy can ridicule. No great writer ever possessed less tact, or cared less to acquire it, in preaching his views. He will mouth platitudes with great parade and solemnity, and fuss interminably over trivialities. He will stifle his virtuous characters with adulation, and crush their humanity by loading them with all the virtues that all the conduct books ever prescribed. There is a smugness and complacency about him which quite blind him to the ridiculous aspects of his own writing.

To perceive the greatness of Richardson requires a greater maturity, and some willingness to give him one's time. The extraordinary power, the almost unbearable tension, of the moral and psychological conflicts in his novels issue from a relentless, dogged analysis that at first seems to move not at all, yet soon succeeds in gripping the reader in a tense drama that stretches every nerve.

It is easy to point out absurdities and a quite deplorable lack of taste in all the three novels of Richardson; but these defects come to matter little when we see them against the originality and power of the moral, psychological and dramatic achievement of this first great English novelist.

5 Greatness, Goodness, Happiness —'A Great, Useful, and Uncommon Doctrine'

HENRY FIELDING

No man enters this gate without charity.[1]

'I dislike his Principles, both Public and Private,' said Richardson about Fielding (*Letters*, 4 Aug 1749). To aggravate Richardson's dislike for Fielding's principles was his aversion to the manner in which these principles were expounded. Fielding's laughing irony, his boisterous jests about matters very serious to Richardson, his urbane manner of watching the absurdities and misdemeanours of the world with detached amusement vexed Richardson greatly. Fielding persisted (at least till he came to write his somewhat grave last novel) in telling 'truth with a smiling countenance', and persisted in laughing at those who would dress it in a 'decent solemnity' (*TJ*, XI, i).

Contemporary readers seemed to divide themselves instinctively into Richardsonians and Fieldingites. Richardsonians declared themselves greatly scandalized by Fielding's principles and the levity of his manner. His first biographer, Arthur Murphy, as well as his cousin, Lady Mary Wortley Montagu, contributed towards distorting the image of his private life. Lady Mary could write very enthusiastically about his art and his zest for life. 'Ne plus ultra', she is said to have written on her copy of *Tom Jones*; but her innuendoes about his private life were very damaging to Fielding's reputation :

His natural spirits gave him rapture with his cook-maid
... Henry Fielding has given a true picture of himself
and his first wife, in the characters of Mr. & Mrs. Booth...
I wonder he does not perceive Tom Jones and Mr. Booth
are sorry scoundrels ...

I cannot help blaming that continued indiscretion, to
give it the softest name, that has run through his life, and
I am afraid still remains. (*Letters and Works*, III, 122-3,
92-4)

Thus the image of an improvident rake, who in his writings made an attempt, as Richardson put it (*Letters*, 4 Aug 1749), 'to make Morality bend to his Practices', grew in the public mind, so that by 1828 Hazlitt had to protest : 'You are asked if you like Fielding, as if it were a statutable offence' (*Works*, XII, 374). Thackeray's colourful and widely read 1853 lecture on the looseness and perverseness of Fielding's own life and the lives of his heroes, fixed the distorted image more firmly in the public mind.

Late nineteenth and early twentieth century critics, like Hazlitt and Coleridge before them, looked with more favour than his contemporaries upon Fielding's novels, but often only by running down Richardson as a solemn, didactic writer who preached a narrow morality and wrote in such poor taste that characters whom he meant to portray as virtuous seemed cunning hypocrites to the reader. In contrast, Fielding began to appear as a great realist, making a vigorous, penetrating study of *l'homme moyen sensuel*, undeterred by delicate scruples about morality, and unconcerned with lofty aspirations. Like Leslie Stephen, who complained of Fielding's lack of delicacy and interest in 'lofty' and 'spiritual' aims, and found a disparagement of philosophy and 'heroic impulses' in his novels, they saw Fielding as a hearty, 'manly', 'English' writer, endowed with robust common sense, a keen eye for sham and a gift for exhilarating comedy.[2] Thus Fielding came to be regarded as the frank realist and Richardson as the frowsy moralist.

Wilbur Cross's three-volume biography of Fielding published in 1918 went a long way towards correcting the misconceptions about Fielding's personal life. Since then, and particularly in the last thirty years, Fielding scholarship has built up a totally different picture of Fielding's writings, including his early plays, as motivated forcefully and consistently by deep moral and religious convictions.[3]

Richardson's and Fielding's contemporaries had not, for the most part, made the mistake of seeing the realist-moralist dichotomy between the two novelists. Many contemporaries hostile to Fielding had perceived that he was trying to convey certain principles about character and morality with just as much zeal as Richardson. It was precisely this that aroused their indignation, for they found the principles pernicious, so pernicious that the newspaper *Old England* singled out *Tom Jones* as the chief among the lewd publications the Bishop of London had referred to in a pastoral letter in which he declared that the vogue of immoral books was responsible for the wrath of God which caused England to be rocked by an earthquake in 1750.[4] It was because Johnson felt that Fielding was preaching subversive principles that he reviled him as a 'blockhead', a term which he went on to explain as meaning 'a barren rascal'; and indicted *Tom Jones* as 'so vicious a book ... I scarcely know a more corrupt work'.[5] Another contemporary, Sir John Hawkins, was more explicit; his indictment neatly sums up the reasons why Fielding's ideals were considered so dangerous:

> 'The Foundling, or the history of Tom Jones,' [teaches] that virtue upon principle is imposture, that generous qualities alone constitute true worth, and that a young man may love and be loved, and at the same time associate with the loosest women. His morality, in respect that it resolves virtue into good affections, in contradiction to moral obligation and a sense of duty, is that of Lord Shaftesbury vulgarised ... He was the inventor of that cant-phrase, goodness of heart, which is every day used as a substitute for probity, and means little more than the virtue of a horse or a dog ...'[6]

Fielding himself had made no secret of the fact that his intention in *Tom Jones* was to preach 'a great, useful, and uncommon doctrine' (XII, viii). Though his ideas about life, as well as his theories about art, unlike Richardson's, did not permit him to create perfect gentlemen and ladies, he did not shy away from presenting exceptionally good men and women. At the beginning of *Joseph Andrews* he declared that a novelist by communicating such 'valuable patterns to the world' does great service to humanity. He chose the universally admired Ralph Allen, 'the best man' (*Amelia*, Dedication), as the model for his portrait of Mr. Allworthy, which he declared was 'a stronger picture of a truly benevolent mind than is to be found in any other' work (*TJ,* Dedication). However, he felt that the 'valuable patterns' presented in fiction ought to seem life-like; they should not turn into abstract patterns drawn from a conglomeration of all the virtues.

Therefore, in his quest for heroes through whose example he could 'recommend goodness and innocence', 'wisdom and virtue', and instruct readers 'in this most useful of all arts, which I call the ART of LIFE' (*Amelia*, I, i), Fielding alighted on Tom Jones; a generous but 'wild' lad of nineteen, who the whole Somersetshire population thought 'was certainly born to be hanged' (III, ii), and on Billy Booth a sensitive but erring young lieutenant, who lands himself three times in jail, leaving his wife and two children to endure poverty and insult.

As foils to these two erring heroes, in whom he finds potentialities for becoming ideal gentlemen, Fielding created two mature gentlemen who have arrived at the stage of living an ideal life. As a foil and mentor to Booth, Fielding chose Dr. Harrison, a good but simple priest, blunt and brusque in his manner; a true and wise Christian, but not too familiar with the ways of the world. To balance Tom's youth, and to strengthen him in goodness and wisdom, he chose a benevolent country gentleman, 'all-worthy' in his moral character, but not all-accomplished in social skills, nor all-wise in worldly matters, unlike the sagacious Sir Charles who can never be taken in by even the cleverest villain.

In a third novel, Fielding chose as his heroes a footman, Joseph Andrews an innocent, ignorant, virtuous lad and a poor, eccentric curate of a country parish, Parson Abraham Adams, a clumsy and comic character. Adams's unpractical idealism is of a kind which makes him appear as quixotic as Cervantes's hero, though it succeeds brilliantly in casting satirical reflections on the inhumanity, corruption and false values of the world. Neither the middle class Richardson, who declared he was revolted by Fielding's 'continued lowness' (*Letters*, 23 Feb 1752), nor the aristocrat Horace Walpole, could stomach such heroes. Walpole wrote to Madame du Deffand who had praised *Tom Jones* : 'Dans les romans de Fielding, il y a des curés de campagne qui sont de vrais cochons.—Je n'aime pas lire ce que je n'aimerais pas entendre' (July 1773).

The reason why Fielding chose six such characters is to be sought in his views about the nature of man, which he frequently elaborated in his novels and periodical essays.

Though at times he criticized Shaftesbury, especially for his deistic leanings, Fielding's intuitive feeling, as well as his reasoned convictions, led him, like Shaftesbury, to the belief that many people (though perhaps fewer than Shaftesbury would admit) were endowed with a natural goodness, and were actuated by naturally benevolent instincts. Fielding developed his own brand of the Shaftesburian philosophy, modified by his Christian beliefs, in which the highest place is given to the virtue to which he, following the Latitudinarian divines, gave the name 'good-nature'. In fact, good-nature is regarded by Fielding not only as the greatest virtue, but as identical with virtue. In the poem *Of Good Nature*, he asks 'What is good-nature ?' and answers : 'Is it not virtue's self ?' In his novels he judges almost every quality and every action of an individual by the test of good-nature, the 'delight in doing good'.

Several times in his miscellaneous writings, Fielding gave definitions of good-nature, but perhaps the two most important and characteristic passages occur in *Tom Jones*—in the chapter 'Of Love' and in Tom's answer to the Man of the Hill's misanthropic diatribe against man. The Man of the Hill, embittered by the treachery of his mistress, and of the person whom he regarded as a loyal friend, looks upon man as a 'vile animal', 'everywhere the object of detestation and avoidance'. Tom disagrees, and supports his view by citing 'an excellent writer', Shaftesbury (VIII, xv). In the chapter 'Of Love', Fielding identifies the philosophers, supposed 'finders of truth', who maintain there are 'no such things as virtue or goodness really existing in human nature', and 'no such passion [as love] in the human breast', with the *finders of gold* (a slang term for latrine-sweepers). He concludes with the assertion: 'there is in some (I believe in many) human breasts, a kind and benevolent disposition, which is gratified by contributing to the happiness of others' (VI, i). Tom, we are told, is characterized by this disposition (III, viii). A few chapters later Fielding asserts that good-nature operates intuitively rather than rationally:

> Mr. Jones had somewhat about him... which... doth certainly inhabit some human breasts; whose use is not so properly to distinguish right from wrong, as to prompt and incite them to the former, and to restrain and withhold them from the latter. (IV, vi)

Fielding's belief in the presence of such an instinctive tendency led logically, as in the case of both Shaftesbury and the Latitudinarian divines, to the belief that an individual experiences supreme happiness by performing benevolent actions. In *The Covent-Garden Journal* (no. 29) Fielding quotes with great enthusiasm from his 'beloved author', Dr. Barrow, (whose sermons lead to Booth's conversion in *Amelia*):

> As nature... to the acts requisite towards preservation of our life, hath annexed a sensible pleasure, forcibly enticing us to the performance of them: so hath she made the communication of benefits to others, to be accompanied with a very delicious relish upon the mind of him that practises it; nothing indeed carrying with it a more pure and savoury delight than beneficence. A man may be VIRTUOUSLY VOLUPTUOUS, AND A LAUDABLE EPICURE BY DOING MUCH GOOD.

The portrayal of Tom relies wholly on this theory. Tom's spontaneous, 'natural' actions are always generous because generosity gives him happiness. Soon after he reaches London Tom gives money, which he himself needs badly, to a starving cousin of his landlady. In answer to her grateful words wishing him 'a glorious reward', Tom tells her:

> 'Your cousin's account, madam,' said he, 'hath given me a sensation more pleasing than I have ever known. He must

be a wretch who is unmoved at hearing such a story; how transporting then must be the thought of having happily acted a part in this scene!' (XIII, x)

The practical utility of the belief in good-nature is not muffled by much rapture, in the Dedication to *Tom Jones*:

Besides displaying that beauty of virtue which may attract the admiration of mankind, I have attempted to engage a stronger motive to human action in her favour, by convincing men, that their true interest directs them to a pursuit of her.

Fielding knew the world well enough to recognize the necessity of appealing to self-interest, if men wished 'to work others to their own purposes' (*TJ*, VIII, ix). Therefore, in working men to his own purpose, which was to make them follow the path of 'goodness and innocence', Fielding offered self-interest as an incentive; but he emphatically denied that he had any desire to support 'the comfortable doctrine' that the virtuous man is rewarded by worldly prosperity and happiness. In *Tom Jones* (XV, i) he goes out of his way to attack such a doctrine which he describes as false, unChristian, and 'destructive of the noblest arguments that reason alone can furnish for the relief of immortality', and proceeds to draw a sharp line between 'those cardinal virtues [prudence, temperance and fortitude], which like good housewives stay at home, and mind only the business of their own family', and the selfless virtues, the social affections.

Though Fielding asserts that the practice of benevolence is 'natural' and provides supreme happiness, he does not suggest that every human being is endowed with benevolent instincts. Therefore, for some individuals there seems to be no possibility of achieving genuine goodness or happiness, for they are entirely devoid of these instincts. Obviously Tom's half-brother, Blifil, is one such. Another is Colonel James in *Amelia*, who 'had not the least grain of tenderness in his disposition' (II, 79).

If an individual is endowed with this disposition, neither a bad education, nor a bad environment, seems to have any influence on his good-nature. Tom, educated by the egregious Thwackum and Square, and keeping company for the most part with Black George, the thieving game-keeper, and with the coarse, money-loving tyrant, Squire Western, is not in the least affected. Nor does Sophia Western's environment, in which the chief influences are her coarse father and worldly aunt, leave any taint on her good-nature. However, in *Amelia* and *The Covent-Garden Journal*, Fielding takes a more orthodox Christian position, attaching greater importance to education and training in moral discipline. Though he is still anxious to assert that 'Nature...must give the Seeds', he finds that 'to improve or depress their Growth is greatly within the Power of Education' (*Covent-Garden Journal*, no. 48).

If then Fielding believes that character is innate and at least to a very large extent fixed, does he imply that the virtuous man acts virtuously by mere instinct, or does he suggest that good actions involve conscious principles, rational judgment and a deliberate striving after virtue?

Fielding's statement, quoted a few pages ago, regarding Tom's having 'somewhat about him', seems to assert that man is led to act rightly or wrongly at the behest of his instincts. But only five lines after that statement, he gives a further exposition of the principle, which seems to refute what he has said before, and, moreover, makes the reader wonder if Tom is a good example of the operation of the principle; for Tom, even if he can be said to possess the requisite 'integrity', certainly does not have the kind of 'penetration' and 'knowledge' described by Fielding:

> ...it may be considered as sitting on its throne in the mind, like the Lord High Chancellor of this kingdom in his court; where it presides, governs, directs, judges, acquits and condemns according to merit and justice; with a knowledge which nothing escapes, a penetration which nothing can deceive, and an integrity which nothing can corrupt. (*TJ*, IV, vi)

In *An Essay on the Knowledge of the Characters of Men*, Fielding stresses that good-nature acts 'without any abstract contemplation on the beauty of virtue, and without the allurements or terrors of religion' (*Works*, XIV, 285). Another definition in *The Champion*, requires at least the operation of the mind; here Fielding asserts that good-nature operates with 'a constant regard to desert', and continues : 'It is impossible for a fool, who hath no distinguishing faculty, to be good-natured' (*Works*, XV, 258).

The ideal character, Mr. Allworthy, at least twice in the novel recommends to Tom a deliberate self-control, a conscious struggle to follow the dictates of 'prudence and religion' (V, vii; XVIII, x). Allworthy himself is guided by rationally formulated ideas about justice, charity, goodness and nobility. In *Amelia*, in all the theoretical arguments at least, the impulses and passions of even good men are shown to require the support not only of prudence, but also 'the allurements and terrors' of the rewards and punishments promised by religion, to keep them under control. The chief philosophical theory criticised in *Amelia*, is that held by Booth, which is not unlike the theory which postulates that some people are 'naturally' endowed with good-nature. Booth believes that the actions of an individual are entirely motivated by whatever happens to be his predominant passion, not by his moral or religious beliefs. He thinks that if benevolence is a man's ruling passion he acts benevolently; on the other hand, if cruelty, ambition or avarice is his ruling passion, he acts unjustly and viciously. Consequently, a man's 'actions could have neither merit nor demerit' (XII, V). This theory is elaborated at length, and criticized again and again, during the course of the novel. At the end of the novel, when he is in prison, Booth comes upon a collection of Barrow's sermons, which convinces him of the truth of the Christian faith. He declares himself converted, and gives up his false philosophical position.

Yet throughout the novel, Booth, in spite of his false beliefs, always displays an essential nobility, while not only the wicked unbelievers, but even clergymen, behave ignobly. Further, though his false beliefs have been at least partly held responsible for his miserable plight, the relief he obtains from it is not due to his conversion from scepticism to faith but to accidental exposures of villains and discoveries of long-lost wills.

Nevertheless, the emphatic insistence on the necessity of belief in Christianity and the attack on false philosophical positions are given so central a place in this novel that one feels that Fielding's religious views changed after he wrote *Tom Jones*.[7] In fact, one cannot help feeling that Fielding is projecting something very like what had been his own philosophical and religious development in the characterization of Booth. Certainly, the spontaneous, creative aspects of the characterization in *Tom Jones*, and even in *Amelia*, do seem to endorse most of the tenets of the philosophical position taken up by Booth before his conversion, however much Fielding may seem to fight it in didactic passages recommending prudence and religion. Virtue is surely a much easier acquisition for men like Tom and Booth and Allworthy with their innate good-nature, than for men like Blifil and Colonel James. In fact, the idea of virtue in Fielding is very like the idea of the gentleman: it is far more difficult, if not impossible, to be virtuous if one is not born virtuous, just as it is almost, if not quite, impossible to be a gentleman if one is not born a gentleman.

In addition to attacking false philosophical theories, in *Amelia* Fielding intends to show that in a society as perversely unchristian and as polluted by political and moral corruption as the one he portrays, there is no chance for a young man as generous, sensitive and susceptible to intellectual ideas as Booth. Such a society will encourage only the moneyed or the morally corruptible who will allow themselves to be 'made a dirty channel to assist in the conveyance of that corruption which is clogging up and destroying the very vitals' (*Amelia*, IX, x) of the country. In such a society brave army officers like Booth will have to linger on half-pay and will be expected to 'maintain the dress and appearance of a gentleman' on an income 'not half so good as that of a porter' (IV, viii). The political corruption, especially the pernicious system of 'touching' without which no preferment was possible, is a persistent theme in *Amelia*. Booth is inveigled into giving fifty pounds, obtained by pawning Amelia's clothes and jewels, to a man who will get him a position from a 'great man'. Not only the system of 'touching', but the fact that the pimps and panders of the 'great' men living in a decadent society had to be kept happy, worked against the honest gentleman. My Lord, who uses the most elaborate schemes to trap married women, in whom he completely loses interest after they have yielded to him just once, obtains a commission for a young sergeant within hours of an offer of help in his nefarious designs on Amelia.

Fielding's attitude towards the political corruption which he exposes in *Amelia* is one of deep pessimism, even of despair. Some historians in recent years[8] have felt that the novels of Fielding (and of Smollett) which seem to depict 'a country in an advanced stage of decay', paint a much darker picture than is warranted by the historical facts; however, there is no gainsaying the fact that Fielding, who was gifted with an uncommonly shrewd and penetrating intellect and a fine sense of humour, and who was prepared to sacrifice his health working as a London magistrate, could feel only a sense of dismay and despair as he studied the governing class of his day.[9]

While Fielding blames society for the disillusionment and consequent apathy and lack of fibre of a man like Booth, his purpose in *Amelia* is to fix the responsibility for an individual's unhappiness on his own self. The technique of the 'Art of Life' which he intends to teach does not consist in shifting the responsibility for one's failures and moral poverty to Society or Fortune. In the 'exordium' to the novel, he comments scornfully on the weak attitude which allows a man to knuckle under and blame Fortune for his plight.

Since Fielding's intention was to demonstrate that life is an art which each individual has to learn, and that men tend to assign an unwarranted importance to Fortune, the question naturally arises whether Fielding succeeds in showing that the happiness and misery of the Booths is not due to Fortune but to the efficiency or inefficiency they display in practising the 'Art of Life'.

The principal cause of the sufferings of the Booths is their miserable financial condition. At the end of the novel, owing to a sudden turn of events which they have done nothing to influence, the estate which they should have rightfully inherited is restored to them. Dr. Harrison then embraces Booth and says:

> 'Your sufferings are all at an end, and Providence hath done you the justice at last which it will, one day or other, render to all men.' (XII, vii)

Several times in the course of the novel Fielding refers to Fortune and Providence; some critics have played much on the distinction between these two words, but there is no significant difference between the events which Fielding ascribes to Providence and to Fortune. Quite often he tends to use the two words quite indiscriminately. Only ten pages after Dr. Harrison attributes the prosperity of the Booths to Providence, in his commentary Fielding pronounces: 'Fortune seems to have made them large amends for the tricks she played them in their youth (XII, ix). Quite early in the novel Fielding deplores 'all the malice of their fate' (IV, v). He speaks of the malicious turn which was given to these affairs in the country, which were owing a good deal to misfortune, and some little perhaps to imprudence' (IX, i).

Because the words, Providence and Fortune, are used interchangeably, the heavy emphasis in 'the exordium' on the 'impropriety' of assigning a role in life to Fortune has to be called irrelevant to the scheme of the novel. However, this is not to be regarded as equivalent to saying that Fielding fails to demonstrate what he considers to be the technique of 'the Art of Life'; in fact he succeeds in demonstrating this with great humanity and moving power. He would say that the ability of the Booths to love each other as ardently as they do and to confer so much happiness on each other in spite of all their troubles is proof that they are masters of the Art of Life; and that except for the disturbances due to the fact that Booth's misleading theories have sapped his moral energy, throughout the novel they do indeed experience genuine happiness. Apart from the temporary distresses caused by some of Booth's indiscretions, the two of them are 'richer . . . than millions of people who are in want of nothing' (III, x). For, as he puts it in *Tom Jones*, 'what happiness this world affords equal to the possession of such a woman as Sophia [or Amelia, for they are both modelled on the same much beloved Charlotte, his first wife], I sincerely own I have never yet discovered' (XVIII, xiii).

As for a gentleman achieving financial prosperity by his own endeavours without the powerful aid of Fortune, the philosophy of the gentleman culture and the realities of the gentleman oriented society, provided little scope for it, the opportunities for gainful employment which he could explore being so few.

If religion and consequently a strenuous moral struggle and a rejection of false philosophical theories are considered necessary for the regeneration of Booth, only prudence is required to keep Tom Jones straight. In several overt, deliberate statements in *Tom Jones* prudence is very strongly recommended. In the *Dedication* to the novel Fielding declares that his aim is 'to teach prudence and discretion' and in a sententious paragraph in the third book he proclaims:

> Goodness of heart and openness of temper ... will by no means, alas! do their business in the world. Prudence and circumspection are necessary even to the best of men. They are indeed as it were, a guard to Virtue, without which she can never be safe. (III, vii)

It is at once noticeable that Fielding refuses to call prudence a virtue; it is 'a guard' which is, 'alas', necessary in a malicious and envious world. He proceeds to compare prudence with 'the outward ornaments of decency and decorum', two qualities of which he almost always speaks pejoratively.

More often than not Fielding uses the term prudence with distaste, almost with aversion. His beloved characters are like Parson Adams, who is described as 'a character of perfect simplicity' (Author's Preface), and who is easily taken in by the wiles of others. Blifil, the odious hypocrite, is from a very young age 'a very prudent lad' (III, x). In order to persuade Sophia to marry Blifil, her aunt reads her what Fielding describes as 'lectures of Prudence' (VI, xiii), and gives her a 'discourse on the folly of love, and on the wisdom of legal prostitution for hire' (XVI, viii). On the other hand, Tom and Booth are a little too frank and ingenuous. The admirable Dr. Harrison has for years been deceived by another clergyman whom he considers a very good friend; if he is called 'wise' Harrison feels insulted. In *Tom Jones* Fielding says of himself: 'If we have not all the virtues, I will boldly say, neither have we all the vices of a prudent character' (XII, xiii). In *The Covent-Garden Journal* (no. 21), Fielding refers to Plato's remark that 'the just Man and the unjust Man are often reciprocally mistaken by Mankind, and do frequently pass in the World the one for the other', and explains that the reason for this is that 'the former are for the most Part Fools, and the latter are Men of Sense'. Several changes are rung on this theory in the novels.

In *Tom Jones,* in the chapter which is devoted to giving 'a Hint or two concerning Virtue, and a few more concerning Suspicion', a difference is sought to be established between 'two degrees' of suspicion. One arises 'from the head' and 'is indeed no other than the faculty of seeing what is before your eyes, and of drawing conclusions from what you see'. About the other, which 'always proceeds from a bad heart', Fielding says with revulsion : 'I cannot . . . help regarding this vast quicksightedness into evil, as a vicious excess, and as a very pernicious evil in itself' (XI, x). However, most of his good characters do not show either degree of suspicion. Allworthy cannot see 'what is before his eyes' and has no suspicion of Thwackum or Square, or of his sister, or of young Blifil, whom even the innocent Sophia suspects; Amelia does not suspect My Lord, who lavishes time and money on her; Tom has no suspicion of the real character of Molly or of Lady Bellaston; Adams 'never saw farther into people than they desired to let him' (II, x); the good Heartfree is absolutely incapable of suspecting anybody.

Because of this characteristic of his good people, Fielding frequently finds it necessary to defend them against the charge of dullness of intellect. Twice he has to defend Amelia; in defence of Allworthy's fine intelligence and 'true wisdom' he is compelled to speak out again and again. The reader listens, but is not always convinced.

It is true that some instances of Allworthy's credulity are necessary to advance the plot, and so Fielding is pushed into them; however, his theory about the gullibility of good men is to a large extent responsible for the failure in characterization which makes Allworthy seem so inadequate as a moral ideal. It is quite clear that he is meant to be the moral centre of the novel, and not a pompous or comically credulous character.[10] The first description of him as 'more glorious' than the rising sun in all its glory (I, iv) is meant to establish the reader's attitude towards him. Fielding seems genuinely to believe that the virtue of open-heartedness cannot be reconciled, except with great difficulty, and only at an advanced age, with prudence.

As it can be seen from the portrait of Blifil, Fielding saw a menacing power in hypocritical men to make good men suffer. Therefore, he wrote *Tom Jones* and *An Essay on the Knowledge of the Characters of Men* to recommend prudence, the 'guard to Virtue', selecting as the hero of his novel the young, openhearted Tom who responds spontaneously to the call of life. The ostensible scheme of the novel is to trace Tom's sufferings to his lack of prudence, and to show that in the course of the novel he has made some progress towards achieving it. Tom's disgust with himself at the thought of having received 'wages' from Lady Bellaston, and his horror at the thought that he has committed incest with his own mother, are designed to push him on the way to prudence. The novel ends with the announcement :

> He hath also, by reflexion on his past follies, acquired a discretion and prudence very common in one of his lively parts. (XVIII, xiii)

But this intended scheme does not receive spontaneous support from Fielding's imagination; there are many other qualities not easily reconcilable with prudence which are much dearer to his heart. Consequently, the general effect of the novel is to make the reader feel a certain antipathy towards prudence and prudent men.

It is necessary to emphasize that Tom is presented as a 'heroe' to be admired and loved, not merely, as some critics have averred, as a realistic portrait of a young man sowing his wild oats. Fielding emphosizes that this 'thoughtless, giddy youth' who 'would often very impudently and indecently laugh', especially at the prudent Blifil's 'decent reverence' towards his superiors (III, v), is a person whom the world ought to admire :

> These two characters [men like Tom and Blifil] are not always received in the world with the different regard which seems severally due to either ... the little respect which I have commonly seen paid to a character which really does great honour to human nature, and is productive of the highest good to society. But it was otherwise with Sophia. She honoured Tom Jones, and scorned Master

Blifil, almost as soon as she knew the meaning of those two words. (IV, v)

Tom possesses, what Blifil lacks—'that generosity of spirit, which is the sure foundation of all that is great and noble in human nature' (XII, x); and for this, Fielding is prepared to forgive faults or, to put it more correctly, he thinks that a man endowed with such 'generosity' is incapable of committing any fault which is really serious.

In fact in the final book of the novel, Fielding makes Tom sound a little too good. Testimony after testimony is given to emphasize his goodness during and soon after the Lady Bellaston episode. When Tom pleads with Allworthy for the villain Blifil who has injured him so cruelly, Mrs. Miller exclaims: 'You are too good, Mr. Jones, infinitely too good to live in this world'—a verdict which Allworthy supports by acknowledging: 'To what goodness have I been so blind ! ... I am equally astonished at the goodness of your heart, and the quickness of your understanding' (XVIII, xi).

It is such pronouncements, perhaps, which encouraged a critic like William Empson to become a little too solemn about Tom's goodness, and to distort the realism and kill the comedy of Fielding's presentation of a sensitive lad, who needs to be protected from his own naive youthfulness, overflowing energy and, even, from his undiscriminating goodness. Empson agrees that Tom needs to learn prudence, but avers in all seriousness:

... the chief idea about Tom Jones ... is that he is planned to become awestrikingly better during his brief experience of the world ... a real Gospel Christian, which is what Tom is turning into as we watch him ... But the end conveys something much more impressive than that these examiners [Allworthy and Sophia] give him a pass degree; he has become so much of a Gospel Christian that he cannot help but cast a shadow even on them ... and when Tom rises above Allworthy he is like a mountain.[11]

This lofty praise is inspired by two incidents in the novel— Tom's forgiveness of Black George when the fact of his having stolen money from him is revealed and Tom's charity towards the pathetic highwayman who threatens to shoot him with a pistol which is not even loaded, and who tells him a heart-rending tale of the hunger and illness of his family. According to Empson these incidents prove that Tom has understood 'the absolute command of Jesus to forgive', and Allworthy has not.

Mr. A.E. Dyson takes a stand similar to Empson's about 'real mercy' *versus* justice, and declares, 'Tom is actually more virtuous than Mr. Allworthy.' Mr. Dyson feels that Fielding's advocacy of 'prudence' for Tom is meant to be ironical; Tom 'always . . . is right about people', Allworthy 'disastrously wrong', because Tom's 'own lack of reputation frees him from convention'.[12]

This kind of estimate makes nonsense of Fielding's presentation of Tom and Allworthy, and of his declared intentions and plans concerning them. Further, it turns a blind eye to the numerous statements which Fielding in his various capacities as novelist, essayist and magistrate made on the subject of justice and the law.

The reasons why Tom takes on Lady Bellaston (to get access to Sophia through her), and the way he gets out of his predicament with her by the trick of proposing marriage, though quite understandable in his circumstances, are not quite in accordance with 'the absolute command of Jesus' about forgiveness, charity and truth. Moreover, there is no justification for Empson's phrase 'planned to become'. The generosity Tom shows at the end of the novel to Black George is no different from the generosity he shows as a child to this same Black George who silently allows him to be mercilessly beaten in order that his own error in trespassing on Western's grounds may remain hidden. In the final paragraphs of the novel Fielding tells the reader that Tom has still much to learn under the wholesome influence of Allworthy and Sophia, who are to 'correct' 'whatever in his nature . . . had a tendency to vice' (XVIII, xiii). In the context of the remarks of Empson and Dyson, it is necessary to study what Fielding has to say on the subject of forgiveness towards criminals. When Tom wants to allow Black George to go scot-free, Allworthy emphatically disagrees :

'. . . you carry this forgiving temper too far. Such mistaken mercy is not only weakness, but borders on injustice, and is

> very pernicious to society, as it encourages vice. The dishonesty of this fellow I might perhaps have pardoned ... but when dishonesty is attended with any blacker crime, such as cruelty, murder, ingratitude, or the like, compassion and forgiveness then become faults. (XVIII, xi)

This stand is much more liberal than the statements which Fielding makes in his own person elsewhere in his writings. Even in an essay on benevolence and good-nature itself, and one written quite early in his career, he declares: 'To be averse to, and repine at the punishment of vice and villainy, is not the mark of good-nature but folly' (*Works*, XV, 258). In *An Enquiry into the Causes of the Late Increase of Robbers* he severely chastises the mistaken kindness which refuses to prosecute criminals. Complete benevolence would, he says, do no harm in 'a society acting according to the rules of Christianity':

> But as it hath pleased God to permit human societies to be constituted in a different manner ... it becomes the good-natured and tender-hearted man ... to restrain the impetuosity of his benevolence ... For want of this wisdom ... notorious robbers have lived to perpetrate future acts of violence, through the ill judging tenderness and compassion of those who could and ought to have prosecuted them ... The desire to save these wolves in society may arise from benevolence; but it must be the benevolence of a child or a fool. (*Works*, XIII, 110-11)

Anyone who has read the above passage will realize why Fielding makes the wise and judicious Allworthy differ from Tom, or why he says about the kind Dr. Harrison:

> It was a maxim of his that no man could descend below himself in doing any act which may contribute to protect an innocent person or to bring a rogue to the gallows. (XII, vii)

In *An Enquiry* Fielding goes much further. At a time when young boys were sentenced to death for thefts of over one shilling, and there were 'one hundred and sixty offences of different degrees of heinousness'[13] for which the death penalty could be given, Fielding defended it, even for minor thefts.

It is true that especially in his earlier works, Fielding writes with moving irony about the harsh punishment meted out for petty theft. In *Joseph Andrews* we have the generous postillion who is the only person who will help the wounded and naked Joseph—'a lad who hath been since transported for robbing a hen-roost' (X, xii); in *The Journey from this World to the Next*, there is a striking moment when the spirit of a man who had been hung for stealing eighteen pence walks up to Minos 'in fear and trembling' and is readily admitted because he pleads :

That he had supported an aged parent, that he had been a tender husband and a kind father—and that he had ruined himself by being bail for his friend. (I, vii)

Nevertheless, early and late in his career Fielding felt it necessary to remind every gentleman, especially every country gentleman who was responsible for administering the law in the countryside, to act as he describes Allworthy acting, not only at the end of the novel, but also at the beginning when he is shown sitting on his 'seat of justice' (II, vi), and voicing the sentiments he reiterates at the end of the book. It could therefore be no part of Fielding's 'planned' purpose to show Tom rising in stature above Allworthy 'like a mountain', and symbolize this by Tom's forgiveness of Black George, or of the pathetic gentleman-turned-highwayman.

In leaning over backwards to defend Tom, critics like Empson and Middleton Murry have given another aspect of Fielding's ethical attitude a slight twentieth-century twist. Today the most widely accepted view about Tom's sexual irregularities is that Fielding presents them as the principal manifestation of Tom's extraordinarily generous, unselfish character. Fielding does link Tom's sexual adventures with his 'good-natured' character, his belief in people, and his tenderness for them. But Fielding certainly would not have used the phrasing now fashionable. Empson would like the term 'holy' for Tom's adventures with women: 'where he is most scandalous, one might instead find him holy, because he never makes love to a woman unless she first makes love to him.'[14] According to

Fielding Tom feels 'depreciated... in his own conceit' (XV, ix) for having accepted 'wages' from Lady Bellaston.

Of Tom's creator, Mr. Murry says, 'he believed that there was a generosity of the body.'[15] Most readers, however, would not find it difficult to realize how Fielding would have reacted if such 'generosity' had been recommended for Sophia or Amelia; he will not permit it even to Allworthy, about whom he goes out of his way to assert, 'this worthy man had never indulged himself in any loose pleasures with women, and greatly condemned the vice of incontinence in others' (IV, xi). It is not as if Fielding wants us to believe that Allworthy is a solemn or sanctimonious person; on the contrary, for he stresses that Allworthy 'had possessed much fire in his youth, and had married a beautiful woman for love' (VI, iv).

Fielding certainly would not want to conceal that Tom is of a very sensual nature, that he has 'the vices of a warm disposition' though he is 'entirely free from those of a cold one' (XII, xiii); that he has 'naturally violent animal spirits' (V, x). It is true that, as Murry puts it, in the case of Tom 'women make the running'. The brazen Molly certainly seduces him; the comment Fielding makes on the situation represents the eighteenth century attitude—Tom 'must have had very much, or very little of the heroe, if her endeavours had proved unsuccessful' (IV, vi). The generosity of Tom's disposition is certainly meant to give a different colour to his behaviour from that of the casual philandering of most men; Tom is not remotely like the rake who seeks pleasure at the cost of women. If he receives something from a person, he cannot help feeling tender and being generous towards that person.

Fielding's purpose in writing of Tom's peccadilloes was certainly to display the sweetness of Tom's disposition; but his purpose was also to show, in defiance of the Puritans, that many other vices, including certain kinds of chastity, are much worse than sexual incontinence, vice though that is. Thwackum, 'strictly chaste' and 'a great enemy to the opposite vice in all others' (V, x), is a far more vicious person than Tom. So is Blifil, whose 'appetites were by nature so moderate' (VI, iv) that there was no danger of his slipping into any forbidden pleasures. Fielding is revolted by people like Blifil who cannot respond to any other human being because their 'affections are solely placed' on themselves (IV, vi). Prudes Fielding detested and ridiculed. There is an illuminating scene in the early *Journey from This World to the Next* in which Fielding's slightly belligerent attitude towards sexual ethics is highlighted. A 'grave lady' steps up to seek entry into Elysium and is promptly rejected by Judge Minos who declares that there 'was not a single prude in Elysium'. Another spirit then steps forward thinking he will gain immediate welcome :

> He likewise represented the great animosity he had shown to vice in others. . .as to his own behaviour, he had never been once guilty of whoring, drinking, gluttony, or any other excess. He said, he had disinherited his son for getting a bastard—'Have you so', said Minos,.'then pray return into the other world and beget another; for such an unnatural rascal shall never pass this gate.'

Then the author himself steps up in trepidation :

> I confessed I had indulged myself very freely with wine and women in my youth, but had never done an injury to any man living, nor avoided an opportunity of doing good; that I pretended to very little virtue more than general philanthropy, and private friendship.—I was proceeding, when Minos bid me enter the gate, and not indulge myself with trumpeting forth my virtues. (I, vii)

In *Tom Jones* also Fielding shows something of this belligerent tendency to quarrel with accepted standards; nevertheless, it is not to be thought that Fielding was prepared to condemn all the prevailing ideas on the subject. The extremely well-written scene at the end in which Sophia and Tom have a little debate about sexual ethics is very instructive. Fielding has all along made it clear that Sophia can take in her stride a few youthful peccadilloes of a man like Tom. Even when the hunting-party of which she is a member, discovers Tom with Molly in the 'thickest part of the grove', Sophia returns home with him quite amicably, and cannot refrain from giving him 'tender looks' (VI, ii). Yet towards the end, when both Allworthy and Western plead with her to marry Tom, finding that he has been at it again in London, she feels, though she is still very much in love with him, that she must refuse, at least till time has given her proof that Tom has abandoned 'these vicious courses, which I should detest you, if I imagined you capable of persevering in'. To the good Mrs. Miller who has come to plead with her on behalf of Tom, Sophia expresses views which Fielding obviously shares, and wishes to make explicit:

> 'She says, she had forgiven many faults on account of youth; but expressed such detestation of the character of a libertine, that she absolutely silenced me...."I once fancied, madam," said she, "I had discovered great goodness of heart in Mr. Jones...but an entire profligacy of manners will corrupt the best heart in the world; and all which a good-natured libertine can expect is, that we should mix some grains of pity with our contempt and abhorrence." (XVIII, x)

A stricter, more Christian, point of view is put in the mouth of Allworthy and, at least once, expressed by Fielding himself. To Jenny Jones, who is brought before him as mother of the bastard Tom, Allworthy reads a kind but very solemn sermon on the 'heinous' nature of her offence against which 'the highest vengeance is specifically denounced' (I, vii). In the middle of the novel, Fielding himself becomes strangely ironical and sharp about a lapse which he has treated quite light-heartedly in the rest of the novel:

> Mr. Jones and his ragged companion had certain purposes in their intention, which, though tolerated in some Christian countries, connived at in others, and practised in all, are however as expressly forbidden as murder, or any other horrid vice, by that religion which is universally believed in those countries. (IX, iii)

Even if this statement is meant to be regarded only as an ironical reflection on the difference between what is professed and what is practised, the treatment of the question of illicit sexual relationships in *Amelia*, leaves no scope to suggest that Fielding's attitude is ironical. In his last novel sexual promiscuity is presented as an appalling and characteristic symptom of the social corruption which he portrays throughout that book with such fierce dismay. In *Amelia* (IX, v) and in the *Covent-Garden Journal* (no. 68) Fielding goes so far as to suggest that adultery, 'this atrocious vice', should be made a penal offence. Dr. Harrison's long letter on adultery, which is thrown among the dissipated revellers attending a masquerade, is the kind of writing one hardly expects to find in a novel, certainly not in one by an author who is prepared to applaud promiscuity, in Mr. Murry's phrase, as 'a generosity of the body':

> 'I need not tell you that adultery is forbid in the laws of the decalogue [and]...in the New Testament.... And sure in a human sense there is scarce any guilt which deserves to be more severely punished. It includes in it almost every injury and every mischief which one man can do to, or can bring on, another.... The ruin of both wife and husband, and sometimes of the whole family, are the probable consequence of this fatal injury. Domestic happiness is the end of almost all our pursuits.... When men find themselves for ever barred from this delightful fruition, they are lost to all industry, and grow careless of all their worldly affairs. Thus they become bad subjects, bad relations, bad friends, and bad men. Hatred and revenge are the wretched passions which boil in their minds. Despair and madness very commonly ensue, and murder and suicide often close the dreadful scene.' (X, ii)

Even more startling is the one and a half page address by the author to his 'young readers' about the power of beauty:

> I am firmly persuaded that to withdraw admiration from exquisite beauty, or to feel no delight in gazing at it, is as impossible as to feel no warmth from the most scorching rays of the sun... To run away is all that is in our power... Since of all passions there is none against which we should so strongly fortify ourselves as this, which is generally called love...[It] sprouts usually up in the richest and noblest minds; but there, unless nicely watched, pruned, and cultivated, and carefully kept clear of those vicious weeds which

are too apt to surround it, it...chokes up and kills whatever is good and noble in the mind where it so abounds. (VI, i)

These direct addresses and letters, and the revolting portraits of unscrupulous philanderers and their panders make the sexual adventurism of this novel very different from that of *Tom Jones*. In *Amelia*, sexual appetite divorced from marital love is represented as repelling and menacing. If Booth's lapse is so casually accepted by Amelia and so readily forgiven, it is not because it is regarded as lightly as Tom's conduct, but because Amelia is that kind of noble and generously forgiving woman, and because living in a degenerate society she is accustomed to look upon such lapses as only too common. It certainly makes Booth 'the most wretched of human beings' (IV, v) and brings a heap of troubles on both of them.

A severe indictment of 'gallantry', the sport so popular among gentlemen, is found in two articles in *The Covent-Garden Journal* published in the same year as *Amelia*. Very instructive is what Fielding has to say about novelists who describe it light-heartedly, or with approval:

Yet certain it is, that thro the Prevalence of Custom, the Ruin of a Woman is far from being regarded...with that Abhorrence and Detestation which it deserves...nay, I am deceived if, instead of being considered on the Man's Side as a Mark of Disgrace, it is not sometimes treated as a Point of Honour... The reason of this, in a great Measure, is the Levity with which this Matter hath been handled by some of our fashionable Authors...tho' many of my gay Readers...have a Vanity in desiring to be thought no Christians, they will at least be ashamed of being no Gentlemen...First then, can any thing be more dishonourable than to engage in a Combat with one who is greatly inferior in Strength...In the last Place...let me apply to the humanity of these Gallants; and this the rather as the Latins often use the Word Humanitas for the chief Qualifications of a Gentleman. (no. 20)

It must be remembered that even in *Tom Jones*, though it brought down so much wrath on Fielding's head, his attitude to promiscuous sex is not only far more thoughtful, but far more strict, than that of most sophisticated aristocrats or rumbustious country squires. Fielding represents the opinion and habits of the contemporary country gentlemen very vividly through the mouth of Squire Western. Advised by the sanctimonious Thwackum to 'put the laws in execution' and 'rid the country of these vermin' (vermin like Molly who is found in the bushes with Tom), the hunting squire, who can think of no greater misery than an England without foxes, retorts:

> I would as soon rid the country of foxes...I think we ought to encourage the recruiting those numbers which we are every day losing in the war. (V, vii)

Poor Parson Supple, if he murmurs a protest, is immediately told off:

> 'Why sorry', cries the squire, 'where is the mighty matter o't? What, I suppose, dost pretend that thee hast never got a bastard? Pox! more good luck's thine: for I warrant hast a done *therefore* many's the good time and often.' (IV, x)

Casual amours were a part of life for the elegant aristocrat in high society, and for the middling gentleman—author, lawyer, or coffee-house-gaming-table frequenter—in London and the popular spas. Fashionable mistresses and their illegitimate offspring were everywhere in high circles. The best proof of his love that the weeping George the Second could give his long-suffering queen, when on her death-bed she urged him to marry again, was to blubber out: 'Non, non, j'aurai des maitresses.' Robert Walpole used his position as head of the ministry to have his illegitimate daughter declared legitimate, and to get a title for her.[16] Boswell picked up many a casual amour on his journeys between Scotland and London, and provided £10 a year for the maintenance of his illegitimate son—for Boswell had succeeded in evolving a theory about the 'harmlessness of temporary likings unconnected with mental attachment'.[17]

It was the moral situation of this society that Fielding was reflecting and combating. In the earlier novel he accomplishes this through the technique of comedy and irony, and with undoubtedly a light-hearted attitude towards sexual peccadilloes, especially of the kind which do not involve, in his phrase, 'the Ruin of a Woman'. In *Amelia* his moral attitude has become incomparably more stiff, as well as more Christian; some would say, his moral arteries have hardened.

However, even in *Tom Jones*, particularly in the final books, Fielding makes an obvious effort to impress upon the reader that Tom has been severely punished for his 'imprudence' and 'vice'. Halfway through the novel he begins to talk of Tom's 'offences, which as is the nature of vice, brought sufficient punishment upon him themselves' (XI, x). He wants the reader to believe that Tom, having been thrown into jail where he is tormented by the thought that he has probably killed the man whom he fought in a duel, and by the horror of the news that he has committed incest with his mother, has suffered so much that 'it would be difficult for the devil to have contrived much greater torments for poor Jones' (XVII, i). That Fielding does not convey the effects of this punishment with genuine pathos, or with a sense of the inexorable consequences of man's conduct, is partly a deliberate effect of his general 'comic' intention, and partly a failure due to his undramatic, external approach to characterization. Tom's suffering is certainly not presented very convincingly, and readers, even in our century, who would like him to be punished are exasperated. Here is Ford Madox Ford thoroughly outraged :

But the high mission of the novelist...is so to draw life that from [his] pages the public may learn at least that life is first of all governed by cause and effect—that if you are lousy, and I use the word on purpose, you will live like a louse and, if there is a hell, go to hell. And what other word could describe Tom Jones—the miserable parasite who was forever wreathed, whining about his benefactor's knees, whose one idea of supporting himself was to borrow money simultaneously from his heart's adored and two mistresses...We gather from it no belief at all that merely by listening to the pious conversation of Mr. Allworthy... he would be converted from a rather crawling rake to a finely erect specimen of *homo sapiens Europaeus*... and 'the best of husbands'.[18]

Such a statement is so extreme that no reader will be influenced by it. It is not Fielding's detractors, it is his defenders, who undermine his stature, both as moralist and creative writer. The solemn disquisitions on Fielding's ideas of sexual morality, the pother about 'holiness', the disproportionate emphasis on Christian beliefs and allegories in his novels, make us lose sight of the writer who claimed that his purpose was 'to laugh mankind out of their favourite follies and vices' (*TJ*, Dedication) and selected 'affectation' as the chief subject of this laughter (*JA*, Author's Preface), of the writer who was always quick to perceive the gap between ideals and action even in his good and beloved characters.

Fielding's treatment of the theme of chastity, for instance, cannot be judged without giving far more importance than is given these days to the great comic scenes in which Tom's major lapses are depicted. Typical is the scene (IX, v) which shows the seduction of Tom by Mrs. Waters—a masterly scene, learned and sophisticated in style and characterization, but hugely hilarious. Similarly, in the scene of Tom's second adventure with Molly (V, x-xi), if due weight (and a great deal is due) is not given to the comic and ironical effects achieved by Fielding's expertise in the mock-heroic technique, one gets a quite distorted picture of Fielding's approach to art and life, to characterization and morality. In such passages the technique and tone are as relevant to the moral intention as in the satires of Pope and Swift. If under the critic's hands this technique is metamorphosed into, 'his prose is like an archangel brooding over mankind'; if 'the tone of the book' starts 'glowing with the noble beauty of its gospel, which Fielding indeed would be prepared to claim as the original Gospel',[19] one is constrained to say, however, distinguished the critic, that the distance between such interpretations and Fielding's own intentions, is scarcely less comic than the distance between Tom's sublime heroics about his love for Sophia and his fall down to earth in 'the thickest part of the grove' into Molly Seagrim's very earthy lap 'bedewed likewise with some odoriferous effluvia' (V, x).

A writer who relishes the ironies of life as much as Fielding, cannot help turning a critical eye on his 'heroe', as on everybody else. The characterization of Tom is an imaginative, honest presentation of a 'good-natured' boy in all his boyishness; a boy who is endearing because he is affectionate and spontaneous, but who needs loving protection and guidance because he has as yet much to learn from life. The boy is appealing because he is full of vitality and good-humour; he is amusing, because he so often vows 'eternal constancy' (X, vii) to his girl, and so often slips into constancy only to his own weakness. He will grow up and settle down into a generous, amiable, cultured but unaffected country gentleman.

It is thus Fielding visualizes Tom's future; but for this, he will have to be the 'favourite of fortune'; thrown into Booth's circumstances, as these circumstances are till the end of the novel, he would act like Booth. The character of both heroes is in essentials the same; given at least some degree of financial prosperity and a good wife, they will be very amiable and worthy examples of the 'good-natured' gentleman. Their love for their family, and their family's love for them, will keep them steady; their feeling for humanity will keep them sensitive, spirited and tolerant, responsive to the needs of their tenants, neighbours and country. For his heroes Fielding visualizes a way of life not exalted, heroic or 'holy', but practical, attainable and domestic.

Like many representative writers of his time, Fielding steps back from 'enthusiasm' of all kinds; from the fervour both of religion and of heroism, from the cold light of reason, as well as from the hot fumes of metaphysics; and turning his back on 'greatness', ambition and sophistication, retreats to the homely, the amiable and the humane.

Through the two decades of his writing life, Fielding kept challenging the idea of 'greatness'. From 1731 when he wrote *The Life and Death of Tom Thumb the Great,* to 1742 with *The Life of Mr. Jonathan Wild the Great* and the *Adventures* of the footman Joseph Andrews and 'his friend', the simple, uncouth Mr. Abraham Adams, on to 1752 when he gave the famous definitions in 'The Modern Glossary' and wrote his last novel, *Amelia,* selecting the humble Sergeant Atkinson, the brusque Dr. Harrison, and the ineffectual Booth as the principal characters, Fielding continued to explore the worth of greatness, placing it in antithesis to goodness.

At one point in the *Preface to The Miscellanies* (containing among other works *Jonathan Wild*), Fielding does state that 'the true sublime in human nature' is a synthesis of greatness and goodness. According to him this is a rare combination, scarcely ever achieved; but here he suggests that it could nevertheless be pursued as an ideal, there being not 'any absolute repugnance among them [greatness and goodness]' (*Works*, XII, 245). However, in *Jonathan Wild* he states :

> Mankind......confound the ideas of greatness and goodness; whereas no two things can possibly be more distinct from each other, for greatness consists in bringing all manner of mischief on mankind, and goodness in removing it from them. It seems therefore very unlikely that the same person should possess them both. (I, i)

A devastating definition of 'Great' is given in 'The Modern Glossary' in which the author has 'endeavour[ed] to fix to each [word] the exact ideas which are annexed to every one of them in the World':

> GREAT: Applied to a Thing, signifies Bigness; when to a Man, often Littleness, or Meanness (*Works*, I, 154-6)

The sustained irony of *Jonathan Wild* stems from the idea succinctly expressed in its third book : 'What a wolf is in a sheepfold, a great man is in society' (III, iii). With greatness Fielding associates selfishness, rapacity, cruelty, hypocrisy and insatiable, ruthless ambition. In the world of the great, 'Worth' is equated with 'Power, Rank, Wealth' and 'Wisdom' with 'the Art of acquiring all [the above] three.' The terms 'Virtue' and 'Vice' stand for 'Subjects of Discourse' and the word 'Fool' is 'a complex idea compounded of Poverty, Honesty, Piety, and Simplicity'. As in Goldsmith and the later sentimentalists, poverty and 'obscurity' tend to be equated with honesty; 'simplicity' of manners, and, it would seem, even of the understanding, is placed against 'refinement'. The beloved character, Parson Adams, is 'as entirely ignorant of the ways of this world as an infant just entered into it could possibly be' (I, iii). From Adams's comical yet glorious inability to contend with the worldliness of the world, the novel of which he is the hero derives its humour, which, rumbustious and genial though it is, casts dark critical shadows on the selfishness and wickedness of society. In a world where all is policy and polished manners, where language and virtue are interpreted according to the meanings of the 'Modern Glossary', such a figure will be found to be odd and eccentric; or, perhaps, only those who do not mind seeming uncouth and ridiculous and quixotic can remain unsullied.

Fielding's ironic insistence on the qualities that great men must develop is so similar to Lord Chesterfield's advice to his son whom he wanted to shape into a great man that one would take it to be a conscious parody, if one did not remember that the letters, though the most characteristic of them were already written, were not published till 1774.[20] The hypocritical old gentleman who pretends to be Dr. Harrison's friend says:

> If thou art wise, thou wilt think every man thy superior of whom thou canst get anything; at least thou wilt persuade him that thou thinkest so, and that is sufficient. Tom, Tom, thou hast no policy in thee. (IX, ix)

Among the several maxims that Jonathan Wild lays down 'as the certain methods of attaining greatness', one is: 'that the heart was the proper seat of hatred, and the countenance of affection and friendship' (III, xv). Put this beside Chesterfield who told his son Philip that a man of the world 'must be able to accost and receive with smiles, those whom he would much rather meet with swords' (*Letters*, 30 April 1752).

To the subject of the good-breeding which gave the great this 'command of the countenance' Fielding returned again and again, drawing a distinction between its 'natural' and 'artificial' varieties. In the *Essay of Conversation* where he selects the Earl of Chesterfield as its best exponent he describes it as 'artificial good nature', though near allied to that great Quality (*Works*, XIV, 249-51). In *The Covent-Garden Journal* he says:

> I have not room at present, if I were able, to enumerate the Rules of good Breeding: I shall only mention one, which is a Summary of them all. This is the most golden

of all Rules, no less than that of doing to all Men as you would they should do unto you . . . Here, however, my Readers will be pleased to observe that the subject Matter of good Breeding being only what is called Behaviour, it is this only to which we are to apply it on the present Occasion, perhaps therefore we shall be better understood if we vary the Word and read it thus: Behave unto all Men as you would they should behave unto you. (*Works*, II, 63-4)

Some commentators choose to read only the first half of this statement, so that Fielding's definition of good-breeding is represented as implying Christian action,[21] whereas he merely gives it the meaning it had in common parlance—smooth, considerate behaviour.

Of course Fielding at all times preferred natural good-breeding to its over-sophisticated aspects. Tom Jones 'had natural, but not artificial good breeding' (XIII, iv). Tom, 'though he had never seen a court was better bred than most who frequent it' (XIII, ii), but he does not have the aplomb of the 'polite', which enables them brazenly to carry off any situation. Thrown into the company of Lady Bellaston and Sophia both together, Tom behaves most awkwardly. Of Sophia we are told:

Sophia was perfectly well bred, though perhaps she wanted a little of that ease in her behaviour which is to be acquired only by habit, and living within what is called the polite circle. But this, to say the truth, is often too dearly purchased . . . its absence is well compensated by innocence; nor can good sense, and a natural gentility, ever stand in need of it. (IV, ii)

Not unrelated to this idea of good-breeding is Fielding's repeated satire on his century's habit of branding all that was not sophisticated as 'low'. It was customary for the supposedly 'polite' to sniff at scenes of domestic happiness, sincere and warm affection and homely pleasures. Fielding himself had to fight a bitter and unsuccessful battle against critics who found *Amelia* too 'low' for their tastes.

The delight he took in idiosyncrasy made Fielding almost lament the tendency of an education in good-breeding to destroy 'humourous' individuality. Men like Fielding and his beloved Hogarth placed a value on eccentricity; for them it enriched literature and art, and gave zest to life. Fielding found 'high life' not only hypocritical but also dull. In *The Covent-Garden Journal* essay on humour there is a little sadness in his tone as he points out :

> For indeed good Breeding is little more than the Art of rooting out all those Seeds of Humour which Nature had originally implanted in our Minds . . . Being the Art of conducting yourself by certain common and general Rules, by which Means, if they were universally observed, the whole World would appear (as all Courtiers actually do) to be, in their external Behaviour at least, but one and the same Person. (*Works*, II, 60-65)

Here we approach that hankering after the 'natural' and primitive, which becomes a prominent tendency in the literature of the second half of this century. Fielding's distaste for the artificial good-breeding of high society does not lead him quite to the point of idealizing the Noble Savage (though even this has been attributed to him)[22] but it makes him, like many other writers of the period, gravitate towards the ideal of the unambitious, uneventful, rural life of the country gentleman. The superiority of this way of life is asserted consistently in all his three novels. The good gentleman, Mr. Wilson, who is discovered to be Joseph Andrew's father, having 'sufficiently seen that the pleasures of the world are chiefly folly, and the business of it mostly knavery', has lived with his family almost twenty years in the country 'with little other conversation than our own'. From this happy, peaceful house, Parson Adams 'departed, declaring that this was the manner in which the people had lived in the golden age' (III, iii-iv). Squire Allworthy has 'not been absent a month at a time during the space of many years' from his country seat (I, iii). 'Mr. Jones and Sophia . . . within two days of their marriage, attended Mr. Western and Mr. Allworthy into the country' and presumably stayed there ever after, showing 'their condescension, their indulgence, and their beneficence to those below them' (XVIII, xiii). After the adventures described in *Amelia*, Lieutenant Booth, apart from one trip to London to pay his debts, 'returned into the country, and hath never since been thirty miles from home', though years have now gone by in this idyllic 'serenity' (XII, ix). Since such idealization of the simple, country life was so prominent a trend, it is worthwhile listening to what the other side has to say:

> Whether for the better or the worse, no matter; but we are refined; and plain manners, plain dress, and plain diction, would as little do in life, as acorns, herbage and the water of the neighbouring spring, would do on the table... Let them show me a cottage, where there are not the same vices of which they accuse the Courts; with this difference only, that in a cottage they appear in their native deformity, and that in Courts, manners and good breeding make them less shocking and blunt their edge. (Chesterfield, *Letters*, 20 Nov 1753, 6 June 1751)

Fielding did not fail to see vices in cottage and country, but he seemed to prefer them in their crude form, rather than have their poison disguised by the hypocrisy of high life.

In fact Fielding's portrayal of 'good' characters and his ethical attitudes towards the antitheses between greatness and goodness, prudence and innocence, sophistication and rough good nature, cannot escape the charge of banality as well as crudity. His attitude, which he shared with other representative writers, is quite understandable as a reaction to an age when the sophistication of the intellect and of manners had been carried to an extreme; but a new form of exaggeration was soon to become fashionable—a consciously cultivated simplicity and innocence and softness of heart, smacking as much of artifice and insincerity as the sophistication against which it reacted.

Fortunately Fielding's irony, shrewdness and virile robustness save him from many of the pitfalls of sentimentalism. Fortunately, once again, by the time he wrote *Tom Jones*, and more so when he wrote *Amelia*, he had got over the rumbustious, facetious technique of *Joseph Andrews*. The hog's blood and the contents of chamber-pots which with great zest he allows to be flung at his comic, but nevertheless idealized and beloved, representative of innocence and charity cannot be said to add, either artistically or morally, to the value of even a 'comic epic poem in prose'. Sometimes one cannot help wishing, as Leslie Stephen did, that Fielding 'had a nose and eyes capable of feeling offence'.[23]

Again, somewhat banal, and a trifle crudely presented, is the ideal of charity that Fielding prescribes in *Joseph Andrews*. Adam's blithe expectations that in a Christian country no man will refuse money to a fellow-creature in need are meant to display, through comedy, his naive innocence; but they are also meant to serve as serious social criticism, indicting the selfishness and cruelty of the world. Yet, in a characteristic scene (II, xiii-xv), we are shown the absent-minded, but jovial, hearty parson pouring in an 'immense quantity of ale' into his vigorous, athletic body, forgetting he has no money in his pocket. Finding himself unable to settle the innkeeper's bill of seven shillings, he wanders about 'lamenting and groaning' that there is no Christian charity left in the world, till he meets a poor pedlar, who has 'no more than six shillings and sixpence in his pocket', but who willingly offers to lend it all to him At this, 'Adams gave a caper, and cried out, It would do; for that he had sixpence himself'. Upon this Fielding comments :

> And thus these poor people, who could not engage the compassion of riches and piety, were at length delivered out of their distress by the charity of a poor pedlar.

Of course, no one will deny that Fielding succeeds in portraying in Adams a character who is indeed very delightful; comic, yet appealing and lovable; nor will any one deny that Fielding is able to invest his ideal parson with some truly admirable virtues. Fielding's mastery of that comic method which enables a writer to criticize yet idealize a character, to eat his cake and yet have it, is undeniable. Unlike Allworthy or Harrison, Adams is of course not presented as an ideal person to be imitated, but is created for the mirth and laughter his character arouses, and the suggestions and shadows it casts on the human situation. Yet, as a human being, he is in many ways Fielding's ideal; a person who is most endearing because of the warmth and sweetness of his temper; and one who is worthy of the highest respect because, in spite of all his comical characteristics, he has genuine courage and dignity.

Poverty and injustice have not soured Adams's spirits, and his enjoyment of life is communicated with a zest that is infectious. This was the most impressive trait in Fielding's own character. The energy and relish with which he could taste the pleasures of life and fight its injustice, even when he knew he was fast dying of a painful and debilitating disease, make the reading of *A Journal of a Voyage to Lisbon* a moving, but most heartening experience. It is this trait which Adams shares with his creator, who obviously loved him and took great delight in depicting him.

Perhaps Adams's most endearing and admirable quality is his ability to identify himself with the joys and sorrows of others. When his friends are fortunate and happy, the true charity of his disposition—the ability to feel for every man as one would feel for oneself—displays itself in its most agreeable and admirable form. When his friends receive good news, we see him dancing and capering about the room feeling their joy as it were his own. Most of us have charity enough to offer some sympathetic comfort to others in their sorrow; but few have enough charity to be actively happy in the happiness of others. It is this characteristic of Adams that makes concretely alive the very fine definition of Charity which Fielding gives in the early *Champion* essay : 'It weighs all mankind in the scales of friendship and sees them with the eyes of love' (*Works*, XV, 272).

In Fielding's opinion charity was the highest and most indispensable of the virtues. The importance he attached to it is summed up in Minos's stern announcement at the entrance of Elysium : 'No man enters this gate without Charity' (I, vii). In the characterization of both his ideal gentlemen, Allworthy and Dr. Harrison, charity, not only in the sense of giving alms, but of brotherly love and forgiveness, finds an important place.

Fielding shows the true magnanimity of Allworthy's temper not only by making him give money freely to the unfortunate, but also by frequently laying stress on his great tolerance, his refusal to allow any scandal-mongering at his table, and his unwillingness to condemn anyone without thoroughly examining his case. One of Allworthy's best described qualities is his 'overlooking disposition':

> Men of true wisdom and goodness... can see a fault in a friend, a relation, or an acquaintance, without ever mentioning it to the parties themselves, or to any others; and this often without lessening their affection. Indeed, unless great discernment be tempered with this overlooking disposition, we ought never to contract friendship but with a degree of folly which we can deceive... Forgiveness, of this kind, we give and demand in turn. It is an exercise of friendship, and perhaps, none of the least pleasant. And this forgiveness we must bestow, without desire of amendment. There is, perhaps, no surer mark of folly, than an attempt to correct the natural infirmities of those we love. (II, vii)

For Fielding charity, or as he preferred to call it, 'good-nature', not only covereth a multitude of sins, it makes ample amends for the absence of many a more dazzling quality. Fielding has no revolutionary ethical system to propagate. The 'great, secret, and uncommon doctrine' that he propounds is 'secret' only because men turn their eyes away from it, 'uncommon' only because in their blindness they refuse to practise it. He writes in the cause of the obvious truisms of morality, propounding the widely-diffused ideas of his day, of Christian ethics and of traditional philosophy. Again and again one will find him pointing out, and quite often without any attempt at subtlety, that the wicked man will find no repose, that there is no happiness except in the comfort of a good conscience.[24] The qualities which all men recognize as virtues—liberality, gratitude, sympathy, constancy, modesty, integrity—are the qualities which Fielding repeatedly recommends as the touchstones by which to test the worth of a human being. The virtues which Fielding's ideal gentleman must cultivate are the virtues preached by moralists in all ages—courage, to face the injustice of men and the vagaries of fortune; equanimity, to endure adversity and to bear prosperity 'without any violent transport' (*TJ*, V, vii, *Amelia*, XII, viii); moderation, 'justly to weigh the worth of all things' (*Jonathan Wild*, III, ii), so as not to be tempted 'to buy at too dear a price' the goods in 'the grand market of the world'—honours, riches, pleasure (*TJ*, VI, iii). To Fielding, there is nothing so appealing as 'the loveliness of an affable deportment' (IX, iii); and nothing 'more glorious' than 'a human being replete with benevolence, meditating in what manner he might render himself most acceptable to his Creator, by doing most good to His creatures' (*TJ*, I, iv). After all there are not many new ethical principles to be discovered more important than those which have been already taught:

[principles of which] no man who understands what it is to love, and to bless, and to do good, can mistake the meaning ... If thine enemy hunger, feed him; if he thirst, give him drink; not rendering evil for evil, or railing for railing, but contrariwise, blessing. (*Amelia*, XI, viii)

Nor are Fielding's ideas on the position of women any different from the ideas of his day. The model gentleman, Allworthy, says of the model lady, Sophia:

'Whenever I have seen her in the company of men, she hath been all attention, with the modesty of a learner, not the forwardness of a teacher ... Indeed, she has always showed the highest deference to the understandings of men; a quality absolutely essential to the making of a good wife.' (XVII, iii)

The advances in science which many of his contemporaries greeted with enthusiasm and excitement, Fielding looked upon with disfavour. He would have felt no hesitation in endorsing what Johnson declared so vehemently:

We are perpetually moralists, but we are geometricians only by chance ... the innovators whom I oppose are turning off attention from life to nature. They seem to think, that we are placed here to watch the growth of plants, or the motions of the stars. Socrates was rather of opinion, that what we had to learn was, how to do good, and avoid evil. (*Life of Milton, Works*, VII, 76)

To the traditional classical and philosophical scholarship, which according to both writers, teaches this science of 'how to do good and avoid evil', Fielding gave as much importance as Johnson. He takes care to emphasize that even Tom and Booth are learned, cultured men (*TJ*, VIII, ix; *Amelia*, VII, v). He himself had 'acquired the largest working library possessed by any man of letters in the eighteenth century, surpassing even Dr. Johnson's'.[25]

Like the traditional teachers, Fielding sees no happiness in 'greatness'; in the life of ambition, power and fame; with them he agrees that happiness is to be found only in contentment and a cheerful disposition; for the wise man has 'discerned, as it were through a microscope (for it is invisible to the naked eye), that diminutive speck of happiness which they [the great] attain even in the consummation of their wishes' (*Jonathan Wild*, I, xiv). The best blessing that Fielding can think of for his readers is :

... to be possessed of this sanguine disposition of mind : since, after having read much, and considered long on that subject of happiness ... I am most inclined to fix it in the possession of this temper. (*TJ*, XIII, vi)

Such then is the considered advice of a man who, as his aristocratic cousin said, 'was framed for happiness' (*Letters and Works*, III, 122). The wise reader will take it, unrevolutionary though it is.

6 Angry Young Gentlemen and 'A Most Risible Misanthrope'

TOBIAS SMOLLETT

I laid claim to the character of a gentleman, by birth, education, and behaviour, but...
...those rotten parts of human nature, which now appear so offensively to my observation... every where we find food for spleen, and subject for ridicule.
Then I launched out into the praises of a country life, as described by the poets whose works I had read.[1]

The three quotations from Smollett's novels placed at the head of this chapter, are in a manner a résumé of the estimate that will be made here of Smollett's idea of the gentleman.

Roderick Random and Peregrine Pickle, the two young heroes who settle down in 'perfect felicity' as country gentlemen on large, prosperous estates at the conclusion of Smollett's first two novels, are regarded by almost every reader as unpleasant persons. Earlier critics were generally agreed that Smollett himself was complacently indulgent towards many reprehensible traits of character in his young gentlemen and therefore did not hesitate to charge Smollett with a certain degree of moral insensibility. In recent years, several critics[2], approaching Smollett from a variety of critical standpoints, have sought to explain away the unpleasantness of Smollett's young gentlemen in such a way that the novelist's own moral perception is exonerated, or even vindicated as being sensitive and profound.

The following discussion attempts to show that if the reader of Smollett's first two novels is left with a distinctly unsatisfactory feeling with regard to the characterization of the heroes, it is not, as it has been suggested, because they are unpleasant or unbalanced persons whom the writer intends to present as such, nor is it merely because of a technical failure due to the novelist's choice of an unsuitable medium for satire. It is because Smollett antagonizes his readers who find themselves unable to agree with the moral appraisal that he makes of the character and behaviour of his young 'gentlemen'. *Ferdinand Count Fathom*, in many ways a much inferior novel, is less antagonizing, because in that work Smollett does not attempt, as in the case of Roderick and Peregrine 'to secure a favourable prepossession' (*RR*, Preface) for characters who are quite uningratiating.

It is not as if Smollett wishes to depict characters from an amoral point of view, or to depict only those characters whom he can satirize. In this matter he differs radically from the traditional picaresque writers to whom he owes his inspiration. A characteristic picaresque tale is a realistic story of the adventures of an underprivileged lad trying to survive as best he can in a world which has little concern for him. The tone of the picaresque tale is generally amoral, and the episodes in which the picaro's struggle for survival is demonstrated are devised mainly for their entertainment or sensational value. In the Preface to *Roderick Random*, Smollett himself points out that, though he admired the picaresque writers, especially Le Sage, and had 'modelled' himself on them, for both aesthetic and moral reasons he considered it very important to make crucial modifications in the picaresque form, particularly in the character and situation of the protagonist. To Smollett the moral function of his writing was fiercely important. He was possessed by an almost frenzied desire to expose 'the sordid and vicious disposition of the world' in order to provoke the reader to be 'indignant' about it. He tells us that he decided that this would be possible only if the hero of the novel was able 'to secure a favourable prepossession'; if he was satirized and became an object of 'mirth' instead of an object of 'compassion', the purpose of the novelist would be defeated. Smollett then proceeds to point out that such a hero must belong to a particular social class in order to engage the sympathy of the reader. Quite unlike the picaro, he must not be a low-born waif brought up on the streets; it is 'the dignity of his birth and character' that according to his creator, makes Roderick a suitable protagonist for a novel. Because of this belief Roderick is made to hail from a very old and well-established Scottish gentry family; at the end he is rehabilitated and restored to his rightful position of a prosperous country gentleman. Peregrine's lineage, though not very ancient, is backed by an uncommonly large fortune. He receives the traditional education of the gentleman (and of the kind that only the wealthiest among them could afford)— Winchester, Oxford and grand tour accompanied by tutor, valet and foot-man. He is certainly not compelled to be nasty in response to the helplessness and nastiness of his circumstances, as the traditional picaro is.

In Smollett's opinion, Roderick and Perry, with all their defects, are much above the common run of men, in mental as well as moral calibre. No moral faults at all are to be ascribed to Roderick; his mistakes and frustrations are to be attributed to his 'want of experience' (Preface) and to the 'iniquity of mankind' (I, xxi). Peregrine is presented as more blameworthy than Roderick, but even his faults are judged to be venial in comparison with his many fine qualities; moreover, by the end of the novel he is supposed to have turned into a wise and admirable gentleman, whom the reader can look upon as justly 'restored to his rightful inheritance, and re-established in that station of life which...he could fill with dignity and importance' (II, civ). The principal characteristic of Perry's nature, his pride, is both deplored and admired. It leads him to 'vanity', which is satirized, but gives him stature and a spirit of independence, which is praised. When he is thrown into prison for debt, this trait manifests itself in a 'savage obstinacy and pride' (II, ci); then he refuses, with an inexcusable fury and sullenness, even the most friendly offers of help from his friends and faithful servants. At this juncture, Smollett laments Perry's conduct, and yet he sympathises with it, attributing it to a sturdy independence which, not without some excuse, manifests itself in insolently proud behaviour and in a sullen hatred of all mankind.

The attitude that Smollett adopts towards his two heroes is indeed not surprising, for in the characterization of both, he is to a large extent drawing a self-portrait. In the dedicatory epistle to *Ferdinand Count Fathom* addressed to Dr.—, by whom he is generally recognized to have meant himself, Smollett attempted an analysis of his own temperament and behaviour. It has a striking resemblance to his analysis of Perry and, to a certain extent, of Roderick.

> Know, then, I can despise your pride, while I honour your integrity; and applaud your taste, while I am shocked at your ostentation. I have known you trifling, superficial and obstinate in dispute; meanly jealous, and awkwardly reserved : rash and haughty in your resentments: and coarse and lowly in your connections. . . . Yet as I own you possess certain good qualities, which overbalance these defects . . .and as they are chiefly the excesses of a sanguine disposition and looseness of thought, impatient of caution or control, you may thus stimulated, watch over your own intemperance and infirmity with redoubled vigilance. . .

The character analysis shows considerable self-knowledge and self-criticism; like many other people, Smollett could see his faults, and yet also cherish them.

Much of Smollett's own temperament is reflected in the irascibility and petulance of Roderick's and Perry's behaviour. Pugnaciousness is a trait which Smollett himself could not quite get over till the end of his life, as his *Travels* make only too obvious. Not only does he show without any disapproval Roderick and Perry exercising their horse-whips 'with such agility about the. . . face' (*PP*, I, xxviii) of anyone who provokes them, but even in the novel written during his last years, he shows the much more endearing and mature character, Matthew Bramble, running on his gouty legs to belabour two negro retainers of a neighbouring lodger who are disturbing him by playing upon the French-horn.

Smollett almost commends the emotions of anger, envy, resentment and revenge. An extreme sense of 'mortification' is invariably felt by the injured ego of his gentlemen, if they are crossed even in matters of not very great importance. He seems to look upon these emotions as spurs, just as necessary to the preservation and continuity of life as the instincts of fear and sex. 'Resentment' is described as the principal feeling that enables Roderick to cling to life. In a letter Smollett speaks in a similar strain about himself—'stupefied with ill-health, loss of memory, confinement and solitude', he is able to keep alive only because of the 'stings' of the malice of his 'grub street friends' (to Dr. W. Hunter, 24 Feb 1767).

Smollett gives hardly any importance to that conquest of the passions which found so important a place in eighteenth century thought. Not by controlling the passions, but only by pitting one violent passion against another equally violent, does man find it possible to persist in the struggle for life. In a characteristic Smollett passage Perry consoles himself in these words:

> If I must be a prisoner for life... let me at least have the satisfaction of clanking my chains so as to interrupt the repose of my adversary; and let me search in my own breast for that peace and contentment, which I have not been able to find in all my scenes of success. In being detached from the world I shall be delivered from folly and ingratitude ... I shall have more undisturbed opportunity to... prosecute my revenge. (II, xcvii)

Smollett did not hide the fact that he felt peeved when he found others behaving more prudently and wisely than him. Referring to Dr. John Armstrong, who had been hesitant in praising his play, *The Regicide*, he wrote:

> ... The truth is I am piqued at the Superiority which the Wariness and Wisdom of such fellows gives them over the Weakness and Leakiness of my own Disposition—Yet notwithstanding I admire their conduct and rejoice at their success.[3]

But the seeming ingenuousness of this confession gives no inkling of the coarse and malicious descriptions of well-known contemporaries in *The Adventures of an Atom*, nor of the scurrilous and cruel attacks, especially in the first edition of *Peregrine Pickle*,[4] on Fielding, Garrick, Akenside, Chesterfield and, perhaps the most barbarous, on the generous and noble Lord Lyttleton, whose monody on the death of his wife, Smollett, no very great poet himself, felt he had a right to ridicule.

With such a temperament, Smollett was naturally contemptuous of the currently popular belief in man's natural benevolence expounded by the neo-Platonists and by Shaftesbury, whom he dismissed as 'that frothy writer' (*PP*, I, xliii). In *Ferdinand Count Fathom* he ridicules 'disciples of Plato and some modern moralists' who ascribe actions to 'the innate virtue and generosity of the human heart' and contrasts them with himself, 'whose notions of human excellence are not quite so sublime' (ch. liii). These notions inspire some unforgettable pictures of man's indifference and inhumanity to his fellowmen. Perhaps the finest is the one which shows how Roderick, badly wounded and having fainted with loss of blood, is 'bandied from door to door through a whole village', and is 'tumbled out like a heap of dung' at every house, because every one wants to avoid the expense of burying him in case he dies (II, ii).

Even in the far more mellow novel, *Humphry Clinker*, written twenty-three years after *Roderick Random*, Smollett's view of life, though presented with much wry humour and much greater balance, has not changed fundamentally. Matthew Bramble is convinced that 'we live in a vile world of fraud and sophistication' (23 April, by Matt). He and his friend, the actor Quin, 'are perfectly agreed in their estimate of life; which Quin says, would stink in his nostrils, if he did not steep it in claret' (30 April, by Jeremy). Matthew is made to wonder if he feels thus about life because he is old and an invalid; but he is made to conclude that it is 'more probable' that, having become wiser with age and experience, he has at last begun to see things more clearly (2 June, by Matt). It is natural that, unlike the splenetic Matt, his romantic young niece, Liddy, should find the new scenes of life which open out to her exciting and beautiful. In this more balanced novel in which Smollett has planned to present the variety of different angles from which life is viewed by men of different temperaments, though he contrives to make the young girl's appreciation sound somewhat naive, he allows the world to seem a very pleasant place in the letters she writes to her friends. But by the end of the novel, he makes even Liddy perceive the incorrigibly foolish and wicked nature of man.

In his introduction to *Humphry Clinker* (Everyman's Library, 1966), Howard Mumford Jones states that in his last novel

'Smollett's anxiety was to affirm that by and large life is good'. It is true that he could now see 'the sordid and vicious disposition of the world' (*RR*, Author's Preface), which had so overwhelmed him in his earlier novels, with amused tolerance. Now, like his Jeremy he was 'determined to enjoy as long as I can', 'the humour in the farce of life', determined to see that what had before 'moved' his 'spleen' should now excite his 'laughter' (30 April, by Jeremy). With such a determination, he was able to effect a most remarkable change from the oppressive, brutal, vindictive atmosphere of *Peregrine Pickle*, and write one of the most refreshing novels of the century. However, one feels that his considered judgment of life is not fundamentally different from his former appraisal of it. In the goodness and benevolence of a few solitary individuals, Smollett had always believed. His view of life was never Mandevillean. Even in *Ferdinand Count Fathom*, he created a large number of characters so completely good and generous, and portrayed them with so much sentimental gush, that they seem merely the illusions of an idealist. Moreover, he seems to share the sentimental view held by Fielding and numerous other writers of the period that good and benevolent men are generally credulous, and find it difficult to prosper in the world. The noble Renaldo, who is so deceived and tormented by the devilishly clever villain, Fathom, is told by his sister:

'Nothing is more easy ... than to impose upon a person, who, being himself unconscious of guile, suspects no deceit. You have been a dupe, dear brother, not to the finesse of Fathom, but to the sincerity of your own heart'. (ch. lix)

All the more because of the existence of such benevolent people who suffer, Smollett believes one ought to feel disgust for the world where the majority are deceitful and malicious.

So in *Humphry Clinker*, Smollett suggests a solution, not very optimistic, for avoiding the worst aspects of a life where 'the longer I live, I find the folly and fraud of mankind grow more and more intolerable' (28 April, by Matt). The only way out is to escape from the haunts and activities of men, and settle down to the quiet life of a country gentleman, keeping company with only 'one or two sensible friends' (8 June, by Matt).

Indeed, already in the conclusion of his first two novels, Smollett resorts to this favourite solution of the eighteenth century. But as yet, in the body of the novels, and in their fierce, destructive tone, the solution offered is anger. As yet anger, and the resultant feelings of mortification, bitterness, revenge and misanthropy (interrupted by a fitful charity shown towards a few individuals) are seen as the only possible reactions to the folly and iniquity of the world. It is with these weapons that the angry young gentlemen of the first two novels slash their way through the world, and their ability to be angry and to hit out is a mark of their superiority to other men. Perry is appreciatively described as 'a child of passion' (II, lxxxvi). Women find Perry very attractive, because of 'an agreeable ferocity' (I, xvii) which characterizes his personality.

The 'ferocity' and 'passion' of these young gentlemen find vent in some strange behaviour. Both Roderick and Perry, if people or circumstances get the better of them in any matter, get 'transported' or 'distracted', and fall into 'the condition of a frantic Bedlamite' (*RR*, II, xxii). Perhaps the culminating illustration of this savage raving is found when the faithful, innocent Pipes tries to console Perry who, having been let down rather badly by a cabinet minister, has locked himself up in his room:

> ... in a most frantic condition, biting his lips so that the blood ran from his mouth, dashing his head and fists against the sides of his chimney, and weeping with the most bitter expressions of woe. (II, xcvi)

Perry warns Pipes that if he tries to enter his room, he will shoot him. In spite of this, Pipes does break in; Perry takes a loaded pistol and shoots straight into his face. 'Happily', something has gone wrong with the pistol and so Pipes is saved.

Nor is the frantic behaviour of Peregrine and Roderick always due merely to lack of self-control; both of them deliberately work themselves up into such 'paroxysms' whenever they want to assert themselves or get something out of their friends. After one such deliberate fit Roderick points out complacently: 'This finesse had the desired effect' (II, xiii). Perry is equally good at this kind of bullying, and continues to practise it even after Smollett has informed the reader that his hero has learnt to 'express himself as became a man of honour, sensibility and politeness' and 'with surprising temperance, affability and moderation' (II, cv). Even at this stage, Perry's behaviour is neither restrained nor honest. When he has no money, his 'pride' enables Perry to keep rejecting Emilia's offer to marry him, though she is pining for him; but, when he becomes rich again, he refuses to postpone the wedding even by a day, though Emilia pleads with him to wait for the arrival of her mother who is away for a few days. So Smollett proceeds to describe the behaviour of this affable gentleman:

> Peregrine, maddening with desire, assaulted her with the most earnest entreaties, representing that ... delay must infallibly make a dangerous impression upon his brain and constitution. He fell at her feet in all the agony of impatience, swore that his life and intellects would actually be in jeopardy by her refusal; and, when she attempted to argue him out of his demand, began to rage with such extravagance, that ... the amiable Emilia was teased into compliance. (II, cvi)

Yet Smollett expects his heroine to enjoy 'perfect felicity' (II, cvi) with such a husband. No writer who has pretensions to sensitivity and seriousness of purpose can describe his hero, as Smollett does, first cunningly planning and attempting rape on the heroine by enticing her into a bagnio, and then on the wedding night, going 'to the delicious scene, where he found her elegantly dished out, the fairest daughter of chastity and love' (II, cvi).

Fortunately, Smollett is able to endow his heroes with a grit and resilience which take the edge off this brutality and bad taste. To Roderick, at least, Smollett is able to impart some of his own tenacity. Like Fielding, Smollett could command a most remarkable will-power and moral strength in times of difficulty. This enabled him, when harassed by a most painful illness, and bereaved by the loss of an only child, not only to go on writing for his living, but to present a highly entertaining picture of life in *Humphry Clinker*. It is this kind of will-power which enables Roderick, at least most of the time, to keep going quite buoyantly in situations of extreme stress to which most people would succumb. Perhaps the most impressive incident illustrating this tenacity occurs during the Carthagena expedition when an epidemic breaks out on board ship. The men are dying like flies, and Roderick himself is asked to take confession, and prepare for death. Consumed by fever and tortured by the inhuman barbarity of his vindictive captain, he lies in the most filthy surroundings, and watches corpse after corpse being flung overboard every day :

> Another in my condition, perhaps, would have submitted to his fate, and died in a pet; but I could not brook the thought of perishing so pitifully, after I had weathered so many gales of hard fortune. (I, xxxiv)

Smollett's admiration for this quality of tenacity is best communicated in the words of the more simple souls among his characters, men like Bowling, Pipes and Trunnion. When Bowling thinks Roderick is succumbing to despondency, he talks him out of it in that idiom of the brave, weather-beaten sailor at which Smollett is so good :

> He comforted me, with observing, that life was a voyage in which we expect to meet with all weathers; that despair signified nothing; but resolution and skill were better than a stout vessel : for why! because they require no carpenter, and grow stronger the more labour they undergo. (II, v)

Because of his courage and tenacity, Roderick is not an unsympathetic character in the earlier part of the novel. He is a callow youth, but not without fine instincts; cast out upon a selfish world, he naturally learns from it what it has to teach him. If he reacts brashly or violently, it is because the world hurts him most cruelly. It is more in the second half of the novel that Roderick's character strikes us as nasty; and, what is more to the point, his creator fails to realize that he is portraying a nasty character. Always 'touchy and impatient of control' as Roderick was (I, xv), now his prickly disposition becomes insufferable. He sets about his adventures with the assumption that society owes him someting. He seems to be under the impression that he has a right to exploit women for their money, and to revenge himself upon them when they refuse to be exploited. If a rich heiress, or her mother, sends him packing, 'inflamed with resentment' (I, xv), he at once sits down to meditate vengeance. Even when he feels he is about to land an heiress, he does not dream of love or happiness, or even of financial prosperity, but only of revenge; in fact his idea of happiness is to possess the power to take revenge. Yet, the reader is still meant to take note of what the Preface calls 'the dignity of his character'.

The situation in which Roderick's, and Smollett's, idea of gentlemanly behaviour is revealed most startlingly is when Roderick feels embarrassed at the thought of having to give an account of his life to his future wife, Narcissa. It is necessary that he should be able to establish himself in her eyes as what he 'laid claim to' be;—'a gentleman, by birth, education, and behaviour' (II, xx). This makes Roderick worry a great deal about certain aspects of his life. The reader, however, is surprised to find that the uneasiness which Roderick feels is due to the 'low situations' in which he has been involved because of his poverty, and not to his behaviour in having tried to trap into matrimony rich heiresses for whom he had felt nothing but scorn or repulsion; nor to the fact of his having pursued them with malicious revenge when defeated in such attempts. Apparently the gentleman feels shame, and is disgraced in the eyes of society, not when he conducts himself like a cad in order to obtain money, but when he is compelled to earn money by working with his hands, to become a footman, and wear 'a servile disguise so unsuitable to my birth, sentiments, and, let me add, my deserts' (II, xx).

Let us now see how 'our hero', Perry, is able to 'maintain the character of a gentleman'. For his behaviour, Perry has not even Roderick's excuse of retaliating upon a world which has been extremely harsh to him. It is true that Perry's mother is portrayed as an incredibly cruel monster with an implacable hatred for her son; but, as Smollett himself says, Trunnion's generosity completely makes up for this; besides, long before his mother begins to hate him, Perry reveals 'a certain oddity of disposition' (I, xi). In childhood, this disposition finds vent in numerous 'jokes', which result in the cruel harassment of the one-eyed, gouty Trunnion, who loves Perry dearly and most generously. Many of the incidents Smollett invents throughout the novel in order to amuse us with Peregrine's pranks, Fielding, who knew what is lovable in human nature, and what is monstrous and destructive in it, would certainly have invented in order to present a vicious and hateful individual.

Whatever the defects of *Roderick Random*, the general tone of that novel is not continuously unpalatable as is that of this novel. For one thing, Strap is a delightful person, whereas Perry's companions, and his mentors during his childhood, Pipes, and even more so Hatchway, have savage, maliciously cruel tendencies. Moreover, because of the seriousness of the issues treated in *Roderick Random* and its brilliant exposure of administrative corruption and inefficiency, that novel achieves a moral power which is quite lacking in the tedious jokes Perry perpetrates on stupid painters, pedantic doctors, and on the husbands and lovers of the numerous 'inamoratas' he requires to satisfy his 'very amorous complexion' (II, lxxxv).

After his return from the grand tour of Europe, for the seemingly high object of what Smollett calls 'practical satire' (II, lxxxii), Peregrine forms a collusion with the misanthrope Crabtree. But their satirical efforts described with great zest over a very large number of pages, result only in paltry ridicule of superstitious curates longing to get benefices by fair or foul means, and of society women of depraved tastes who spend their lives cheating their equally depraved husbands.

It is of course Smollett's own personal urge to satirize the world that leads him to create within the framework of his novel a character who will perform the role of a satirist. So he is led away into endowing Perry with a 'talent for raillery' (I, xxi) and setting him up as a 'castigator' (II, lxxxv) of 'the villainous pests of society' (I, lxviii), as a judge qualified to punish 'offenders against...humanity and decorum' (II, lxxxv). Since Peregrine's own conduct is so arrogant, shabby and base, the reader naturally questions the propriety of assigning him such a role.

Smollett praises Peregrine for the shrewd study of character he has made by establishing his 'court of ridicule' (II, xcii), and goes so far as to wish that 'the executive power of the legislature [had] been vested in him' (II, lxxxv). Yet all that Smollett manages to select as the most philanthropic or intelligent example of his satire is that he can trick and put down a gang of sharpers. The rest of his conduct has shown that he is very good at beating up and persecuting the husbands and lovers of the women whom he chases and that he has an itch to indulge incessantly in 'jokes'. A tiresome number of these, puerile, and at the same time viciously cruel and offensively excremental, fill the pages. There is, for example, the tomfoolery of hoaxing people into believing that they have eaten cat's meat, so that they 'retched with convulsive agonies' and 'mutually defiled them as they lay' (I, xlviii). There is the sadism of the 'joke' when Perry wants to 'make himself merry' at the expense of a gull who is already maddened out of his wits because, as a result of Perry's foolery, he has been confined to the Bastille. So he practises his talent upon the tormented creature, till he is convinced that the only way to escape the penalty of being locked up for ever in the horror of the Bastille, is to undergo the horror of an operation which will 'reduce' him to 'the neuter gender' (I, xlvii)—rollicking fun for the school-boy and as much scatological adventure as he wants; and one concedes Smollett's right to cater for the school-boy; one only questions the critic's right to give such writing a serious philosophical aura.

When Peregrine sets up as a fortune-teller in co-operation with Crabtree, we see that he can manage to worm out the secrets of society women and their maidservants, to use the information against them, and to use the women themselves for 'the purposes of gallantry' (II, lxxxv). And yet Smollett informs the reader, obviously with the intention of impressing upon him Perry's attribute of generosity, that the 'profit' accruing from the conjuration scheme is used, after deducting the expenses on spying on women, etc., for the poor and for hospitals! The reader is appalled by schemes so unbefitting the character of a gentleman, capped by such peculiar philanthropy. At a fairly late stage in the novel, Peregrine is set up as 'a patron of the arts' so that his magnanimity may be revealed; with much admiration for him in his tone, Smollett applauds the discernment with which he combines both justice and mercy in his satirical schemes, for he 'chastised' only the arrogant writers and actors, but the humble, even though they were insipid, he protected with 'generosity and compassion' (II, lxxxv). It is particularly this consistent attribution of generosity to this selfish puppy that antagonizes the reader.

In addition to attributing generosity to him, from the beginning of the novel, Smollett talks of Peregrine as displaying numerous virtues, accomplishments and sensitive qualities that are normally ascribed to a refined and honourable gentleman. Quite a few of these qualities, the reader is astonished to find being associated with him. He is said to have a fine intelligence, a strong 'appetite' for knowledge and naturally good taste, which has been refined by learning and observation (II, lxxxviii); he shows 'a very promising poetic talent' (I, xvii); he is a political writer of such acumen and force that he manages 'to raise the character of the paper' for which he writes (II, xcvii).

The chief fault of Perry, as Smollett sees him, is his pride. This pride manifests itself in much arrogant or ostentatious behaviour which, according to Smollett, is not altogether unforgiveable in a young gentleman of his qualifications. It manifests itself also in one action which is condemned as altogether dishonourable—the attempt to rape Emilia, made in Lovelace style by decoying her to a bagnio and preparing her with 'cordials'.

Already when but a schoolboy at Winchester, Perry had to 'struggle between his interest and love' when after making inquiries about 'the situation and pedigree of his new mistress', Emilia, he had felt that the straitened circumstances of her family would 'derogate from the dignity of his situation' (I, xviii). When he returns home after his rampage on the Continent, he begins to entertain ideas of subduing Emilia to his will without damaging his chances of making a brilliant marriage. 'Sorry I am,' says Smollett, 'divulging this degeneracy in the sentiment of our imperious youth, flushed with the consciousness of his own qualifications' (I, lxvi).

But Perry's chief characteristic has always been, and always remains, the desire to subdue everyone, and particularly every woman, to his will. When Perry pursues a woman, it is never out of affection, even temporary; it is seldom even only for the gratification of his 'turbulent and unruly' (I, lii) physical appetite; the gratification of his vanity and egoism is always a powerful incentive. Indeed, Smollett quite often says so, and yet fails to take it into account in his total estimate of Perry's character. There is a singular lack of affection in Perry's nature. No two heroes could be more different in this respect than Fielding's Tom and Smollett's Perry. What Perry most enjoys is to set women by the ears. When impressed by his handsome appearance and ostentatious behaviour all the fashionable women contend with each other for his favours, he gets considerable pleasure in exasperating the contention among them 'by an artful distribution of his attention among the competitors' (I, lxx). 'Our hero', 'our gentleman', is a cad; but Smollett does not see it. He is without generosity or compassion though Smollett so frequently attributes these qualities to him. It is true that in the description of some of Perry's encounters with women there is much droll fun, and much effective satire, especially on female folly and perfidy. It is also true that Smollett ridicules with considerable irony the vanity of 'our gallant' and that he talks with some disapproval of his 'caprice and whim' (II, lxxx). But his vanity is never really cut down to size, and his egoism, self-sufficiency, peevishness and brutality remain the same even at the end, when his heart is supposed to have been 'softened' (II, xc), and he is supposed to be able to behave like a 'man of honour, sensibility and politeness' (II, xcvi).

However, it must be said that, though some critics give a great deal of emphasis to this 'reform', Smollett himself is rather casual about it. From time to time after the prison episode, he certainly throws about phrases which imply that Perry has attained 'philosophical resolution' (II, cv); but he is still sometimes quite cynical about Perry's behaviour. It would therefore be perhaps unfair to accuse Smollett of this additional error of regarding the supposedly chastened Perry as very different from his previous self. It is just that the author has as yet neither the ability nor the inclination to take a consistently serious, moral and refined view of man's personality, nor, for that matter, a consistently shallow one.

As the central incident of the novel, Smollett presents

Perry's long-planned, treacherous contrivance to rape Emilia. After he manages so far as to lure her into a bagnio and ply her with liquor doctored with opiates, Emilia's presence of mind enables her to see through him, and to escape from his clutches. When he finds that all his attempts to cajole and bully her are of no avail, he decides to carry her away by force. So he embarks upon 'a most fatiguing adventure' (II, lxxviii) during which in various disguises he pursues Emilia across the country, and lies hiding in inns and thickets upon the highway in order to abduct her. The adventure is described in exhaustive detail and often with much energy, but it is not a patch on the brilliant pages in which Richardson presents Lovelace's pursuit of Clarissa. Not only does Smollett not come anywhere near the human and moral power of Richardson's narrative, but he falls much below him even in humour and sardonic ability. Richardson's dramatic presentation of his hero makes Lovelace's letters glitter with the laughter of a perceptively satirical analysis of himself and the world. One has only to compare Perry's fatuous pranks as 'satirist' with Lovelace in this comparable aspect of his role, to realize the power of Richardson's writings even in matters where he is commonly thought to have no talent at all.

Frustrated in his attempts to kidnap Emilia, Perry falls ill. This tames his 'fury'; and like the proverbial devil when ill, he becomes penitent. He writes a remorseful letter to Emilia's mother offering marriage; but, as soon as he receives a refusal, resentment again rises uppermost.

So it goes on; Perry 'mortified', or wanting to mortify Emilia; Perry hungering with desire and offering reparations; Perry 'nettled' and revengeful as soon as any offer is rejected. Such behaviour he considers 'atonement', of which he declares he has done sufficient, when in his class-conscious, money-conscious way he says to Emilia's brother:

> As for your sister, I have once in my life affronted her in the madness and impetuosity of desire; but I have made such acknowledgements, and offered such atonement, as few women of her sphere would have refused. (II, lxxxvi)

He of course knows that he had planned the rape carefully,

over a long period of time. After this Perry begins to lose his money. Now 'the consciousness of his decayed fortune, by adding to the sensibility of his pride, increased the horror of another repulse' (II, xc). At this time Emilia inherits £10,000 from her uncle and Perry is imprisoned for debt. Now, she writes to him agreeing to marry him. He is most touched and very full of 'love', but he refuses, 'determined to sacrifice the interest of my passion to my glory', and hoping she will do justice to his 'self-denial' (II, ciii). In his remarks on this, barely fifteen pages before the end of the novel, Smollett seems to go out of his way to deprive his supposedly regenerate hero of our sympathy; is it just that he, like his Crabtree, cannot conceive that any man, even a wise and reformed hero, can be less egoistic and wilful ?

> Nature could not have held out...had not the pride and caprice of his disposition been gratified to the full in the triumph of his resistance...Perhaps he might have overshot himself in the course of his perseverance...But all these possibilities were providentially prevented. (II, ciii)

Providence prevents these mishaps by again showering money on Perry. His father, from whom he had no hopes of getting any money, dies intestate, so that he can inherit a second estate, having already run through his uncle's. Now again richer than Emilia, and so having the upper hand, he goes to her, insists on having the wedding that very day and falls into a 'paroxysm' when she says she would like to wait for her mother's arrival. She has to give in and it all ends in the 'perfect felicity' of possessing Emilia on the wedding night; and possessing, moreover, the monied power to treat with 'ineffable contempt', 'with the most mortifying disdain' all 'those against whom his resentment had been kindled' (II, cvi). In all this where is the 'love [of] his fellow men' that Mr. Paulson[5] and others declare it is Smollett's intention to teach Perry before he can gain Emilia ? How can Smollett teach it when he himself has not yet learnt how to love them or what qualities to value in them ?

The extravagance and brutality of Peregrine's conduct make the reader wonder whether it was Smollett's temperament and personal experiences which inspired his peculiar idea of the gentleman, or whether his observation of contemporary life and manners gave him such an idea. In the historical accounts which have come down to us, the kind of ruffianly behaviour in which Perry revels is associated not only with adolescent bucks of 'good' families but also with some brilliant and highly attractive courtiers.[6] The riotous orgies of the notorious gangs of Mohocks are by no means the only instances of violent and unscrupulous behaviour. Fashionable gentlemen could go about London, breaking windows, thrashing the guard, slitting the noses of innocent passers-by, gouging out their eyes, rolling women downhill in tubs, hanging them upside down, and cutting grossly coarse Rabelaisian capers in order to outrage the citizens. More of these incidents are recorded of Restoration times, but even as late as the last decades of the eighteenth century the circle which gathered round the Prince of Wales at his fabulously expensive residence, the famous Brighton Pavilion, was notorious for its wild extravagance. The prince himself, when well past his youth, sitting in the banqueting room on the ostentatious decorations of which he had spent the equivalent of a million dollars in modern money, thought it was a feather in his cap if he could boast that he had thrashed a Brighton butcher within an inch of his life.

Many of the traits of character ascribed to Perry, as well as several characteristic episodes in the novel, are associated in historical accounts with the celebrated John Wilmot, Earl of Rochester.[7] Rochester set up as an Italian mountebank and delighted as much as Perry and Crabtree in the opportunities that the disguise gave him to worm out their secrets from women. There are resemblances also between Perry's experiment in making a lady out of a beggar girl and Rochester's making an actress out of one of his mistresses; even the famous bath given to the girl has its origin in the *Memoirs*. Like Perry, the gay, light-hearted, cynical debauchee, Rochester, was a gifted poet. In spite of his indulgence in numerous coarse and obscene frolics, he could prove singularly attractive and charming. But the charm soon fizzled out, and at thirty-three he died a decrepit old man, suffering the agonizing pains of venereal and other diseases. But Smollett imagines that his fictional hero, in spite of all his dissipation, will settle down as a progressive country gentleman, healthy and robust in body and mind.

Fortunately, Smollett's own mind and temper became considerably more healthy and mature in the interval between the publication of *Peregrine Pickle* and his last two novels. Moreover, surprisingly, the farouche satirist developed into a most winningly charming writer. Not to succumb to the charm of *Humphry Clinker* is as impossible as it is not to be put off by the virulent, callow tone and the brutal, puerile jokes of *Peregrine Pickle*. It was to take Smollett eleven years from his second novel to master the engaging tone of the satirical phantasy of *Sir Launcelot Greaves*, and another nine to achieve the sane, balanced humour and amiable wisdom of *Humphry Clinker*. Even now, the carping sullenness and the insensitiveness of taste remain in parts of both novels, but such elements fall so properly into place in their structural scheme and dramatic characterization, that any reader not familiar with the early novels would place Smollett among the most engaging and affable writers of a century which gave to literature the charm of Steele, Goldsmith and Sterne.

Though Smollett's reading of life and people did not change in his maturer years, his anger with the world passed away and, with it, the unbalanced ferocity that would fight it on its own ground, and pay it back in its own selfish and savage currency. Even in the earlier novels, the harsher qualities of revenge and ferocity are partly due to his frustrated idealism. Smollett's anger with life, and his brutality in giving vent to this anger, are obviously not the expression of a callous, cruel temperament, but of a man who feels too keenly and is too thin skinned, always to preserve his balance and equanimity. He himself studied this aspect of his nature, as is often recognized, in the character of Matthew Bramble. Like Matthew, Smollett could express his hopes for the amelioration of man only in satire, with gruffness and pugnacity. Fortunately, especially in later life, Smollett could laugh at this aspect of his character, and he allows Matt's nephew, Jeremy, to make fun of Matt's eccentricities. This ability to laugh at himself made it possible for him as he advanced in age to become, like Matthew, a 'most risible misanthrope' (30 April, by Jeremy).

In spite of his pessimistic view of human nature and the

implacable invective of his writings, at heart Smollett remained a generous humanitarian, actively concerned with the betterment of the conditions of man's life. In this respect also, he is like his Matt. Matt bitterly disowns man, saying: 'What have I to do with the human species? except a very few friends, I care not if the whole was—' (28 April, by Matt). And yet Matt continues to help whoever he finds in trouble, is constantly generous even towards worthless tenants and servants, suffers an insufferable sister with wry humour and affection, and gives refuge even to oddities like the petulant Lismahago. Similarly, Smollett went on reviling the race of man, and yet worked with a burning zeal to expose the misery of man's condition. To the horde of Grub Street 'authorlings' he employed to do the hack-work for his *History* and his translations of the European classics, he gave free dinners; he endured their backbiting and sycophancy and contrived to forget his irritation with them in the amusement provided by their folly. Indeed, like Matt, he was 'a Don Quixote in generosity' (12 Sept, by Jeremy).

As with Matthew, Smollett's frustrated idealism not infrequently found vent in sentimentality instead of in feelings of anger and revenge. In the novels of this growling satirist, there is much of that absurd excess of emotionalism characteristic of the sensibility cult discussed in the next chapter. Matt is often put to a great deal of trouble trying to hide his tears and charitable deeds from the stares of a cruel and jesting world. When *Humphry Clinker* was written the sensibility cult was at its height; therefore this display of sensibility may, to a large extent, be put down to the current fashion; but it must also be regarded as a manifestation of the writer's own psychological need, as in fact the whole sensibility movement itself was; like an epidemic it broke out upon the emotional starvation that the age of reason had sought to impose on writer and reader. But much before the sentimental disease reached epidemic proportions, the contagion had affected Smollett's earlier novels. *Ferdinand Count Fathom*, in particular, is full of preposterous scenes contrived in order to applaud the most fantastic exhibitions of feeling. Like the sentimental writers, in such scenes Smollett repeatedly gives emphasis to the pleasure, the 'woeful enjoyment' and the 'pleasing anguish' that is obtained by wallowing in grief and tears.

Even Roderick and Peregrine are required to display sensibility. Roderick has been steeled by the most tormenting experiences, and brutalized by them too; but, since he is the hero, Smollett feels compelled to endow him with the laudable ability to weep with a weeping heroine in the theatre. The love-scenes in the novels are freely strewn with conventional sentimental phrases; in such scenes even Emilia, who shares much of the hardness of Peregrine, is portrayed in the vocabulary of the sentimental writers. The forceful exposure of the political and military system in the first half of *Roderick Random* challenges comparison with the most powerful satire of the century, but any of the literary hacks whom Smollett employed would have been able to dish out the pallid love story told in the second half of the novel. In *Peregrine Pickle* the intrusion of the sentimental school-girl romance upon the brutal and farouche satire, makes the total effect more unsavoury than it would be if the fierce tone had been maintained consistently.

But curiously, when he came to write his last two novels, the sentimental trend in literature, then at its strongest, proved favourable to Smollett; it brought out the most amiable side of this fierce satirist, though it was responsible for much weakness and fatuity in even some of the best contemporary writers. The sentimental idealism which inspires the conception of the protagonist of *Sir Launcelot Greaves* governs the tone of the satire in that book, and gives it, in spite of the sharpness of its criticism of social wrongs, an amiable quality. Similarly, the engaging comedy and the balanced tone of *Humphry Clinker*, are to a considerable extent due to the fact that Smollett could here cast his protagonist in the mould of the 'benevolent misanthrope', creating the best example of a 'type' which was already popular in the literature of this period.[8]

Literary historians generally dismiss *Sir Launcelot Greaves* in a line or two, dubbing it 'preposterous', or 'an oddity', or describing it as the product of a 'very low level of inspiration'.[9] Judged strictly by the standards of the realistic novel, the central situation, which presents an idealistic youth prone to fits of melancholia, who decides to wear the armour of his forefathers and challenge social evils like a knight of old with lance and shield, is of course far-fetched; but, once this situation is accepted as a satirical device, the individual episodes are by no means preposterous or remote from the concerns of life. In fact, in its exposure of the evils of parliamentary elections, private madhouses, the system of guardianship and of appointing country magistrates, this novel has as close a relevance to contemporary problems as the most purposeful novels of the time. Justice Gobble, his wife, and their numerous victims in Launcelot's second adventure do not suffer in the least by comparison with Fielding's finest satire of social monsters.

The hero of this novel is not meant to be regarded as a man who is completely deranged; except for his determination to wear armour, he acts more sanely and effectively than the supposedly sane heroes of the contemporary sentimental novels. Launcelot is an extremely sensitive youth who falls into melancholia, and even suffers a temporary spell of insanity, because he is badly shaken by the brutal treatment he receives from the uncle of the girl he loves and by the supposed scorn of the girl herself. After some time his fit of frenzy passes and he returns to 'calmness and acts of benevolence' (ch. iv). When his father dies he gets sufficient hold over himself to manage the estate. But the lad who had always been disgusted with the trivial social demands of fashionable society, and had always felt a philanthropic urge to protect the weak and punish wrongdoers, now chooses to take refuge in his so-called madness, and knowingly adopts the eccentric role of a knight errant. Where Don Quixote presents a puny and ridiculous figure, Launcelot with his winning personality, presents a most imposing and striking appearance, sitting on a noble steed, clad in a brilliant suit of black armour. Equipped with the armour both of his ancestors and of madness to protect him, he can effectively set up as 'a general redresser of grievances' (ch. iv). Mad men and angels can rush in where the ordinary person fears to tread.

Before the blight of madness falls upon him, Launcelot distinguishes himself at the Inns of Court. When his father falls ill and his political rivals try to wrest his Parliamentary seat from him, Launcelot proves himself a most effective orator and brings the seat home for his father. According to Smollett, this young squire has all the right ideas and principles. Though he mingles freely with the country swains, like Matthew Bramble, he detests social climbers, and treats with contempt the rich yeomen and their families who 'assume the dress and manners' of the gentry (ch. iii). Though so charitable, he has the right ideas about the giving of alms, and never encourages idlers. Though so benign, he is extraordinarily peremptory with scoundrels. He horse-whips husbands who continue to ill-treat their wives even after he has given them a warning—a very Smollettian conception, indeed, of the man of feeling!

As befits a country gentleman whose family has sent a representative to Parliament for many generations, Sir Launcelot has done much serious thinking on political problems; he has strong views on party controversies and the selection of parliamentary candidates. These views are vividly presented in the once-popular anthology piece which shows Launcelot trying to persuade an unruly crowd at an election meeting not to vote for either of the two candidates, one a Tory squire who is 'an illiterate savage' and the other a Whig who is a cunning, sycophantic 'plebian'. But the electorate itself is composed of 'a pack of rascals who deserve to be sold', and Launcelot is pelted with dirt and stones (chs. ix-x).

Launcelot is able to put his purposeful thinking and chivalric courage more successfully to use, when he succeeds in rescuing a whole crowd of 'living monuments of inhumanity' from the clutches of a monster of 'a modern magistrate' and his dragon-like wife. Here Smollett wishes to expose the tyranny and terror of a judicial system controlled by the powerful gentlemen of the land who, if it will serve their own ends, will put a whole district at the mercy of an ignorant, villainous brute, investing him with the power of magistrate. Justice Gobble, the son of a tailor, worked as a journeyman-hosier till he married the widow of his master and acquired a petty fortune. Then one day, backed by Lord Sharpington, who was indebted to him, he was metamorphosed into a justice of the peace. As is to be expected from their antecedents, the Gobbles are both servile and snobbish; they tyrannize over the poor and lowly, and connive at the vices of the great. Sir Launcelot liberates the tormented victims of this monster, and starts legal proceedings against him so that he can be 'expunged from the commission with disgrace' (chs. xi-xii).

Having thus, with the force of his armour and his principles, performed these actions symbolic of the public duty of the gentleman, Launcelot decides to cast aside his chivalric dress when, mid-way in the novel, he has a chance meeting with Aurelia Darnel and the misunderstanding between them, which had been caused by the machinations of her uncle, is cleared. But Aurelia is captured again by her uncle who has appropriated all her money; now, to avoid being called to account he wants to marry her off to one of his accomplices, or to do away with her in some manner. So Launcelot has to go to London in search of Aurelia. He traces her to a madhouse into which he himself is trapped by the uncle. Fortunately, Launcelot's friends succeed in rescuing the couple from this appalling fate, so that 'the accomplished Sir Launcelot Greaves and the enchanting Miss Darnel' can get married. As is usual with such conclusions in the eighteenth century novel, the two settle down in the ancestral home, an ideal country gentleman, supported by an ideal lady, admired by their equals and doing their duty by the common people.

Sir Launcelot Greaves was Smollett's first experiment in blending satire with sentiment, a dose of quixotism and quizzical humour. The formula obviously suited his genius and he used it again in *Humphry Clinker*. For this novel he also hit upon another happy device—the currently popular epistolary form of fiction writing. As Matthew Bramble and his entourage travel over England and Scotland, they write letters reporting their impressions of people and places. To the same people and the same places each of them reacts differently, according to his own personality and moods. The resulting variety of reports gives the novel a stimulating and piquant quality. Since the opposing opinions of differing personalities are all accorded attention, the novelist's own personality emerges as urbane, tolerant and understanding. Now Smollett can write both slashing satire and boisterous farce without spoiling either by the former cruelty, brutality and coarseness. But though the tone is genial, and even boisterous, though there is a bland tolerance of stupid and even mean people, the prevailing inspiration of the book is the urge to express dissatisfaction with almost all of life, at least as it is commonly lived.

The Welsh squire Matthew Bramble, in whom Smollett is presenting an idealized portrait of himself is continuously captious and seems to be a surly, uncouth misanthrope; but he proves to be most intelligent, understanding and endearing, when one gets better acquainted with his quizzical humour, his acute criticism of affairs, his large-hearted charities and his accommodating ways. Though a grumbling eccentric, Matt is well-read, appreciates learning and the arts, and has spent his life thinking over the problems of his country, particularly the problems of the lives of country gentlemen like himself and his friends.

Wherever he goes Matt 'picks up continual food for ridicule and satire' (24 April, by Jeremy). Extremely fastidious, even snobbish, in his tastes, Matt squirms at the vulgarity of the nouveaux-riches and the impertinence of the social-climbers who swarm into the fashionable resorts of Bath and Harrowgate. His extraordinarily sensitive nerves and his delicate physical constitution make it impossible for him to stand the noise and stench of London and the fetid atmosphere of the pump-rooms at Bath. For Matt is a typical victim of 'the spleen' or the 'English disease'—a physical and nervous ailment recognized by medical observers as peculiarly common among the English upper class of the time.[10]

Among the many aspects of life and of his own character and temperament that Smollett is interested in exploring at this period, is the relation between the health of the body and the condition of the mind. Both Matt and Jeremy frequently make reference to the reciprocal connection between bodily and mental health. Wracked by the gout and afflicted by the spleen, Matt becomes peevish or uncontrollably furious and gives a public demonstration of bad temper on occasions when, as Jery says, 'a sensible man should rather laugh than be angry' (28 Sept, by Jeremy).

However, in spite of his extreme fastidiousness, and his misanthropic remarks, Matt possesses 'a heart warmed with beneficence and compassion' (23 June, by Jeremy). His avaricious sister, who grudges every penny and every ounce of meat to the servants, is constantly grumbling that Matt will 'ruinate the family with his ridiculous charities' (26 April, by Tabitha).

Matt is so generous and so sensitive to other people's misfortunes, that it is necessary for him, as it is for Goldsmith's Mr. Drybone, the Man in Black,[11] to wear the forbidding mask of misanthropy and surliness in order to protect himself from imposition. This gruff, misanthropic pose is very commonly adopted by benevolent characters in eighteenth century literature. Referring to this peculiarity in Matt, L.M. Knapp makes a shrewd observation that can be applied to all the 'benevolent misanthropes' in the literature of the period :

> Indoctrinated in the Augustan age of rationalism, Smollett felt that it was more decorous to appear misanthropic than to succumb to a Shandean emotionalism.[12]

Obviously a good and sensitive person cannot go out into the harsh and hypocritical world without sheltering himself behind some sort of mask, whether of eccentricity, or madness, or misanthropy. But the remedy is not much better than the disease; it can hardly be said to be a very efficacious or a very attractive one for facing the conditions of real life; and as for sentimentalism, it smacks even more of that than straight-forward 'Shandean emotionalism'.

If a perfidious world thus compels men to adopt artificial postures, is there no normal, happy and beneficent existence possible for the good and sensitive man ? The answer would seem to be—yes, if he is a gentleman, has a landed estate, and can retire into the countryside, with some financial backing, to live the life of a sensible and benevolent squire.

It is significant, though perhaps not very surprising, that, going in quest of the right values and the good, happy life, even Smollett, who is ever ready to cock a snook at society, should arrive at this conservative and conventional destination where the century's quest so often comes to a halt. One gets rather tired of this esquire-errantry that always ends at the gates of a wooded park; a stately mansion in the distance, further back, fields and pasture lands, humming with the enthusiasm of the current revolution in agriculture, cultivated by the healthy and thriving tenants and the grateful labourers, 'under the auspices of' (8 June, by Matt) the beneficent, honest gentleman who presides over it all, usually with an ideal companion at his side, his virtuous lady, sober and wise and a model of refined sensibility.

This conservative ideal of the century is elaborated at length in many of the warmest and most deeply felt pages of Smollett's last two novels; in fact, the opportunity to expound it seems almost to be the *raison d'etre* of his last and best piece of writing. Throughout *Humphry Clinker* the principal intention behind Matthew Bramble's critical remarks is to contrast 'town grievances' with country pleasures. Early in the novel a long, trenchant letter (8 June, by Matt) gives a remarkably incisive as well as picturesque expression to Matt's disgust with 'the enormities' of London—its noise, dissipation and foul air; its stale, insipid, adulterated food, mixed with 'the vermin that drops from the rags of the nasty drab that vends' it; its water taken from 'open aqueducts, exposed to all manner of defilement' of which 'human excrement is the least offensive part'. From the noisome dirt and vulgarity of London and the fashionable spas, Matt and his entourage travel to the rural north of England and finally to Scotland. Having studied Edinburgh critically but lovingly, they move to the highlands and the farthest Hebrides. The grim sardonic laugh refuses to play upon this scene. Now the letters glow with the feeling not only of Smollett's nostalgia for his Scottish birthplace, but with the feeling of the poet in him for the Scottish mountains and lakes, 'the most picturesque and romantic prospect I ever beheld' (3 Sept, by Jeremy). Lough-Lomond strikes Matt with a beauty that 'even partake[s] of the sublime' (28 Aug, by Matt).

In addition to exalting rural life and denigrating town civilization, Smollett makes a purposeful and persistent effort to examine the principles and duties of the life of the country gentleman, and to advocate the conditions in which he can find genuine happiness. The general reader will perhaps feel that all this is hardly the stuff of which novels are made, but Smollett with his incisive style and trenchant satirical observation is at least able to give a far more effective expression than many poets to the ideal of the honest, independent, philanthropic life of the country gentleman—to that ideal which almost every representative writer of this period felt it obligatory to stress in verse and prose.

With the purpose of advocating this ideal, Smollett reserves a large number of pages to describe the miserable ruin of Matt's friend, the sensitive but weak gentleman, Mr. Baynard. In contrast to him is presented the ideal country gentleman, Charles Dennison, in whose life may be studied 'the theory of true pleasure reduced to practice'.

Mr. Baynard's story (30 Sept and 26 Oct, by Matt) is meant to be a representative illustration of the lives of the 'nineteen out of twenty' country gentlemen whose lives are ruined because they are too weak to resist the importunities of their vain, extravagant wives and daughters. To repair a fortune, much of which he had lost in not very wise pleasures and investments, Baynard made what he thought a 'prudent marriage' with the rich daughter of a 'citizen'; from then onwards everything went sliding along the downward path. Her caprice and vanity, rendered the more insupportable because of her shallow, upstart tastes, incited her to have the front of the venerable Gothic mansion pulled down and give it a 'screen of modern architecture; so that all without is Grecian, and all within Gothic'. The magnificent old oak trees were felled; corn-fields, pastures, and 'streams that afforded the best trout in the country' were all exterminated to provide 'pleasure grounds' with 'a great basin in the middle', suited to her new-fangled ideas of landscape architecture.

Very different from the unfortunate Mr. Baynard is Charles Dennison, a model country gentleman whose example is used to illustrate the opportunities available to a gentleman for doing good to his neighbours and country, and for achieving his own happiness (8 Oct and 11 Oct, by Matt, ? 7 Oct and 14 Oct, by Jeremy). Dennison, acknowledged throughout the district as both 'a person of great learning' and 'the best farmer in the country', succeeded to an impoverished estate after the death of his dissipated elder brother. Though he had been 'bred to the law, and even called to the bar', as soon as his brother died, he gave up his profession, preferring to live upon his estate even though it would afford him almost no income. He spent his days hedging, ditching, draining bogs, burning heath, planting trees, raising poultry, breeding cows, growing on his own farms all the corn and vegetables he needed. His mind open to new ideas about agriculture, he studied its theory in the writings of the contemporary experts and managed to get practical instruction from an intelligent farmer in his neighbourhood.

The aspirations that impel a man to shape his life in such a manner are plain, unsophisticated and essentially humane; they arise from the basic and universal hunger of the human spirit for peace, comfort, good health and domestic happiness; from the need to give and receive kindness, friendship, fidelity and love. The happiness of such a life derives from the glow of satisfaction experienced in making the earth yield of its best, in reaping the fruits of one's labour, in spreading prosperity and kindness among neighbours and dependents. 'Unspeakable delight' (8 June, by Matt) is Matt's reward when he views the effects of his schemes of 'improvement' on his own estate.

Though these pages on the life of the country gentleman are warm with feeling and rich with vivid detail, communicated in that fine, forceful English which is one of Smollett's most splendid assets, any reader familiar with the literature of the period will notice that the criticism of the Baynard household and the praise of the Dennisons is but an echo of ideas expressed repeatedly in innumerable essays, poems and novels all through the century. The harassed existence of a writer striving to earn a respectable income gave Smollett little time to taste the 'rural felicity' of a life such as that of the Dennisons, or even to bring any original thinking to bear upon it. But a nostalgia inspired by his reading and his personal hankering for peace led him to champion, with a genuine fervour, this ideal that had found such universal favour among his contemporaries. Indeed, in this matter Smollett reacts much as he tells us his Roderick reacted when he was consulted by a man about a small legacy he had just received. Himself plunged in the bitter struggle for existence in London, Roderick immediately responded by urging the man to buy a small piece of land and establish himself upon it as a country gentleman. 'Then,' says Roderick, 'I launched out into the praises of a country life, as described by the poets whose works I had read (I, xvi). Peregrine also reacts in the same manner; in spite of the fact that so much emphasis has been laid on his interest in the study of the characters of men, his passion for satirical observation, his remarkable social gifts and his ability to shine in the political sphere, as soon as he retrieves a small part of his lost fortune, he is shown to be strongly drawn towards the life of 'pastoral felicity' (II, cii-ciii). His friend condemns his plans of retirement, 'as a scheme that would blast the fairest promises of fame and fortune, and bury his youth and talents in solitude and obscurity'. But these arguments have no effect on Peregrine. The conventional language of the passage makes the conventional nature of the ideal it expresses even more obvious :

> He even parcelled out his hours among the necessary cares of the world, the pleasures of domestic bliss, and the enjoyments of a country life; and spent the night in ideal parties with his charming bride, sometimes walking by the sedgy bank of some transparent stream, sometimes pruning the luxuriant vine, and sometimes sitting in social converse with her in a shady grove of his own planting.

A reader who has not sensed the ethos of this period would note with surprise that this life of the benevolent, hard-working country gentleman is posited as the ideal even by a writer like Dr. Smollett, who was by training, a physician and linguist; by profession, a very successful novelist, critic, translator and historian; an author whose 'income from writing was greater than that of any other eighteenth-century writer with the exception of Voltaire.[13] Only when he is left absolutely without any money and is thrown into jail, is Perry allowed to attempt any serious writing of poetry or to try his hand at the work of translating the classics. Only then does he think it natural 'to profit in some shape or other, by those talents which he owed to nature and education' (II, iv). Smollett will attribute brilliant intellectual and literary gifts to his hero, but when it comes to visualising a good and happy life for him, he will not dream of suggesting for him the career of a great and successful poet or man of letters, interested in propagating truth, disseminating knowledge and making men more enlightened and understanding. Pope, so proud of his use of the 'sacred weapon' of satire 'left for truth's defence' (*Epilogue to the Satires*, II, 212), so confident of maintaining 'a Poet's dignity and ease' with the financial independence he achieved by writing poetry (*Epistle to Dr. Arbuthnot*, 1.263), yet posited this same ideal. One must remember that though during the course of this century the writer's position may on the whole be said to have steadily improved, as yet, in the mind of the general public as well as the writer, the life of a poet or of a scholar was irretrievably linked with 'toil, envy, want, the patron, and the jail' (*The Vanity of Human Wishes*, 1.160). For his nephew Jeremy, Matthew Bramble will consider 'no profession but that of a country gentleman' (26 June, by Matt), though as such, he will of course sit in Parliament, as Matthew himself sat for many years, always as a politically independent member, voting according to the dictates of his conscience (2 June, by Jeremy).

Throughout his life Smollett remained in contact with a distinguished circle of medical friends; though he gave up the practice of medicine while he was still quite young, till the end of his life he showed keen interest in the causes and manifestations of diseases, particularly those which we now call psychosomatic ailments. It is therefore ironical that in his novels his interest in medicine should manifest itself only in a large number of amusing portraits of medical charlatans, and that none of his heroes should be projected as a respectable physician or man of science. The autobiographically projected Roderick, trained as a surgeon, practises medicine only when in serious financial straits, whereas he is continuously obsessed with the idea of establishing himself as a 'gentleman'.

And yet this century of the country gentleman valued the man of letters and the scientist sufficiently to elect Samuel Johnson deferentially as its 'great Cham' (Smollett to John Wilkes, 16 March 1759); sufficiently to enable its greatest poet to say of its greatest scientist :

> Nature and Nature's Laws lay hid in Night :
> God said, 'Let Newton be !' and there was light !
> (Pope, *Epitaph for Newton's Tomb*)

But the star of the country gentleman was still in the highest ascendant, and Smollett could not do otherwise than steer by its light.

7 'The Heart Rather Than the Head'

OLIVER GOLDSMITH, HENRY MACKENZIE, LAURENCE STERNE

> ... The race is not to the swift, nor the battle to the strong, neither yet bread to the wise, not yet riches to men of understanding, nor yet favour to men of skill.
> —*Ecclesiastes.*

An urge to repudiate accepted contemporary values, a reaction against the preference given by certain sections of contemporary society to rational thought and intellectual sophistication, to elegance of manners and the refinement of urban civilization, led to the creation of a number of idealized characters in the novels of the second half of the eighteenth century. The warm-hearted man, innocent in the ways of the world is now exalted, 'simplicity' and 'honesty' being contrasted with two types of currently prevailing modes—with the luxury, sophistication and artificiality of 'high life', and the rationalism, scepticism and materialism of Enlightenment civilization. Pope singled out the 'honest man' as 'the noblest work of God' (*Essay on Man*, iv, 248); Edward Young asserted :

> Th' Almighty from His throne, on earth surveys
> Nought greater, than an honest, humble heart.
> *Night-Thoughts*, viii, 475-6.

Against such an 'honest' man, Young placed the 'man of the world' (1.8); Goldsmith described 'luxury' as 'curst by heaven's decree', and declared :

> To me more dear, congenial to my heart,
> One native charm, than all the gloss of art.[1]

As has been shown in earlier chapters, the theories of the Shaftesburian school of philosophy had promoted a faith in the 'natural goodness' of man which could lead to the cult of primitivism and the exaltation of 'the noble savage'. The philosophy which postulated benevolence as the highest virtue fostered the growth of philanthropy; but it also fostered the habit of seeking sensuous gratification from the exercise of the compassionate feelings, so that, for a time, the titillating pleasures of 'sensibility' became the most sought-after effect in literature.

In the novel of the period, different aspects of the tendency to idealize the simple warm-hearted man can best be studied in the characterization of Sterne's Uncle Toby, Goldsmith's Vicar and Sir William Thornhill (*alias* Burchell), and Mackenzie's William Harley and Richard and Edward Annesly. In the earlier chapters on Fielding and Smollett it has been shown that this tendency also underlies the characterization of Parson Adams and Sir Launcelot Greaves.

Though in the portrayal of almost all these men, the worth and lovableness of a simple, warm-hearted character is communicated with a delightful blend of humour and pathos, there is an obvious danger in the attempt to present such men as ideal characters. Too often such idealization tends to identify intelligence with cunning, and politeness with falsehood, while naivete and imprudence tend to be associated with generosity and a good heart. A sentimental equation gets established between true worth and inability to prosper in this world, between wickedness and knowledge of the world. As already shown, even Fielding, in spite of his vigorous mind and shrewd realism, does not quite escape the danger. Goldsmith is often trapped into this snare, though he was quick to perceive a similar limitation in the values of the contemporary sentimental comedy, and though he was endowed with a delightful gift of irony and a whimsical humour, which he does not discard in portraying his simple men. Only Sterne manages to steer clear of the pitfall of such a confusion of values, though 'sentiment' is the very impulse of his art.

However, if the 'simple' character involves its creator in certain inherent difficulties, it provides splendid opportunities to the writer of the 'comic-epic-poem in-prose' for humour, pathos and irony, and for the creation of lovable and memorable eccentrics. With the opportunities that the form affords for comment, ironical or serious, and for creating a multiplicity of differing kinds of characters, the ingenious comic writer, like Fielding or Sterne, can present the appeal and the greatness of his simple, good-hearted man, and yet, at the same time, can laugh shrewdly and knowingly at his simplicity. The eighteenth century novel thus establishes the English tradition of presenting the simple man as amusing, and even as ridiculous, but with an underlying heroism in his character, so that, at crucial moments, he assumes, quite spontaneously, an imposing and noble stature.

The preference given by many writers during this period to the 'simple' man, and the difficulties as well as the advantages of presenting such a man as the hero of a novel, can perhaps be demonstrated most clearly from *The Vicar of Wakefield*. In this novel, as well as in his poems, plays and essays, wherever Goldsmith attempts to examine the criteria for attributing merit and worth to the individual, or to study problems of personal happiness and social good, he concentrates his attention on the predicament of the simple, good-natured man, who is too generous to be prudent, too trusting to see through the deceit of the cunning.

Goldsmith's purpose in telling the story of Dr. Primrose, the Vicar of Wakefield, is to present a good and noble person struggling against adversity. The Vicar is simple, generous and deeply attached to his family; he is cheerful and courageous in adversity and has a deep and unquestioning trust in God and in his fellow-men. To make him human, he is given a touch of vanity; to make him endearing, he is given a delightful sense of humour—kind, whimsical, and even shrewd; this he directs gently at the harmless foibles of his wife and children and, most endearingly, at his own.

The Vicar's honesty and trusting nature make him an easy prey to the wicked and deceitful; he loses his whole fortune of £14,000 when the merchant whom he has trusted declares himself bankrupt; his daughter is abducted by the neighbouring squire whom he allows into his house though he is aware of his bad reputation. A series of unlucky chances, and the cunning and villainy of the world, reduce him and his family to bankruptcy. His house and all his worldly goods are reduced to ashes in a fire; the false squire, who has ruined his daughter, has him arrested for debt, and in knee-deep snow the old, ailing pastor is driven to prison in the face of a protesting 'crowd... consisting of about fifty of my poorest parishioners' (ch. xx); his elder daughter, betrayed and ruined, lies dying; his younger daughter, innocent and beautiful, is abducted while the Vicar remains locked up in prison. Though such overwhelming misfortunes fall on his devout head, he does not forget his duty as a priest. In prison he sets himself the task of reforming and consoling his fellow-sufferers, and of reconciling them to God. In spite of the pleadings of his wife and the threats of the squire, he remains firm in his refusal to acquiesce in the sinful marriage of the squire, betrayer of his daughter, to another woman. This refusal, it is made clear, is not dictated by pride or resentment, or by a spirit of vengeance, but by a noble conviction that he must prevent a moral wrong, whatever the cost to himself. In all these misfortunes, even when his aged, feeble body has almost succumbed under the strain, his cheerful temper and the calm faith, which he had avowed at the beginning of the story, remains with him : *I have been young, and now am old; yet never saw I the righteous man forsaken, or his seed begging their bread*' (ch. iii).

To some modern readers the Vicar seems exasperatingly stupid, culpably imprudent and complacently garrulous. Such readers find every sort of fault in him, from 'fecklessness', to 'verbal attitudinizing', to 'spiritual snobbery'.[2] Goldsmith's presentation of Dr. Primrose does not escape the usual dangers of portraying a good man, and he does not always succeed in getting the intended response from the reader. Moreover, at some points in the story, the Vicar is sacrificed to the novelist's desire to weave a complicated, sensational plot, which requires the hero to be completely naive and unperceptive; on other occasions, Goldsmith's desire to convey his thoughts on social and political abuses makes him put into his hero's mouth undramatic and unseasonable sermons; sometimes the first person narrative makes him appear unduly complacent.

What is more significant, the portrayal of the Vicar suffers from that characteristic ambivalence which we find in Goldsmith's presentation of all his good-natured, benevolent heroes. The writer seems to be torn between his desire to criticise the Vicar's naiveté, imprudence, irresponsible optimism and sermonising garrulity, and the desire to admire unstinting generosity, courageous optimism and simple trust in God and man.

Goldsmith was a naturally affectionate and generous man, ever willing to give away the little money he had to any one who claimed to be in distress. But, as has often been recognized, far from being a typical sentimentalist, he was in many ways a typical classicist, opposing the theories about man's natural goodness and the superiority of primitive civilization. Refuting the philosophy of the sentimental school, he asserted :

> Custom and necessity teach even barbarians the same art of dissimulation that ambition and intrigue inspire in the breasts of the polite... for one man who is virtuous from the love of virtue... there are ten thousand who are good only from their apprehensions of punishment. (*The Citizen of the World*, letter x)

Goldsmith's attacks on the theory and practice of the sentimentalists, added to the weaknesses in the characterization of the Vicar and his ambivalent attitude towards him, have led some critics to advance the view that his intention in writing *The Vicar of Wakefield* was satirical. According to them the characterization of the hero is an attack on sentimental idealism; such critics believe that Goldsmith at least set out to present the Vicar as an embodiment of culpable imprudence and facile optimism. Ernest A. Baker was among the first to put forward such a view. Baker feels impatient with those who take the opposite view :

> Prof. Doughty speaks of a certain intellectual stupidity which Goldsmith, like Fielding before him, apparently

considered a necessary concomitant to that elemental goodness which springs from the unsophisticated heart rather than fromt he head.... There is a sort of conspiracy among critics to ignore the irony which was assuredly Goldsmith's intention, though he found it difficult to sustain.[3]

Going several steps farther than Baker, a recent critic contends that Goldsmith 'created Dr. Primrose to satirize the complacency and material corruption of a type of clergy'. According to this critic, the Vicar's character is marked by 'hypocrisy' and 'a petty practicality'; he is a 'fortune-hunter'; 'his complacency is nauseous'. Goldsmith makes the Vicar call his children his 'treasures' in order to expose his 'reliance on his children to provide eventually for his future happiness by marrying into money'.[4]

In the 'Advertisement' he appended to *The Vicar of Wakefield*, Goldsmith describes his own attitude to his hero in clear and unambiguous words :

The hero of this piece unites in himself the three greatest characters upon earth, he is a priest, an husbandman, and the father of a family. He is drawn as ready to teach, and ready to obey; as simple in affluence and majestic in adversity. In this age of opulence and refinement, whom can such a character please ? Such as are fond of his life will turn with disdain from the simplicity of his country fireside; such as mistake ribaldry for humour will find no wit in his harmless conversation; and such as have been taught to deride religion will laugh at one whose chief stores of comfort are drawn from futurity.

Though intellectually Goldsmith feels compelled to condemn credulity, imprudence and undisciplined benevolence, he instinctively presents prudence as at best a pedestrian and unlovable virtue. Almost always, he equates caution with meanness : 'One virtue he had in perfection, which was prudence, too often the only one that is left us at seventy-two', is the comment on the stingy, calculating Mr. Wilmot, who breaks off his daughter's engagement with the Vicar's son on hearing that the Vicar has lost his money (ch. ii).

What is the reader to make of the heading given to chapter twenty-eight in which the sufferings of the Vicar and his family reach a pathetic climax ?

> Happiness and misery rather the result of prudence than of virtue in this life; temporal evils or felicities being regarded by heaven as things merely in themselves trifling and unworthy its care in the distribution.

Here 'prudence' seems to be regarded as opposed to 'virtue', not as a manifestation of it. Goldsmith seems to trace the accumulating miseries of the Vicar and his family to their lack of prudence; he seems to lament that, as the world goes, they must suffer for this lack; but he is confident that no just power would blame them for such a venial deficiency. Their virtue is extolled; it is bound to find reward in heaven, and also in a well-conceived fable.

A similar attitude towards simplicity and prudence is adopted in the characterization of The Man in Black in letter twenty-seven of *The Citizen of the World*.[5] In the first half of the letter, Goldsmith seems to condemn and ridicule the 'simplicity' and easy-going nature of the man, which land him in prison; but then the tone turns appreciative as he describes the good-temper that sustains him in the most difficult circumstances. He makes the Man in Black describe his conversion to prudence and cautiousness. But instead of describing a transformation into an admirable character, he proceeds to paint himself as a cunning hypocrite.

In the characterization of Sir William Thornhill (*alias* Burchell), of the Man in Black and his father, and of 'young' Honeywood in *The Good-Natur'd Man*, Goldsmith examines the problem of benevolence and good-nature. According to him, when in youth the 'passions' are strong, in those young men in whom these are 'all upon the side of virtue', as in the case of Sir William in his younger days, there is a tendency to carry good-nature to a 'romantic extreme' (ch. iv).

In all these sketches of 'benevolent' heroes, Goldsmith's ostensible purpose is to expose and chastise a sentimental indulgence in 'good-nature'. Such men, as the Man in Black is made to say, become mere 'machines of pity' (letter xxvii), unable to distinguish between the genuinely deserving and the indolent impostor. A 'sickly sensibility' prompts them to an impractical idealism. In spite of their own narrow finances, they respond to every call upon their generosity. This soon reduces them to that same miserable plight from which they try to succour the indigent. Such benevolence Goldsmith sternly describes as 'an effect of appetite rather than reason' (letter xxvii), it being tainted by selfishness, self-indulgence and vanity. A susceptibility to flattery, a fear of offending people, a desire to stand well with everybody, are shown to be the unpleasant motives that prompt all these characters to generosity. Sir William Woodville, Honeywood's uncle, condemns his nephew's good-nature as a 'prostitution' of the mind (act v).

Goldsmith was himself afflicted by this 'good-nature'. Unsuspicious and indiscriminating in his generosity, impelled by an almost uncontrollable urge to respond to every tale of distress. real or fictitious, 'tracked by bailiffs and reproachful creditors, running from a hundred poor dependents, whose appealing looks were perhaps the hardest of all pains for him to bear',[6] he tries to administer a warning to his own impulsive nature by making a severe appraisal of the characters of his heroes.

Intellectually Goldsmith perceives that unless disciplined and governed by reason, benevolence is rather a vice than a virtue. The Man in Black shows how the education in the principles of 'universal benevolence' which his father gave to his children, left them exposed to the wiles of the world, and to their own hypersensitive feelings. On the death of their father, they found themselves 'shoved from shore, without ill-nature to protect, or cunning to guide' (letter xxvii).

But emotionally Goldsmith finds himself unable to condemn the 'good-natured man'. In the characterization of all his 'benevolent' men he sets out to expose their self-indulgence and folly, but the criticism evaporates very quickly and only praise is left behind. Fortunately, his genial irony, playful humour and droll sense of the absurd in the human situation save his writing from mawkishness or any outrageous defiance of reality.

Time and again in *The Citizen of the World* and *The Bee*,

and even in *The Life of Beau Nash*, Goldsmith stops to examine the problem of generosity and justice, and to determine the quality of the benevolence which is genuinely altruistic, as well as socially beneficial. In the essay 'A Life of Independence Praised' (*The Citizen of the World*, letter c), Goldsmith lays stress not only on 'the ignominy of receiving', but shows how charity is 'injurious even to the giver', since the gratitude and flattery of recipients shut him off from any real knowledge of himself or of the world. In the essay 'On Justice and Generosity' (*The Bee*, no. 3) he asserts :

> The qualities of candour, fortitude, charity, and generosity ... are not, in their own nature, virtues; and, if ever they deserve the title, it is owing only to justice, which impels and directs them.

This of course invites comparison with what Fielding has to say on the relationship between justice and good-nature. In the essay 'Upon Political Frugality' (*The Bee*, no. 5), as well as in 'Justice and Generosity', Goldsmith goes so far as to call misers 'the very best members of society', for 'with an avaricious man we seldom lose in our dealings; but too frequently in our commerce with prodigality' (*The Bee* no. 3).

When Goldsmith died, his creditors together lost £ 2000 which the prodigal owed them; but helpless widows and orphans stood on the staircase leading up to the room where he lay dead, and wept the loss of their only benefactor. All his life his mind had perceived the benefits of being coldly rational, but his heart had refused to comply.

The debate between the mind and the heart is therefore carried over into the writings, and ultimately in these, as in his life, the heart gets the vote.

Sir William Thornhill and The Man in Black, who are represented as having been schooled by experience out of their youthful good-nature, still retain, judged by normal standards, a certain excess of generosity and sensibility. Sir William, we are informed, early in life realized the indiscriminating and self-indulgent nature of his generosity, so that when the action of *The Vicar of Wakefield* begins, 'his bounties are more rational and moderate than before' (ch. iii). And yet, on our first introduction to Sir William, we find him in trouble with an innkeeper. He has stayed at an inn for two days, but has no means to pay his reckoning, having given three guineas the day before to the town beadle in order to save an old soldier from being whipped for dog-stealing. Fortunately he meets the Vicar, who has just arrived at the inn on his way to Wakefield, having lost his whole fortune. The Vicar is filled with admiration for a man who can demonstrate such selfless generosity, and without knowing anything about the antecedents of this stranger whom he has just met, he settles the account with the angry landlord. The Man in Black, like Smollett's Matthew Bramble, is ashamed of his 'natural benevolence' and afraid of being imposed upon; so he pretends to be a misanthrope, and is heard professing himself 'a man-hater while his cheek was glowing with compassion' (letter xxvi).

In the characterization of all these men whom Goldsmith loves, what is ultimately favoured, is not the discipline imposed by the mind, but the morality dictated by the heart.

Goldsmith's conception of Sir William Thornhill, as the ideal gentleman ('he is Goldsmith's Allworthy', as E.A. Baker points out)[7] is essentially sentimental. Sir William is supposed to be a distinguished, wise, learned, able, understanding, versatile, statesman. He wanders about the countryside in the character of a 'poor gentleman' in order to find 'a woman, who a stranger to my fortune could think that I had merit as a man' (ch. xxxi). During the course of the action, he frequently acts the part of a saviour. He protects simplicity from being imposed upon, and virtue from being contaminated, besides rescuing pretty girls from drowning. He helps farmers in their harvesting and haying, and in return accepts whatever hospitality they offer. At even-tide he sings old ballads, the fresh beauty of which he contrasts with the turgid style of contemporary poetry. He prefers the company of children, 'harmless little men', to that of grown-ups, and always carries in his pocket 'a piece of ginger bread or an halfpenny whistle' for them (ch. vi). Having known life at court, he prefers the Vicar's 'little dwelling'.

In *The Vicar of Wakefield* (ch. xv) there is an interesting argument, in which the characters debate whether 'the honest man' is, indeed, 'the noblest work of God'. The Vicar, who mistakenly suspects Burchell of guile and treachery bursts out angrily :

> 'Both wit and understanding,' cried I, 'are trifles, without integrity: it is that which gives value to every character. The ignorant peasant without fault, is greater than the philosopher with many; for what is genius or courage without an heart ? *An honest man is the noblest work of God.*'
> 'I always held that hackney'd maxim of Pope,' returned Mr. Burchell, 'as very unworthy a man of genius, and a base desertion of his own superiority. As the reputation of books is raised not by their freedom from defect, but the greatness of their beauties; so should that of men be prized not for their exemption from fault, but the size of those virtues they are possessed of. The scholar may want prudence, the statesman may have pride, and the champion ferocity; but shall we prefer to these the low mechanic, who laboriously plods on through life without censure or applause ? . . .'

This is as categorical and rational an answer as any; but we find Mr. Burchell (or Goldsmith) soon sinking into sentimentalism and distortion of facts :

> I have ever perceived that where the mind was capacious, the affections were good. And indeed Providence seems kindly our friend in this particular, thus to debilitate the understanding where the heart is corrupt, and diminish the power where there is the will to do mischief. This rule seems to extend even to other animals; the little vermin race are ever treacherous, cruel, and cowardly, whilst those endowed with strength and power are generous, brave, and gentle.

One wonders where Goldsmith picked up all this animal and human lore, but it is certain that he had only to consult his own instincts, to despise the corrupt heart and the mischievous will, joined though these may be to the most brilliant mind, and to recognize the greatness and strength of the 'generous, brave, and gentle'.

To Goldsmith, the spontaneous generosity that gives without waiting to examine merit or desert, and to weigh the risks, was better than the cold justice that will not excuse the least fault. Gentleness and forgiveness he put high above strenuous discipline and clarity of judgment; amiability and geniality high above urbanity and suave manners. In his approach to the characterization of the men whom he loves and admires, it is easy to see his conviction that the pardonable laxities of their good-nature, are the inevitable accompaniment of their nobility. Sir William Woodville, exasperated though he is by his nephew's good-nature, is conscious of this :

> Yet we must touch his weaknesses with a delicate hand. There are some faults so nearly allied to excellence, that we can scarce weed out the vice without eradicating the virtue.
> (*The Good-Natur'd Man*, act I)

It is these convictions about life that Goldsmith attempts to vindicate in the character of the Vicar, though after some characteristic preliminary hesitations, and with an ironic awareness of the ridiculous reverse side of the picture. The good and noble Dr. Primrose, with his gentle, accommodating temper and indulgent humour, is too tolerant to be a strict disciplinarian. He is too unworldly not to be duped by the cunning and the malicious. Like the other beloved parson from 'the deserted village', he is 'more skilled to raise the wretched than to rise' (*The Deserted Village*, 1. 148). But, in his affections, he is shown as not only generous, but as truly 'skilled'; not only kind, but genuinely able to understand the difficulties of others. To his daughter who is in trouble, he can show not merely tenderness and love, but can also give sustaining comfort and perfect understanding. His charity and love for his fellow-men, his sweetness and whimsical humour make him a genuinely lovable person. It is his creator's conviction that such men alone can rise above their individual interests to that true generosity and genuine faith, which are the ultimate test of wisdom and worth in man. But the stern realist, or the sophisticated intellectual, will dismiss him and the story of his life, as Dr. Johnson dismissed them :

"No madam, it is very faulty; there is nothing of real life in it, and very little of nature. It is a mere fanciful performance."[8]

If in an age of cruel satire and callous sophistication, Goldsmith felt compelled to assert the right of indulgent good-nature and warm-hearted simplicity, even at the risk of sounding a little 'fanciful', his somewhat exaggerated reaction has an undoubted value when directed at certain opposite exaggerations which enjoyed much prestige in the society in which he lived. What his servant says about 'young' Honeywood in the first dialogue of *The Good-Natur'd Man* can aptly be said about Goldsmith himself :

But here comes the strange, good-natur'd, foolish, open-hearted—And yet, all his faults are such that one loves him still the better for them.

The preference for 'the heart rather than the head'[9] is declared much more unambiguously in Henry Mackenzie than in Goldsmith. Unlike Goldsmith, Mackenzie does not feel drawn towards the other side of the question, at least in his novels, though, in his later writings he felt compelled to point out the dangers of hyper-sensibility.

Mackenzie regards simplicity and guilelessness as among the most blessed of the virtues. Like Parson Adams, the hero of *The Man of Feeling*, William Harley, is 'a child in the drama of the world' (ch. xiii). However, for Mackenzie, a virtue greater than even simplicity is sensibility; Harley is characterized as a man of 'extreme sensibility' (ch. xiii).

Mackenzie's reaction against the rationalism and sophistication of contemporary civilization is far more pronounced than that of the other novelists of these decades. He advocates the cultivation of a feeling heart with a much more abandoned fervour. A warm, generous heart is no longer sufficient equipment; a bursting, overflowing one seems to be necessary. Moreover, proof of such a heart is required to be given by the weeping eye. The heroes of Mackenzie are endowed with the most freely functioning lachrymose glands among the heroes of fiction.

Much more often than in the case of the other novelists discussed in this book, one feels that Mackenzie is not so much depicting life as reacting somewhat violently against certain trends in contemporary society, and intrusively preaching an attitude to life which is exaggeratedly sentimental. The humour and the vitality, the shrewd observation of life, and the deep understanding of it, which entitle the other novelists to rank among the greatest delineators of life in English literature, and which make their 'simple' characters so endearing, are not to be found in Mackenzie. The others rank among the masters of irony in English; this irony, together with the intellectual verve and the great gusto we find in their writings, saves their novels from mawkishness; in Mackenzie these qualities are almost completely absent. In consequence of the exaggerations in his attitude, and his comparatively mediocre technique, he fails to convince the reader of the worth of the ideal he places before him.

At the time he was writing his novels, Mackenzie was greatly attracted to the optimistic-sentimental trends in contemporary philosophy which were becoming increasingly popular in certain quarters as the century advanced. Idealistic and emotional people, as well as those who liked to believe that they were keenly sensitive, felt the attraction of a philosophy which asserted that man was by nature good, and would act humanely and justly, if he was allowed to behave as his instincts urged him, undeterred by the artificiality imposed by 'civilization'.

Mackenzie can think of no severer castigation of a man than to call him a 'man of the world', and of no greater compliment than to call him a 'man of feeling'. He takes every opportunity to pour execration upon the luxury, corruption, depravity and hypocrisy of 'the world', of 'high life'. In 'the world' where success is the only value that is cherished, virtues are called vices, and vices virtues. Thus generosity of heart is called imprudence; narrowness of heart, sagaciousness. The impertinence of a coxcomb passes for social poise, but modesty is termed 'rusticity'. William Harley's worldly guardians disapprove of his manners and continually urge him to develop 'a happy forwardness' (ch. xii). They are incapable of understanding his sensitive 'bashfulness', which is not 'the awkwardness of a booby, which a few steps into the world will convert into the pertness of a coxcomb', but that 'consciousness, which the most delicate feelings produce, and the most extensive knowledge cannot always remove' (ch. xi). Indeed, all the virtues which a successful man of the world requires to practise, and which are expounded so brilliantly in the letters of Chesterfield, are anathema to the man of feeling. It is natural, therefore, to find a number of diatribes against the Chesterfield letters in *The Mirror* and *The Lounger*, the two Edinburgh periodicals over which Mackenzie presided from 1779 to 1787.[10] Quite distinct from the 'art of politeness' taught by Chesterfield, is true politeness which is characterized not by flourishes and formalities, but by 'sentiment'. One remembers Rousseau who said that the 'laws of politeness' are 'to be found in a kindly heart' (*Emile*, bk. iv).

Not only 'politeness' but all virtuous inclinations and actions issue from feeling. The altruistic and virtuous feelings are, moreover, considered to be 'naturally' present in all men not corrupted by civilization. Consequently, intellect, moral discipline and religion are assigned a very minor role, if any, in a good man's life. Of Miss Walton, the heroine of *The Man of Feeling*, we read:

...for her humanity was a feeling, not a principle: but minds like Harley's are not very apt to make this distinction, and generally give our virtue credit for all that benevolence which is instinctive in our nature. (ch. xiii)

A similar emphasis on 'natural feeling', and a similar condemnation of 'the world', is found in the stories in serial form which Mackenzie wrote for *The Mirror* and *The Lounger*; these tales achieved an amazing popularity, being printed again and again in Scottish and English periodicals till the end of the century. A very popular tale, the story of Louisa Veroni (*Mirror*, nos. 108-9), is meant to illustrate the absence of 'natural feeling' in the 'higher ranks of society'. Of La Roche, the noble and suffering clergyman living amidst the 'sublimity' of the Swiss mountains we are told: 'La Roche's religion was that of sentiment, not of theory'; of his story (*Mirror*, nos. 42-4) the author says: 'religion is introduced as a feeling not a system, as appealing to the sentiments of the heart, not to the disquisitions of the head.' The influence of the section on the Savoyard Vicar in *Emile* is obvious.

Writers like Mackenzie who exalted 'natural feeling' saw the noble, characteristically human, virtues shining in those whose natures are not blighted by the artificiality of civilization, those whom the world unthinkingly calls savages. The 'noble savage' idea, which was then becoming fashionable, had a considerable appeal for Mackenzie. In *The Man of Feeling* the story of the old soldier Edwards's pathetic plight in the British army stationed in the American colonies is meant to illustrate the vicious cruelty of civilized people, as opposed to the nobility, generosity and wisdom of primitive people. A poor Red Indian prisoner is most mercilessly flogged for several days by the British in order to make him reveal the secret of his hidden treasure. Old Edwards, who helps him to escape from his tormentors, is sentenced to three hundred lashes by a court-martial and is then dismissed from the army. Turned out of the camp without any pity, Edwards meets the Indian he has helped. The reader is meant to take note of the magnanimity of the Indian, and of the poetry of his speech:

> He pressed me in his arms, and kissed the marks of the lashes on my back a thousand times... When we parted he pulled out a purse with two hundred pieces of gold in it... He embraced me:—'You are an Englishman,' said he, 'but the Great Spirit has given you an Indian heart; may He bear up the weight of your old age, and blunt the arrow that brings it rest!' (ch. xxxiv)

In *The Man of the World* several pages are devoted to giving an account of William Annesly's life in America among the Cherokees. Annesly describes the horrifying tortures to which the Cherokees subject the prisoners taken from a neighbouring tribe. The tortures are indescribably brutal, yet Mackenzie's intention seems to be to give an idealized picture of them. The 'noble savage' prisoners bear all the tortures with great courage, and even ask for more, so that they can prove their fortitude, 'an indispensable virtue among the Indians'. Describing 'the festival of their revenge', Annesly comments: 'You can hardly conceive a species of inventive cruelty which they did not inflict on the wretches whom fortune had thus put into their power' (II, xviii). Annesly himself has to undergo the trial of his fortitude by suffering without a groan the most ingenious Indian tortures before he is accepted as one of them: 'He only is worthy to lift the hatchet with the Cherokees, to whom shame is more intolerable than the stab of the knife, or the burning of the fire' (II, xviii). After he has thus proved his courage, he is adopted by a 'noble red man'. There follows a long description of the fineness of 'this rude and simple state of society'. In the course of this description the greed, cruelty and dishonesty of European society are contrasted, through several pages and incidents, with the nobility of the red men: 'My imagination drew, on this side, fraud, hypocrisy, and sordid baseness; while on that seemed to preside honesty, truth, and savage nobleness of soul' (II, xix). After the description of the cruel tortures, this praise of the savage state is not merely sentimental, it proves a shocking lack of sensibility in the writer.

But if sensibility can make Mackenzie insensitive in some matters, it does arouse him to think humanely and justly on many questions. Almost every novelist of the century brings in, as Mackenzie does, the problem of debtor's prisons, of the eviction of poor tenants, of women who are forced to become prostitutes, and of the abuses and cruelty in the army and navy; but 'the man of feeling' alone is aroused, by his sensibility, to think justly of the problem of military conquests and colonialism.[11] Seventeen years before the commencement of the seven-year trial of Warren Hastings for 'high crimes and misdemeanours' against the people of India, Mackenzie wrote:

'Edwards', said he, 'I have a proper regard for the prosperity of my country: every native of it appropriates to himself some share of the power, or the fame, which, as a nation, it acquires; but I cannot throw off the man so much, as to rejoice, at our conquests in India... What title have the subjects of another kingdom to establish an empire in

India to give laws to a country where the inhabitants received them on the terms of friendly commerce ? You say they are happier under our regulations than the tyranny of their own petty princes. I must doubt it, from the conduct of those by whom these regulations have been made... When shall I see a commander return from India in the pride of honourable poverty? (*Man of Feeling*, ch. xxxvi)

Similarly, it is the importance that he attaches to sentiment that enables Mackenzie to take a just stand on the question of slavery. He is among the first creative writers who stress the cruelty of the system; it is one of his principal didactic motives in writing his last novel, *Julia de Roubigné*. What is more, his insistence on the cultivation of sensibility enables him to perceive, what every abolitionist was not able to see, the soul-destroying nature of the system on master as well as slave : 'for the master of slaves has seldom the soul of a man' (*Julia de Roubigné*, letter xxxviii).

Once again, it is the value he attaches to sentiment that makes Mackenzie, like the poets of the Shaftesbury school, more sensitive than most of his contemporaries to the influence of nature, and leads him to postulate a theory about the ministry of nature which foreshadows Wordsworth and the other great writers of the Romantic period. In the story of the Swiss priest La Roche (*Mirror*, nos. 42-4), we hear of the 'sublimity of ideas' experienced by the contemplation of 'those astonishing mountains'. In *Lounger* no. 87, which shows the 'moral use' of the countryside, we hear of the 'purity of mind' inspired by country scenes. The 'rural sentiment', we are told in a quite Wordsworthian phrase, 'stills...the tumult of desire'. In the same essay we come upon the Aeolian harp image which was to become a favourite image of the Romantic poets.

Like the Romantic poets, and essayists, Mackenzie advocates an attachment to the past, to things and places, and praises this attachment for the pensive, melancholy mood it inspires; a mood that stifles vicious instincts and encourages the humane. benevolent ones (*Mirror*, no. 61). The young hero of *The Man of the World* finds 'something that pleased him in the melancholy of lonely recesses and halfworn paths' (II, iii).

Such idealization of nature, natural feelings and natural people, easily leads to a denunciation of those who feel at ease in the sophisticated, artificial world created by civilization, and achieve what the world calls 'success'. In Mackenzie's novels, the men of true worth, 'ill-suited to the rude touch of sublunary things' (*Julia de Roubigné*, letter xlii), more often than not founder and give up the struggle of contending against a wicked world. A premature death seems to be the only solution for the story of the life of the good gentleman, Harley. He catches a fever while nursing a suffering old soldier, and has no urge to recover. His beloved Miss Walton tries to dissuade him from giving up so easily, but Harley finds it best to stop breathing in a world so wicked. And yet, it is made clear, if one is a man of feeling, one will not hate the world. The lesson that is finally taught through the 'narrator' of the story is the lesson that is taught to Rousseau's Emile (bk. iv)—not to hate the world in spite of its folly and wickedness, but to 'pity the men of it' (ch. lvi).

If the man of feeling is incapable of achieving worldly success, the man of the world is incapable of attaining true happiness; for such happiness can be obtained only by exercising the natural instinct of benevolence, which is innate in every man, but which is stifled by the world that has cynically adopted the false philosophy of self interest. On the contrary, the man of feeling, though he achieves no worldly success, and is always getting into scrapes because of his guileless nature, experiences moments of supreme happiness; he feels a glow within himself when he rescues an unfortunate being from misery. For such a benevolent man not only are eternal rewards kept in reserve; he also experiences the highest kind of happiness here below.

In dramatizing the sensitiveness of his heroes who are distinguished from the common herd by their exquisite sensibilities, Mackenzie gives some quite grotesque demonstrations of emotion. Suffering beneficiaries are pictured as 'crawling forward on the ground', and 'clasping the knees' of their generous benefactors (ch. xl). A film of 'beamy moisture' (ch. xxxvi) covers the eyes of the grateful. Hearing that his unmarried daughter is with child, Annesly falls senseless to the floor. His faithful servant 'threw himself down by him, tearing his white locks, and acting all the frantic extravagances of grief' (I, xxvii). The modern reader needs to be reminded that he is meant to admire this conduct.

More distasteful than this hypertrophy of the feelings is the suggestion that there is a pleasure to be derived from witnessing scenes of misery, a luxury to be enjoyed in shedding tears. When the beautiful Harriet Annesly mistakes the libertine who has driven her brother to crime for his benefactor and falls at his feet to bless him, the 'unfeeling, brutal' rake 'feasted the grossness of his fancy with the anticipation of her undoing'. At this the author is aroused to comment that 'there is a truer, more exquisite voluptuary' than the libertine :

Had virtue been now looking on the figure of beauty and innocence I have attempted to draw—I see the purpose of benevolence beaming in his eye !—its throb is swelling in his heart ! he clasps her to his bosom—he kisses the falling drops from her cheek—he weeps with her :—and the luxury of his tears—baffles description. (*Man of the World*, I, xviii)

Even in his later essays, when he had realized the affectation and hypocrisy in which the sensitive can indulge, Mackenzie harps on the 'delight' that is to be obtained from the contemplation of suffering. In *The Mirror* essay, entitled *Advantages to be drawn from Scenes of Sorrow* (no. 72), he asserts : 'There is a sympathetic enjoyment which often makes it not only *better*, but more *delightful, to go to the house of mourning, than to the house of feasting.*' This thought is occasioned by the writer's presence at the funeral of a beautiful young girl; he almost revels in the proud fact that he can feel : 'I think I would not have exchanged my feelings at the time for all the mirth which gaiety could inspire, or all the pleasure which luxury could bestow.'

Poets and preachers in all ages have underlined the value of 'the house of mourning', of 'frequent sights of what is to be borne', as Wordsworth put it ('Elegiac Stanzas', 1.58); but they have not blatantly extracted enjoyment from affliction. If it were not for the fact that the emphasis on the delight to be obtained from suffering is not at all uncommon in many of Mackenzie's contemporaries, one would look upon it as a psychopathological tendency in this particular writer. But the same attitude is to be found in numerous sentimental writers (and also in writers supposedly realistic, and even rough, like Smollett), since Prévost started the fashion in Europe. In the person of his Man of Quality, Prévost wrote :

> If tears and sighs are not to be described as pleasure, it is true nevertheless that they have infinite sweetness for a person in mortal affliction. The moments that I devoted to my grief were so dear to me that to prolong them I abstained from sleep.[12]

The most celebrated example of the literature of sensibility is of course the *Héloise* of Rousseau, who in passages of lyric fervour made the world drink 'la coupe amère et douce de la sensibilité' (VI, xi).

But it would be unfair to suggest that the curve of sensibility is to be traced from the French Prévost to the French Rousseau. As we have seen, Fielding's admired teachers, the Latitudinarian divines, as well as Shaftesbury, had given a religious and philosophical basis to sentiment. In *The Covent-Garden Journal* (no. 29) Fielding himself quoted with approval from the Latitudinarian theologian and professor of Mathematics, Isaac Barrow, a passage emphasizing the 'savoury delight' to be obtained from the exercise of beneficence, enabling a man to 'be VIRTUOUSLY VOLUPTUOUS AND A LAUDABLE EPICURE BY DOING MUCH GOOD'. In the Dedication to *Amelia* Fielding suggests that his reader ought to 'pardon many faults for the pleasure he will receive from a tender sensation'. *Amelia*, of course, is commonly recognized as slightly affected by the sensibility trend, but even in the early *Joseph Andrews*, the writer, in the characteristic sensibility style, reminds 'the hard-hearted villain . . . that there is a pleasure in the tender sensation beyond any which he is capable of tasting' (III, xii). Nor is sensibility absent from the 'comic-epic' of *Tom Jones*. The thirteenth book begins with an invocation which has the true flavour of sensibility :

And thou, almost the constant attendant on true genius, Humanity, bring all thy tender sensations ... the tender scene ... and all those strong energies of a good mind, which fill the moistened eyes with tears, the glowing cheeks with blood, and swell the heart with tides of grief, joy and benevolence. (XIII, i)

The 'affecting' scenes 'of distress', picturing the starving Anderson family (XIII, viii), and the Miller family's hysterics when the daughter is found to be carrying an illegitimate child (XIV, vi), do not fall much short of Mackenzie's excesses. Fielding demonstrates his heroine's amiable disposition by describing her taste in reading : "Ay, and do you love to cry then ?" says the aunt. "I love a tender sensation," answered the niece, "and would pay the price of a tear," (VI. v). When the heroine herself is harassed by her family, she finds compensation in the 'luxury' of grief : 'Sophia, then retired to her chamber of mourning, where she indulged herself (if the phrase may be allowed me) in all the luxury of tender grief' (VII, v).

If so much could be 'allowed' to the great ironist and 'healthy' comic writer, naturally more was expected of 'the man of feeling'. The fatuity of Mackenzie's sentimental passages at once strikes any modern reader, but a whole generation of readers and writers enthused over and imitated his novels and short stories. One such contemporary was the poet Burns, who referred to *The Man of Feeling* as 'a book I prize next to the Bible'.[13]

A revealing letter by Lady Louisa Stuart, then a young girl, to Sir Walter Scott, shows how much of a fashion tears were at this period; it also shows how quickly such fashions pass away :

One evening a book was wanted to be read aloud, and what you said of Mackenzie made the company chuse *The Man of Feeling*, though some apprehended it would prove too affecting. However we began : I, who was the reader, had not seen it for several years, the rest did not know it at all. I am afraid I perceived a sad change in it, or myself—which was worse; and the effect altogether failed. Nobody cried, and at some of the passages, the touches I used to think so exquisite—Oh Dear ! They laughed ... Yet I remember so well its first publication, my mother and sisters crying over it, dwelling upon it with rapture ! And when I read it as I was a girl of fourteen not yet versed in sentiment, I had a secret dread I should not cry enough to gain the credit of proper sensibility.[14]

Mackenzie's own standpoint on the question of sensibility shifted within a few years after the publication of his novels. One of the frequent themes of his later essays is the danger of hypersensibility and of adopting a false sense of values in the enthusiasm of emotion. In an essay entitled 'On Novel Writing' (*Lounger*, no. 20, 18 June 1785), he attacks novels which weave their plots from 'entanglements of delicacy' and represent a 'rivalship of virtues and duties'. However, even in his essays he came down very heavily on Sheridan, who in *The School for Scandal* presumed to expose and ridicule the advocates of sensibility by showing how useful and profitable it is to adopt sensibility as a pose. Entitling his essay *The Moral Effects of Comedy* (*Lounger*, no. 50), Mackenzie lashes out at Sheridan and his kind, whom he considers worse even than the Restoration writers :

... a kind of licentiousness in which some of our latest comedies have indulged, still more dangerous than the indelicacy of the last century : those sometimes violated decency, but these attack principle; those might put modesty to the blush, or contaminate the purity of innocence; but these shake the very foundation of morality, and would harden the mind against the sense of virtue.

After this strident piece of criticism which is quite incomprehensible to anyone who does not know the contemporary sensibility-promoters, Mackenzie embarks on a panegyric on sentimental comedy :

The people, indeed are always true to virtue, and open to the impressions of virtuous sentiment. With the people, the comedies in which these are developed still remain favourites; and corruption must have stretched its empire far indeed, when the applauses shall cease with which they are received.

The 'people', the patrons of the circulating libraries, indeed preferred gusts of emotion to the Restoration writers' hard brilliance and disconcerting lack of concern with morality. The generation which had set such store by 'esprit' had given way to a generation which found nothing appealing that was not muted by the soft haze of sentiment. To realize the measure of the distance that has been travelled, one has only to study the qualities of appearance and temper, so unMillamant-like, that Mackenzie and the sentimentalists select for praise in their women. The descriptions of the two heroines, Miss Walton and Miss Wilkins, from Mackenzie's two novels are typical, and call to mind Rousseau's descriptions of Sophia, the ideal girl whom he selects for his ideal boy, Emile (bk. v) :

> Her complexion was mellowed into a paleness, which certainly took from her beauty; but agreed, at least Harley used to say so, with the pensive softness of her mind. Her eyes were of that gentle hazel-colour which is rather mild than piercing . . . Her conversation was always cheerful, but rarely witty. (*Man of Feeling*, ch. xiii)

> She was not handsome enough to attract notice; but her look was of that complacent sort which gains on the beholder . . . Nor was her mind ill suited to this 'index of the soul'. Without that brilliancy which excites the general applause, it possessed those inferior sweetnesses which acquire the general esteem : sincere, benevolent, inoffensive, and unassuming. (*Man of the World*, I, i)[15]

An exaggerated emphasis on sensibility leads not only to this sort of depreciation of the sharper, more intellectual qualities in literature and life, it also inevitably leads to melodrama, and, ironically, to an astounding lack of artistic as well as moral sensibility. Perhaps the most glaring example of such insensitive sensibility is the conclusion of *The Man of the World* (II, xxi-xxiv). Sir Thomas Sindal, whose characterization throughout the novel is a typical example of the pictures of aristocratic dissipation and villainy in eighteenth century fiction, is about to rape the foundling, Lucy Sindal, who has been living in his house since infancy. At the last precarious moment Lucy's lover rushes in and saves her. In the ensuing struggle Sir Thomas receives a wound. Just then a strange women bursts in to proclaim that Sir Thomas is Lucy's father. Sir Thomas is horrified and, feeling the pain of his fatal wound, also feels repentant. Now Lucy kneels at Sir Thomas's feet :

> 'Talk not, sir', said she, 'of the errors of the past; methinks I look on it as some horrid dream, which it dizzies my head to recollect. My father !—Gracious God ! have I a father ?—I cannot speak; but there are a thousand things that beat here ! Is there another parent, to whom I should also kneel ?' Sir Thomas cast up a look to Heaven, and his groans stopped for a while his utterance.

It is this same Sir Thomas whose machinations tempted Lucy's uncle into crime, and who drugged and raped her mother. But, during his last few days on earth, he is tortured by the memories of his vicious crimes and sheds tears of repentance. This expiation is enough for the author to declare—'of those who have led his life, how few have closed it like him !'

The philosophy which elects sensibility and 'simplicity' as the highest attributes of a human being, in any case inadequate as an appraisal of life and character, seems even more inadequate, and, almost absurd, because of Mackenzie's artistic inadequacy. The weakness and implausibility of Mackenzie's novels (and of the other even more mediocre examples of this genre), are due not so much to the fact that the novelist puts his faith in a false ideal as to his failure to present his convictions with psychological perception, intellectual strength, emotional balance or felicity of style. Mackenzie's belief in his ideal would not have produced such mediocre novels, if he had possessed the ability to communicate with more artistic power his and his century's psychological craving for something precious in life which had been destroyed by contemporary fashions. The appeal and charm of this ideal as expressed in the novel, its capacity to move the reader to genuine feeling, are amply demonstrated by Sterne's portrayal of Uncle Toby and his world.

However, after this harsh appraisal one must emphasize a point which critics have not stressed sufficiently, that in Mackenzie's presentation of the children, Harriet and Billy

Annesly, we have the first really sensitive and appealing studies of children in the history of the English novel,—and that this fine achievement is probably a direct result of the qualities of simplicity and emotional sensibility that he admired so much.

It is perhaps unfair to make Mackenzie stand comparison with Sterne, for Sterne reaches one of the high peaks of the art of the novel. The feeling that the most appealing and humane ideal of character is to be found embodied in the simple, innocent, warm-hearted man, is projected more artistically, as well as with a morally morei mpressive result by Sterne than by any other novelist of the century. In the characterization of My Uncle Toby the presentation escapes those dangers to which the idealization of the simple, 'feeling' man is only too prone, and attains a piquancy, buoyancy and convincingness seldom to be found in a portrayal of ideal goodness. Sterne achieves an unusually subtle combination of idealism and irony, of sentiment and intellectual brilliance, of pathos and hilarity.

Sterne shows a more refined understanding than Goldsmith and Mackenzie of the problem of presenting simplicity as the highest ideal of character. He is much more subtle in showing how the sophistication which blunts the feelings should be cast aside, to give place to that true graciousness which comes from the heart, that *politesse du coeur*, which inclines men more to humane actions, than courteous ones' (*SJ*, 'Character, Versailles'). Fielding's desire to portray the guilelessness of Parson Adams involves the parson in a series of boxing bouts; he is sent rolling down into the mire of a pig-sty; the contents of chamber-pots are sent streaking down his face. Toby gets involved in no such skirmishes. Toby may not have learnt to practise the airs and bows and studied formalities of fashionable society, but one is made to notice that he possesses a spontaneous graciousness and courtesy 'independently of all modes and customs' (VI, ix). Toby carries 'his cane like a pike' and, even when he goes to woo the Widow Wadman, wears an ill-fitting, awkward uniform and a rumpled wig, but 'Nature had......wrote Gentleman with so fair a hand in every line of his countenance' (IX, ii) that he could not be mistaken for anything but a gentleman, unlike Fielding's parson who is mistaken for a pedlar by the gay squires, and for a dealer come about the pigs by Parson Trulliber.

Toby, his brother Walter says, does not know 'so much as the right end of a woman from the wrong'; he has never gazed into a woman's eye 'excepting once that he was beguiled into it by Mrs. Wadman' who pretended something had got into hers; yet with a woman in sorrow or distress he is perfectly at ease, 'nor would the most courteous knight of romance have gone further, at least upon one leg, to have wiped away a tear from a woman's eye' (IX, iii).

In contrast to the usual simple character, Toby is never culpably foolish, nor do his idiosyncrasies make him a nuisance to others. Parson Adams, Goldsmith's Vicar, and Mackenzie's Annesly are the victims of all sorts of deceptions. But Toby is never shown as stupid or credulous; he falls into no traps except when the wily widow, 'daughter of Eve' (VIII, viii), traps him into falling in love—but which son of Adam has ever escaped that trap ?

It often passes unnoticed that Toby, in spite of his guileless innocence and his hobby-horse, represents the point of commonsense and reasonableness in the midst of all the exaggerations and freakishness and pig-headedness of the other characters in the novel. When the learned and knowing ones of the world do or say something particularly absurd or insensitive, Toby starts whistling *Lillabullero* and brings the situation back to normality and good sense :[16]

> You must know it was the usual channel thro' which his passion got vent, when anything shocked or surprised him :— but especially when any thing, which he deemed very absurd, was offered. (I, xxi)

The subtleties of learned discourses lead the schoolmen to arrive at queer though seemingly logical conclusions like 'the mother is not of kin to her child'. Analysis fascinates the philosopher who, in his zeal to decide that 'there are two different kinds of love, according to the different parts which are affected by it—The Brain or Liver', never learns how to love. But Toby, with his 'plain sense of things' (I, xxi), is both more down to earth and more humane:

> What signifies it, brother Shandy, replied my uncle Toby, which of the two it is provided it will but make a man marry, and love his wife, and get a few children? There is at least, said Yorick, a great deal of reason and plain sense in Captain Shandy's opinion of love; and 'tis amongst the ill-spent hours of my life, which I have to answer for, that I have read so many flourishing poets and rhetoricians in my time, from whom I never could extract so much. (VIII, xxxiii)

With the subtlest delicacy Sterne thus contrives to depict a character who is utterly innocent without being obtuse or stupid. Moreover, Sterne makes us recognize that Toby, in spite of his eccentric preoccupation with his hobby-horse, does not ride it so hard that he cannot climb down at once at the call of life, to give his time and attention to the suffering. Unlike his brother's eccentric absorption in abstruse learning, the world of make-believe fortifications which Toby creates for himself never becomes an inhuman preoccupation.

Another noticeable difference between Sterne and his contemporaries is that Sterne is hardly ever overtly didactic. In fact, he seems to squirm at the brazen didacticism of the writers of his century:

> Writing, when properly managed (as you may be sure I think mine is) is but a different name for conversation. As no one, who knows what he is about in good company, would venture to talk all;—so no author, who understands the just boundaries of decorum and good breeding, would presume to think all : The truest respect which you can pay to the reader's understanding, is to halve this matter amicably, and leave him something to imagine, in his turn, as well as yourself. (II, xi)

Toby himself, unlike the Vicar and Parson Adams, suffers from no didactic zeal; he never harangues the suffering in order to preach endurance and fortitude; nor does he, like Mackenzie's heroes, indulge in sentimental effusions and profuse weeping. There is no self-righteousness, no rhetoric, no noise at all, about Toby. When he hears of the pathetic plight of Le Fever and his little boy, he decides at once to do all in his power to help them, but all that he says when the situation becomes too tragic is, 'I wish, Trim, I was asleep' (VI, vii). Yet critics will accuse Sterne of having fathered Mackenzie and his school, and will even say that Mackenzie is a better writer than Sterne, because he is more 'sincere'.[17]

Sterne's frisky humour, unflagging sense of fun, and mild but ever-present irony have an astringent effect on the sentimentality and exaggeration to which idealization is only too prone. Toby's worth and charm are proved against the background of everyday life with its normal ups and downs. Yet no reader will doubt that Toby has all the reserves of strength to bear any misfortune, and all the generosity of heart to forgive any injury. Sterne needs no odious villains, no unscrupulously clever schemers, to prove the greatness of his simple man. No execration is poured upon successful men of the world; we are spared the usual blunt attacks against the vice, cruelty and worthlessness of fashionable people, and the tedious and repetitious scenes of balls, masquerades, seductions, brothels, duels and the rest of the paraphernalia of the eighteenth century novel. Instead, the ideal of simplicity is set off by devising for it a background which makes the book original, refreshing and provocatively witty. Innocence and warmth of heart are projected against the arrogance and perversity of reason, and the blindness of learning, impressing upon the mind the distance between learning and life, between knowledge and understanding.

Toby's brother, Walter Shandy, is 'a philosopher in grain,—speculative,—systematical' (I, xxi); he is a victim to that disease of theorizing and dogmatizing in which truth is the greatest sufferer. Walter with 'his systems and opiniatry' (VII, xxvii) twists and tortures 'every event in nature into an hypothesis, by which means never man crucified Truth at the rate he did' (IX, xxxii). Among such learned men, as Shakespeare phrased it, simple truth is miscalled simplicity (Sonnet lxvi). Sterne sums up the problem, as he sees it, in *A Sentimental Journey*: "When the heart flies out before the understanding, it saves the judgment a world of pains' ('The Remise Door, Calais'). The mistrusting intellect misshapes the forms of things; when he cuts through the knots of theory and reasoning with an instinctive generosity of heart, man arrives at a true understanding of life and its problems. Corporal Trim, Toby's loyal servant and spiritual brother to him in innocence and generosity, is so little used to habits of learning and reasoning that he can remember the fifth commandment only if he is allowed to start at the first, and reel off all of them till he comes to the fifth. According to Walter, he has not 'one determinate idea annexed to any one word he repeats'. Yet Trim proves the best commentator on the commandments :

—Prythee, Trim, quoth my father, turning round to him—What dost thou mean by 'honouring thy father and mother'? Allowing them, an' please your honour, three half pence a day out of my pay, when they grew old.—And didst thou do that, Trim ? said Yorick.—He did indeed, replied my uncle Toby.—Then Trim, said Yorick, springing out of his chair, and taking the corporal by the hand, thou art the best commentator upon that part of the Decalogue; and I honour thee more for it Corporal Trim, than if thou hadst had a hand in the *Talmud* itself. (V, xxxii)

The callousness and loss of contact with life to which the pursuit of reason can lead the speculative is illustrated in the brilliant scene (V, ii-xiv) in which Shandy Hall receives the news of the death of Walter's son, Bobby. Walter, in spite of the fact that he is a 'frank and generous' man, is so completely carried away by his enthusiastic memories of philosophy and literature that as he harangues the company on life and death, he 'absolutely forgets' Bobby. He brings his eloquent disquisition on death to a close with this incredible peroration :

If my son could not have died, it had been matter of wonder,—not that he is dead......'tis terrible no way—for consider, brother Toby,—when we are—death is not;—and when death is—we are not. (V, iii)

The scene is a masterpiece of uproarious humour, strengthened by the author's learning, wit and sprightliness. It is brought to a moving conclusion by the realization of the meaning and pathos of life, and of the variety of the characters of men. No mere sentimentalist, nor any mere wit, could attain the superb quality of these chapters.

Though Sterne was gifted with a sparkling intellect, and though he was steeped in abstruse learning, for him man is most truly man, and most God-like, not when he thinks, but when he feels. The most emphatic assertion of this belief is the famous apostrophe to 'Dear Sensibility' in *A Sentimental Journey* ('The Bourbonnois'). Sensibility alone makes man generous, and enables him to respond to the joys and sorrows of his fellow-creatures, man or beast. The only way to forget one's self and one's petty miseries is to rejoice and suffer with others :

> *Surely, this is not walking in a vain shadow,—nor does man disquiet himself* in vain *by it*—he oftener does so in trusting the issue of his commotions to reason only.— I can safely say, for myself, I was never able to conquer any one single bad sensation in my heart so decisively as by beating up as fast as I could for some kindly and gentle sensation to fight it upon its own ground. (*SJ*, 'The Passport, Versailles')

One is reminded of Keats's wish, 'O for a Life of Sensations rather than of Thoughts !'[18] It is from reason and from that 'understrapping virtue of discretion' (*TS*, VI, xvii), that the vices of avarice, caution, cowardice, hypocrisy, meanness and pride emanate, and 'encompass the heart with adamant' (*SJ*, 'The Remise Door, Calais'). Similarly reason leads one away from Nature into sophistication and artificiality : 'I wish she may ever remain a child of nature—I hate children of art', Sterne said, referring to his daughter who was on her first visit to Paris (To Lady D —, 9 July 1762). Nevertheless, no judgment could be more fantastic than that of his biographer Wilbur L. Cross, who said about Sterne, 'reason. . . . he had none'.[19]

Though he idealises feeling, Sterne, especially the Sterne of *Tristram Shandy*, is certainly not a sentimental writer, in the usual meaning of this phrase. Though the duty of feeling, and of trusting to the impulse of the moment, is an important part of his creed, he can always stand at a distance from himself and his writings with an amused awareness, ready to intervene as soon as feeling turns to excess, or to mechanical gesticulation. His attitude is described in a very apt phrase by Miss Margaret Shaw, who speaks of 'his diffidence in the presence of pathos'.[20] To realise this, one need only compare his technique in emotional passages with the uninhibited way in which Shelley and Byron, and even Lamb, proclaim their feelings and turn on the pathos. Sterne can feel very sincerely, and yet can laugh at the attitudinizing to which feeling drives some people. It is this combination in Sterne which is so delightful.[21] (An exception, however, must be made of his last work, or rather his intimate communion with himself, *The Journal to Eliza*, which he wrote when that disease which he had so gaily defied all his life, after having completely mastered his body, was beginning to break his mental resistance.) Perhaps the most delightful illustrations of this genuine participation in the feelings of others, and yet triumphant objectivity and artistic control, are the scenes of the donkey and the macaroon in *Tristram Shandy* (VII, xxxii), and the Grisette scene in *A Sentimental Journey* ('The Pulse, Paris', 'The Husband, Paris').

Of course no writer seeks, and savours, a sentimental moment as much as Sterne does. The sensation of sentiment is sweet upon his nerves, and he consciously enjoys it, and recommends that his reader go in search of similar experiences. Yet his sentimental experiences were genuine and deep enough to exhaust his frail body; and to make him 'wretched':

> He [Yorick, i.e. himself] has worn out both his spirits and his body with the Sentimental Journey—'tis true that an author must feel himself, or the reader will not—but I have torn my whole frame into pieces by my feelings. (to the Earl of—, 28 Nov 1767)

Though Sterne thus ardently praises sensibility, savours the sensations it produces, and exhausts himself savouring them, unlike the sentimental novels of the period, *Tristram Shandy* far from being drenched with tears, is a rollickingly funny novel.

Of course Sterne believes enough in the goodness and efficacy of tears to make Toby assert, 'Tears are no proof of cowardice, Trim. —I drop them oft-times myself' (IV, iv). Trim, at times, sheds a few quite justified tears; though we are made to notice, that 'he had often cried at his master's sufferings, but never shed a tear at his own' (VIII, xix). More characteristic of Sterne, and so much more purposeful and artistic in arousing sympathy and emotion, are passages where sorrow is suffered quietly; in intimate, but silent, communion with another : 'the heart, both of the master and the man, were alike subject to sudden overflowings; —a short silence ensued' (VIII, xix).

Unlike the run-of-the-mill sentimentalist, Sterne can make use of the literary devices of pathos and sentiment to a purpose. As he wrote to Mr. and Mrs. James (12 Nov 1767), his aim in *A Sentimental Journey* was 'to teach us to love the world and our fellow creatures better than we do'. The statement applies equally to *Tristram Shandy*. Perhaps the most striking example of this purposive pathos and sentiment is the conversation about a negro girl between Toby and Trim. It was written partly in response to a plea : a negro, Ignatius Sancho, having read a 'truly affecting passage' on slavery in Sterne's Sermon, *Job's Account of the Shortness of Life, Considered*, and also having been charmed by 'that soul pleasing character of your amiable Uncle Toby', realized what power Sterne had to move the heart to pity, and sent an appeal to him to stir the world against slavery. Sancho, who perceived the range of Sterne's sympathies, proclaimed in a telling phrase : 'Very sure I am, that Yorick is an Epicurean in Charity.'[22] Sterne wrote back (27 July 1766) saying that when he received Sancho's letter, by coincidence, he had been writing 'a tender tale of the sorrows of a friendless poor negro girl'. He promised to try and 'weave the Tale' into *Tristram Shandy*. The result was not a 'tale', but a three-line description of a negro girl, followed by a brief conversation-piece between Toby and Trim, exquisite in its artistry and much more effective than a long diatribe against slavery. The description presents 'a poor negro girl, with a bunch of white feathers slightly tied to the end of a long cane, flapping away flies—not killing them'. This is, of course, slightly 'sentimental' in the pejorative sense of the word. But the dialogue that follows is developed with a delicate touch that is characteristic of Sterne:

> —'Tis a pretty picture ! said my uncle Toby—she had suffered persecution, Trim, and had learnt mercy—
> A negro has a soul? an' please your honour, said the corporal (doubtingly). I am not much versed, corporal, quoth my uncle Toby, in things of that kind; but I suppose, God would not leave him without one, any more than thee or me—
> —It would be putting one sadly over the head of another, quoth the corporal.
> It would be so; said my uncle Toby.—Why then, an' please your honour, is a black wench to be used worse than a white one ?
> I can give no reason, said my uncle Toby—
> —Only, cried the corporal, shaking his head, because she has no one to stand up for her—
> —'Tis that very thing, Trim, quoth my uncle Toby,—which recommends her to protection—and her brethren with her; 'tis the fortune of war which has put the whip into our hands now—where it may be hereafter, heaven knows !—but be it where it will, the brave, Trim, will not use it unkindly.
> —God forbid, said the corporal. (IX, vi)

It is thus that Sterne contrives to 'teach us to love ... our fellow-creatures better than we do', by prodding the world, ever so gently, to stop and think, as well as by moving it to pathos. In the face of such writing critics can say : 'but he does not think, nor has he any appreciation of moral values.'[23]

But masterly as Sterne's pathos is, it is only one aspect of his art, even of his art in depicting Toby. Sterne believed that the duty which he had taken upon himself, of making his reader 'love the world', was to be performed not only by moving him to tears and compassion, but also by moving him to laughter, and by impressing upon him the high merit of the virtue of Joy. He explained his purpose in writing *Tristram Shandy* :

—If 'tis wrote against anything,—'tis wrote, an' please your worships, against the spleen ! in order, by a more frequent and a more convulsive elevation and depression of the diaphragm, and the succussations of the intercostal and abdominal muscles in laughter, to drive the *gall* and other *bitter juices* from the gall-bladder, liver, and sweet-bread of his majesty's subjects, with all the inimicitious passions which belong to them, down into their duodenums. (IV, xxii)

It is the morose, the disgruntled, the splenetic, who are the enemies of life. Such people Sterne pitied more than he pitied the unfortunate :

I pity the man who can travel from Dan to Beersheba, and cry, 'Tis all barren,—and so it is; and so is all the world to him, who will not cultivate the fruits it offers . . . Was I in a desert, I would find out wherewith in it to call forth my affections—If I could not do better, I would fasten them upon some sweet myrtle, or seek some melancholy cypress to connect myself to . . .
The learned SMELFUNGUS[24] travelled from Boulogne to Paris—from Paris to Rome—and so on—but he set out with the spleen and jaundice, and every object he pass'd by was discoloured or distorted . . .
—I'll tell it, cried Smelfungus, to the world.— You had better tell it, said I, to your physician. (*SJ*, 'In the Street, Calais')

To relish life, and to be interested in all its manifestations, is a part of virtue. Therefore Sterne regarded 'every fair being as a temple, and would rather enter in, and see the original drawings and loose sketches hung up in it, than the transfiguration of Raphael itself' (*SJ*, 'The Passport, Versailles').

The fashionable traveller inquires about the heights of church steeples and the dimensions of palaces, and carefully notes them down in his book; Sterne would rather hasten to measure with his appreciative eyes a beautiful girl, for in her is the joy and the vitality, as also the transience, of life. The urge to stress the importance of this, results in the marvellous Janatone interlude in *Tristram Shandy* :

> —And as Janatone withal (for that is her name) stands so well for a drawing—may I never draw more, or rather may I draw like a draught-horse, by main strength all the days of my life,—if I do not draw her in all her proportions, and with as determined a pencil, as if I had her in the wettest drapery.—
> —But your worships choose rather that I give you the length, breadth, and perpendicular height of the great parish-church, or drawing of the facade of the abbey of Saint Austreberte which has been transported from Artois hither—every thing is just I suppose as the masons and carpenters left them,—and if the belief in Christ continues so long, will be so these fifty years to come—so your worships and reverences may all measure them at your leisures—but he who measures thee, Janatone, must do it now—thou carriest the principles of change within thy frame; and considering the chances of a transitory life, I would not answer for thee a moment; ere twice twelve months are passed and gone, thou mayest grow out like a pumpkin, and lose thy shapes—or thou mayest go off like a flower, and lose thy beauty—nay thou mayest go off like a hussy—and lose thyself. (VII, ix)

In *Tristram Shandy* Sterne wages constant war against that instinct of 'cabbage-planters' (VIII, i) to go blindly along one straight line, to judge life and literature by rules and systems, 'cooly, critically and canonically'. Such habits must be rooted out to give place to laughter, and to the freedom, generosity and balance that laughter alone can give. However, it is only the generous, healthy laughter that clears away malice and cant and pomposity, and produces joy and happiness, that Sterne permits. In the sermon *The Levite and his Concubine*, he points out the distinction between such laughter and the laughter that arises from bitterness :

> Whatever be the degree of its affinity, it has helped to give wit a bad name, as if the main essence of it was satire:

> certainly there is a difference between Bitterness and Saltness,—that is,—between the malignity and the festivity of wit,—the one is a mere quickness of apprehension, void of humanity,—and is a talent of the devil; the other comes from the Father of spirits, so pure and abstracted from persons, that willingly it hurts no man : or if it touches upon an indecorum, 'tis with that dexterity of true genius, which enables him rather to give a new colour to the absurdity, and let it pass. (*Sermons*, I, 299-300)

'Let it pass'; do not be venomous about it, nor let it embitter you; but enjoy it, and ponder over it; for 'everything in this world ... is big with jest,—and has wit in it, and instruction too,—if we can but find it out' (*TS*, V, xxxii).

Sterne's delight in eccentricity and whimsicality is an aspect of this belief in the necessity of laughter and joy, and of relishing life with zest, instead of taking refuge in pessimism and despondency, or in rigidity. Sterne had lived with a miserably ailing body, and a complaining wife, with zest and 'festivity' enough to assert confidently the value of the philosophy that he practised and preached :

> True Shandeism, think what you will against it, opens the heart and lungs, and like all those affections which partake of its nature, it forces the blood and other vital fluids of the body to run freely through its channels, makes the wheel of life run long and cheerfully round. (*TS*, IV, xxxii)

Such Shandeism is the best support in one's own difficulties, and it gives the best help to others in their sorrows :

> ... We must bring three parts in four of the treat along with us—In short we must be happy within—and then few things without us make much difference—This is my Shandean philosophy. (to Robert Foley, 16 Nov 1764)

It is such a Shandean philosophy that gives a man courage and zest enough to enable him, as it enabled Sterne, to twit death even when that old 'scare-sinner' threatens most menacingly, and to outwit him by sheer determination. One remembers the delightful dialogue between Eugenius and the ailing Tristram who stands with difficulty upon 'two spider legs', but is still bubbling with high spirits, and sends death, 'this son of a whore [who] has found out my lodgings', scurrying away to 'break his neck' (VII, i).

Uncle Toby who can whistle *Lillabullero,* so pertinently and with so perfect a sense of timing, to prick the bubble of absurdity and exaggeration, is surely a humorist—the most quiet and sweet and unoffending of humorists. Similarly, another favourite with Sterne, the Yorick of *Tristram Shandy,* is a humorist of a 'mercurial and sublimated' composition, 'with as much life and whim and *gaité de coeur* about him as the kindliest climate could have engendered'. Perpetually merry and frisky, Yorick blows away nonsense with 'the brisk gale of his spirits'. Yorick is like Toby, in that he is 'utterly unpractised in the world, and at the age of twenty-six, knew just about as well how to steer his course in it, as a romping unsuspicious girl of thirteen' (I, xi).

Sterne believed in joy and laughter firmly enough to venture to startle his congregation by standing in the pulpit to 'deny' the traditionally accepted Christian teaching of *Ecclesiastes.* With a superb flourish he brushed it aside (*Sermons,* I, 19-33):

> *It is better to go to the house of mourning than to the house of feasting. That I deny —*

and he proceeded to describe the attitude that passes by the beauty and joy of the world and looks at only the deserts, as 'a nonsensical piece of saint-errantry':

> ... But let us hear the wise man's reasoning upon it—*for that is the end of all men, and the living will lay it to his heart: sorrow is better than laughter*—for a crack-brain'd order of Carthusian monks, I grant, but not for men of the world: For what purpose, do you imagine, has God made us? for the social sweets of the well-watered valleys, where he has planted us, or for the dry and dismal desert of a Sierra Morena?... Do you think, my good preacher, that he who is infinitely happy, can envy us our enjoyments?

Yet, the Sterne who said, 'I am never so perfectly conscious of the existence of a soul within me as when I am entangled' in 'melancholy adventures' (*SJ*, 'Maria, Moulines'), ended the sermon by stressing the value of 'the house of mourning' in making the heart 'pensive ... soft ... susceptible ... full of religious impressions'. What he fought against was austerity and solemnity for its own sake. The Yorick of *Tristram Shandy* 'had an invincible dislike and opposition in his nature to gravity—not to gravity as such ... but he was an enemy to the affectation of it' (I, xi).

Sterne believed in laughter with conviction enough to defy, while still at the threshold of his ecclesiastical and literary career, the great Bishop Warburton, who wrote to him[25] to restrain his propensity to laugh :

> Be assured, my Lord, that willingly and knowingly I will give no offence to any mortal by anything which I think can look like the least violation either of decency or good manners, and yet, with all the caution of a heart void of offence or intention of giving it, I may find it very hard, in writing such a book as 'Tristram Shandy', to mutilate everything in it down to the prudish humour of every particular. I will, however, do my best; though laugh, my Lord, I will, and as loud as I can too. (to Dr. Warburton, 19 June 1760)

He once again affirmed his belief in the virtue of laughter in the letter to William Pitt, dedicating to him the second edition of *Tristram Shandy* in 1759 :

> I live in a constant endeavour to fence against the infirmities of ill health, and other evils of life, by mirth; being firmly persuaded that every time a man smiles,—but much more so, when he laughs, it adds something to this Fragment of Life.

Not only on 'the road between Nismes and Lunel', but all over *Tristram Shandy*, one hears the song :

> Viva la Joia !
> Fidon la Tristessa ! (VII, xliii)

If sorrow and gravity are not good for man's soul, neither is solitude. Man was not created to be a recluse. So in the sermon on *The Levite and His Concubine*, in a strikingly beautiful and impassioned passage, Sterne brought his congregation to a sympathetic understanding of the Levite's search for his concubine :

> For notwithstanding all we meet with in books . . . *'it is not good for man to be alone.'* . . . in midst of the loudest vauntings of philosophy, Nature will have her yearnings for society and friendship . . . . Let the torpid Monk seek heaven comfortless and alone—God speed him ! For my own part, I fear, I should never so find the way : let me be wise and religious—but let me be MAN. Wherever thy Providence places me, or whatever be the road I take to get to thee— give me some companion in my journey, be it only to remark to, how our shadows lengthen as the sun goes down; to whom I may say, how fresh is the face of nature ! How sweet the flowers of the field ! How delicious are these fruits ! (*Sermons*, I, 289-90)

Man is not meant to live alone; he lives in society, supported by the love of his fellow-men. Consequently, the most important of the virtues is love for one's fellow-men—'philanthropy, and those kindred virtues to it, upon which hang all the law and the prophets' (*Sermons*, I, xlviii). Love for one's fellow-men leads one to pity and comfort them in their sorrows, leads to 'this one virtue of compassion' (*Sermons*, I, 50). Compassion, Sterne selected as the 'one virtue' because, as he explained in the sermon on *Philanthropy*, compassion is the foundation on which all the other virtues rest :

> . . .a charitable and benevolent disposition is so principal and ruling a part of a man's character, as to be a considerable test by itself of the whole frame and temper of his mind, with which all other virtues and vices respectively rise and fall, and will almost necessarily be connected.—Tell me therefore of a compassionate man, you represent to me a man of a thousand other good qualities—on whom I can depend—whom I may safely trust with my wife—my

children, my fortune and reputation—'tis for this, as the Apostle argues from the same principle—"that he will not commit adultery—that he will not kill—that he will not steal—that he will not bear false witness". That is, the sorrows which are stirred up in men's hearts by such trespasses, are so tenderly felt by a compassionate man, that it is not in his power or his nature to commit them. (*Sermons*, I, 50)

In the sermon on *Elijah*, he asked the congregation:
Let any number of us here imagine ourselves at this instant engaged in drawing the most perfect and amiable character, such as, according to our conceptions of the Deity, we should think most acceptable to him, and most likely to be universally admired by all mankind. (*Sermons*, I, 86)

He then proceeded to select the generous, compassionate man as embodying the highest and most universal ideal.

In his sermons, Sterne concentrates so much on the 'one virtue of compassion', and on that quality of 'Joy' which he repeatedly recommends, and is so little bothered about dogma and doctrine, or any thing specifically Christian, that Walter Bagehot was disconcerted to find that 'there is not much of heaven and hell' in them: 'they would be just as true if there was no religion at all...and the "valuable illusion" of a deity were omitted from the belief of mankind.'[26]

In the sermon *Vindication of Human Nature*, touching upon one of the most debated ethical controversies of his age, Sterne condemned the philosophers who malign man by representing him as a selfish animal, and declared, 'there is scarce anything which has done more disservice, to social virtue, than the frequent representation of human nature under this hideous picture of deformity' (*Sermons*, I, 112-3). In *Philanthropy* he insisted that compassion is so basic to human nature, that 'we express that sensation by the word *Humanity*, as if it was inseparable from our nature'. Not that Sterne was unrealistic enough to believe that it was 'inseparable' from man's nature, but he was convinced that 'a man must do great violence to himself, and suffer many a painful conflict, before he has brought himself to a different disposition' (*Sermons*, I, 48-9). As early as 1740 courting Miss Lumley, his future wife, he wrote to her: 'Nature never made an unkind creature—ill usage, and bad habits, have deformed a fair and lovely creation' (to Elizabeth Lumley, ? 1739/40; *Letters*, pp. 17-18).

Compassion and generosity are of course the two virtues which pre-eminently characterize Uncle Toby : 'For each one's sorrows, thou hadst a tear,—for each one's need, thou hadst a shilling' (II, xxxiv). Toby's very appearance inspired confidence in the unfortunate : 'there was something in his looks, and voice, and manner, superadded, which eternally beckoned to the unfortunate to come and take shelter under him' (IV, x).

Toby's sympathy and generosity are universal. He will not abuse any one, not a parson nor a papist, not the French nor the Chinese. When the sarcastic remarks which Yorick's curate makes about soldiers provoke Trim to refer to the 'fuss and hypocrisy' of parsons, Toby gently reproves him : ' "Thou shouldst not have said that, Trim,—for God only knows who is a hypocrite, and who is not" ' (VI, vii).

Toby's 'unmistrusting ignorance' (IX, xxiii) is the result of his generosity, not of his stupidity. It is this generosity of temperament that determines the relationship between him and Trim. Though Toby is a gentleman and an officer, and Trim is a mere servant, and though Trim is by nature so respectful that he exasperates Toby by insisting on standing on his injured knee joint when in his presence, Trim rambles on in Toby's company as if they were equals, and Toby thinks it quite natural that Trim should contradict him whenever he differs from him : '— Now if I might presume, said the corporal, to differ from your honour—Why else do I talk to thee, Trim ? said my uncle Toby, mildly' (VIII, xxviii).

Not only are compassion and generosity the highest and most amiable among the virtues, they also lead to the other Christian virtues of forgiveness, meekness, humility and patience. All these receive frequent emphasis in the sermons and are exemplified in the character of Toby. Toby is 'a man patient of injuries; not from want of courage. . .nor did this arise from any insensibility or obtuseness of his intellectual parts' (II, xii), but from the generosity and greatness of his heart. In fact, forgiveness goes hand in hand with courage, for only the brave have the courage to forgive. It is the characteristic of a coward that he never forgives. As Sterne says in *Joseph's History Considered,*

'Cowards have done good and kind actions,—cowards have even fought—nay sometimes even conquered;—but a coward never forgave' (*Sermons*, I, 205).

Toby, so meek and patient, is, surprisingly, a soldier not surpassed by any in his bravery in fighting for his country :

> There never was a better officer in the King's army,—or a better man in God's world, for he would march up to the mouth of a cannon, though he saw the lighted match at the very touch-hole, and yet, for all that, he has a heart as soft as a child for other people. (V, x).

As he himself says to Trim, '—The best hearts, Trim, are ever the bravest.'—And the greatest cowards, an' please your honour, in our regiment were the greatest rascals in it' (VI, xiii).

But the best and bravest men, unlike the knowing ones of the world, do not rise to greatness in the world's sense of the term. When Yorick lies dying, still jesting in his characteristically 'Cervantic vein', he says : 'should I recover, and "Mitres thereupon be suffered to rain down from heaven as thick as hail, not one of them would fit it [his head]" ' (I, xii). This is an idea which is emphasized in different ways from Fielding to Mackenize, but nowhere more delicately than in Sterne.

But if the worthiest men do not achieve greatness in the eyes of the world, they possess the power to endure the pains the world inflicts on them. The 'best hearts', brave as well as meek and humble, derive the virtues of patience and endurance from their courage, as well as from meekness and humility. In four years of a trying illness, Toby 'never once dropped a fretful or discontented word;—he had been all patience,—all submission' (II, iv).

From this patience and meekness derives Toby's calm and unruffled temper. His erratic brother falls into fits of exasperation the moment he is crossed, but Toby sits with poise and without any rancour in his heart for the fit to blow over. His complete sincerity, his complete lack of artificiality, enable Toby to feel confident in any society, and to give assurance to those who need it.

It is because Sterne is able to embody all these essentially humane virtues with such sympathy, humour and artistic power in the character of his 'simple', warm-hearted man, that the portrait of My Uncle Toby still remains, what Hazlitt called it one and a half centuries ago, 'one of the finest compliments ever paid to human nature';[27] which, of course, is a deservedly handsome compliment to Sterne's genius and his understanding of life.

8 'A Young Lady's Entrance into the World' of the Gentleman

FANNY BURNEY

> I am never better pleased than when good girls write clever books.
> —Mrs. Thrale.[1]

'A scheme of happiness at once rational and refined soon presented itself to her imagination', when Fanny Burney's heroine, the elegant and virtuous heiress Cecilia, sat thinking how to organize her life (I, vii). An identical scheme had presented itself to the imagination of Addison and Steele, seventy years before *Cecilia*, when they started planning a campaign to organize the morals and manners of the English people. They had felt that their task must be 'to enliven morality with wit, and to temper wit with morality' (*Spectator*, no. 10); to effect a harmonious union of elegant manners, virtuous conduct, sensitive feelings and rational thinking; in short, to place before the public the idea of 'a finished gentleman'.

It has been shown in previous chapters that as the century advanced, many writers tended to consider it more important to assess the qualities of 'the heart rather than the head' when determining the worth of an individual. Fanny Burney favours the rational compromise that the *Spectator* essayists had evolved. In her novels, praise is reserved only for those who combine the best tendencies of the head and the heart, manifesting both sense and sensibility at their finest. 'The man of feeling', the appellation chosen by the sentimental school as the most noble to commend a man, changes to 'a man of sense and of feeling', which she chooses for her perfect gentleman, Lord Orville (*Evelina,* I, xxiv).

The most noticeable change is that the hero and heroine are once again required to move with ease in fashionable society; in fact, the ability to do so with 'elegance' and 'propriety', an accomplishment possible only to those who have been privileged to receive a highly 'polite' education, and to gain admittance into the 'best company', itself becomes the test by which to recognize the superior human being. The superiority of the character of Lord Orville, the hero of *Evelina,* is revealed by the graciousness of his manners at balls and operas. Though Orville impresses the beholder as 'a character so quiet, so reserved' (II, xxi) when seen as a foil to the fops and libertines who amuse the society women with their glib conversation, he is by no means the shy, retiring hero of the Mackenzie novel; he is always to be found in parks, assemblies and theatres in the company of fashionable ladies and gentlemen; his conversation is animated, sparkling and even gay; he can chat amusingly about plays, operas and museums, and is accomplished in the art of pleasing the ladies with well-turned, gallant compliments.

Awkwardness and bashfulness, especially in the presence of fashionable company, which writers like Mackenzie select as the token of the sensitive gentleman, are now regarded as excusable only in the very young :

> Cecilia was yet no stranger to company . . . since for some years past she had presided at the table of the Dean, who was visited by the first people of the country in which he lived. . .his parties, which were frequent, though small. . . had taught her to subdue the timid fears of total inexperience, and to repress the bashful feelings of shame-faced awkwardness; fears and feelings which rather call for compassion than admiration, and which, except in extreme youth, serve but to degrade the modesty they indicate. (I, iii).

Into Fanny Burney's own life three years before she published *Evelina,* there entered a Mr. Barlow. Recording the episode in her journal she said :

> Mr. Barlow is rather short but handsome. He is a very well-bred, good tempered and sensible young man. . .and he is highly spoken of for disposition and morals. (*Early Diary*, 8 May 1775)

Barlow was wealthy, and sufficiently in love to persist in his offers in spite of her coldness. For a girl like her, without 'fortune' and not particularly good-looking, the prospects in the eighteenth century were dismal. A position as a governess or house-keeper was the best she could expect. Her father and friends tried to show her the path of wisdom; but how could a man like Barlow, who seemed 'to know but little of the world' and had 'no elegance of manners' have any appeal for her ?

In the characterization of the seventeen-year-old heroine of *Evelina*, Fanny Burney may seem to be extolling innocence and unsophisticated manners. Evelina is said to be 'artless as purity itself' (I, v); as her creator points out in the *Preface*, 'her ignorance of the forms, and inexperience in the manners, of the world, occasion all the little incidents' which constitute the plot of this novel which deals with the problems of 'a young lady's entrance into the world' (*Evelina, sub-title*). Ignorance betrays Evelina into many a *faux pas*, and fills her with shame and consternation. She is easily discomfited by the offensive gallantry of the fashionable libertines of London society and panics every time one of them gets too near her. But Fanny Burney is far from desiring for her heroine the outlook or manners of a naive village belle; her values and criteria of judgment are made clear when she makes Lord Orville speak in defence of Evelina as 'extremely well-educated, and accustomed to good company'. In fact, Evelina is perpetually covered with confusion because of her extreme anxiety to be socially correct and behave strictly according to propriety. The importance that she and her creator attach to an acquaintance with 'the forms' finds expression in a characteristic wish :

> But, really, I think there ought to be a book, of the laws and customs *a-la-mode*, presented to all young people, upon their first introduction into public company. (I, xx)

It is necessary to notice that shy and unsophisticated though Evelina is, much of the embarrassment and dismay she suffers is not due to her own ignorance or gaucherie; the unfortunate predicament in which she is placed because of her family history, obliges her to be seen in London in the company of vulgar, low-bred relations, involving her in painfully embarrassing situations. Evelina is 'extremely vexed' at the thought that Sir Clement Willoughby, Bart., might see her with the cits at the opera and 'that he wou'd hear Miss Branghton call me *cousin*' (I, xxi). She finds it agonising to give her unfashionable address to my Lord Orville : 'What was the mortification I suffered in answering, "My lord, I am—in Holborn !" ' (II, xxi). In fact, especially in *Evelina*, so much value is placed on 'elegance', and so much humiliation is associated with an absence of it, that the reader is disturbed by a snobbishness in the tone of the novel and suspects a confusion of values in the novelist's outlook on life and her judgment of people.

Undoubtedly Fanny Burney's most outstanding achievement in *Evelina* is the study of the manners of the two divisions of the London society of the time, the town and the city. Few novelists or dramatists have excelled her in capturing those idiosyncrasies of manners, tone and attitude which bring a social type alive in a few descriptions and speeches. 'Oh, you little character-monger, you !' Johnson greeted her affectionately (*Diary*, I, 71), relishing this most brilliant aspect of her genius. Her keen sense of the ridiculous, be it the ridiculous in the posturings of the modish upper class, or the pretensions of the lower class would-be genteel, enables her to create some of the most effective scenes in the history of the comedy of manners in English. Ever alert as she was to absurdity, as well as to the least infringement of good form, all the current affectations of the fashionable world are unforgettably captured in her novels. For the historian of the reigning modes in late eighteenth century England, there is no happier hunting-ground than *Evelina* and *Cecilia*. A variety of youthful crazes, the passing phases in styles of affectation, are preserved in her highly diverting sketches of assorted members of 'the ton', who follow with concentrated devotion the reigning follies of the season till, the next season, they are driven out by others.

In the late seventies and early eighties when her first two

novels were published, apparently the stage was held by 'the voluble' and 'the insensiblists'. In *Cecilia* the two types are most divertingly satirized in Miss Larolles, who airily sustains a continuous unthinking chatter, and Miss Leeson who lounges pensively in all companies and cuts off conversation with one languorous monosyllable. Of the pretenders to fashion among the men, the most memorably drawn is Mr. Meadows, an 'ennuyé', 'now in the very height of fashionable favour' (*Cecilia*, IV, ii). Meadows never deigns to give any attention to the company; he 'yawns in one's face every time one looks at him' (II, iv), or indolently picks his teeth holding a pocket 'tooth-pick-case glass' in front of him (IV, ii). In spite of this insulting apathy, Meadows is 'courted' by all the ladies for, as the voluble Miss Larolles points out, 'one is never affronted with an ennuyé, if he is ever so provoking, because one always knows what it means' (II, iv).

The sprightly dialogue by means of which these social types are created is a new achievement in the English novel. Fanny Burney displays an enviable gift for mimicking the speech of a multiplicity of characters; whether it is the inconsequential chatter of society drawing-rooms, or the coarse prattle of the shop-keeping classes, the dialogue has the authentic ring of actual conversation and the crisp movement and humorous characterization of comic art at its best.

Behind the creation of this dialogue there were years of experience in recording conversation. From a very early age, in her private diary, and in the letters she sent to the family friend, Samuel Crisp, Fanny Burney had transcribed, almost verbatim, the conversation of the large assortment of people, high society and bohemian, that frequented her father's house in London. Though he was only a music-master, Dr. Charles Burney's drawing-room was perpetually crowded with visitors; writers, artists, society lions, notabilities and curiosities of every kind, English and foreign, passed in and out of the house at all times of the day. Before she discovered the identity of the author of the anonymously published *Evelina*, Mrs. Thrale felt, 'that it was written "by somebody who knows the top and the bottom, the highest and the lowest of mankind"' (*Diary*, I, 21).

The plot of *Evelina* seems designed to enable the author to prove this knowledge. From her secluded home in Berry Hill where she lives with her guardian, Evelina goes to London with Mrs. Mirvan, whose 'town acquaintance are all in the circle of high life' (I, iv). Evelina's gentleman grandfather had made a runaway marriage with a waitress, and had died soon after, leaving this coarse woman a large fortune; however, he had been wise enough to commit his infant daughter to the care of his former tutor, the Rev. Mr. Villars. This daughter, who grew up to be a model of beauty and virtue, made a rash, secret marriage with a libertine, Sir John Belmont, because she was pressed by her vulgar mother to marry a relation of her second husband, the Frenchman Duval. Thereupon her enraged mother disinherited her; Sir John, finding her penniless, disowned the marriage. The unfortunate girl then sought protection from the good Villars and died while giving birth to Evelina. Thus legitimately heiress to two large fortunes, her father's and her maternal grand-father's, Evelina can be confident only of inheriting the clergyman's humble fortune. The novel ends with Sir John acknowledging Evelina as his daughter. She finds a further deserved good fortune, as she is told, 'in becoming, at once, the wife of the man you adore,—and a Countess !' (III, xviii).

When the novel opens, her grandmother, Madame Duval, whom she has never seen before, suddenly decides to come to London to claim her. Madame has relations in the city. Her cousin, Mr. Branghton, keeps a silversmith's shop up Snow Hill, in the heart of the unfashionable quarters of London. As is the way of his kind, he lives above the shop, up 'two pair of stairs', with a son and two daughters; a more spacious room, up only one pair of stairs, is let to a young Mr. Smith (II. ix).

The Branghtons, father, son and daughters, are all ever 'so low-bred and vulgar' (I, xxi); the father 'does not want understanding but...is very contracted and prejudiced' (I, xvii). The son presumes to send a marriage proposal to Evelina, and thereafter, every time she looks at him, she finds 'his mouth was wide distended into a broad grin' (II, xvi). The Branghtons are, of course, socially quite impossible. A piquant scene presents them haggling about the price of opera tickets; the father is taken aback at the demand of half-a-guinea for *one* seat in the pit, and loudly complains about the 'theft'; the son, who prides himself on being more knowledgeable than his father, proclaims he was all along aware of the stiff prices, but had assumed that 'they'd take less, as we're such a large party' (I, xxi).

Every word that falls from the mouth of these cits makes Evelina squirm; when she is being taken around by them, she has but to glimpse her high society acquaintances in the distance to be seized with agitation. Once when they are all caught in the rain, the Branghtons use her name to borrow Lord Orville's coach; as it mounts Snow Hill, where the coroneted coach has never been driven before, 'plump we comes against a cart', and the coach is damaged. Thereupon Branghton junior decides to go to Berkeley Square to appease Lord Orville, for he fears Orville will 'prejudice them in their business'; but, finding him extremely civil, he is encouraged to ask 'for his custom'! Driven so hard, even the timorous Evelina quivers with anger : ' "You'll drive me wild," cried I' (II, xxiii). The meals at the Branghtons are badly cooked and badly served; this, Evelina writes, she would not mind, if the family had 'been without pretensions' (II, xi); and indeed, Fanny Burney is never so diverting, and never so scathing, as when she is exposing the pretensions of the vulgar who aspire to be genteel. Characteristic is the veiled barb that crowns Miss Branghton's vulgarity, when she loudly acclaims her own good taste with the observation : 'For my part, I like it because it is not vulgar' (II, xv).

After nearly two centuries, and after repeated readings, the comedy of these Branghton-Smith scenes still remains surprisingly fresh and piquant; in fact, at times the suavely unsparing observation of this first great feminine satirist lays the complacency of the vulgar almost uncomfortably bare. Seldom in literature has vulgarity been caught with such authenticity. There is some equally sharp and diverting satire on the mercantile vulgar in *Cecilia*, where Messrs. Simkins and Hobson, two London merchants, are drowned in ridicule

Perhaps the most unforgettably portrayed of these cits is Mr. Smith, who lodges with the Branghtons up that one pair of stairs. His showy dress, upstart airs and rude remarks laying claim to a gentility superior to theirs, establish him as a gentleman in their dazzled eyes. But Evelina, who is used to the company of gentlemen, finds it easy to sort out the counterfeit from the genuine mintage. Dr. Johnson was hugely delighted with this portrait of the 'Holborn beau' drawn by his 'little Burney'; joyfully Fanny recorded the great man's praise in her diary :

'Oh, Mr. Smith, Mr. Smith is the man !' cried he, laughing violently. 'Harry Fielding never drew so good a character ! —such a fine varnish of low politeness !—such a struggle to appear a gentleman ! Madam, there is no character better drawn anywhere—in any book or by any author.'

I almost poked myself under the table. Never did I feel so delicious a confusion since I was born ! (*Diary*, I, 54).

Spoilt by the wondering admiration of the Branghton girls, Smith incessantly brags about how he outwits women who have designs on him; however, his conceit and complacency are visibly deflated to a silent, peeved chagrin when Sir Clement Willoughby, with his expensive clothes and baronet's easy self-assurance, descends on him. The gentle Evelina, who to a large extent is the author's portrait of herself at seventeen, observes him with delighted malice : 'he gazed at him [Sir Clement] with envious admiration, and seemed himself, with conscious inferiority, to shrink into nothing' (II, xv). If Smith's complacency deserves this devastating exposure, Sir Clement's unscrupulous levity deserves even more scathing ridicule. Indeed, the baronet, and the other erring ones among the 'quality', are not spared strictures on their moral and social behaviour; most of the members of 'the ton' have, like Pope's witling, 'a brain of feathers and a heart of lead' (*The Dunciad*, ii, 44); nevertheless the feeling persists that, in Fanny Burney's judgment, fashionable appearance and social poise, available without struggle to the rich and well-born, lend a saving grace even to the most raffish and cruelly snobbish among the upper class, while the Smiths, who insist on aspiring to be gentlemen in spite of their Holborn background, deserve to be covered with ridicule and contempt. Sir Clement who, whenever he finds her unprotected by her chaperons, makes objectionable proposals to Evelina under the cover of high flown compliments, is throughout treated with disapproval; but, unlike Smith, he is hardly ever ridiculed; the behaviour of the ladies and gentlemen is shown as abominably shallow and cruel; but, however coarse and brutal, it is never characterized as 'low and vulgar'. Lord Merton and Mr. Coverley arrange a race between two old women 'more than eighty years of age'. 'The whole company' lays bets on them and gaily urges them to run faster; when one of the women slips and falls, Mr. Coverley who has laid a hundred pounds on her, 'swore at her with unmanly rage, and seemed scarce able to refrain even from striking her' (III, vii). Yet Evelina would feel most humiliated if this elegant company heard the Branghtons call her 'cousin'.

It is not that Fanny Burney does not attempt to show the value she places on virtue, morality and 'sensibility'; in fact, there is an almost tedious emphasis on these, particularly in *Cecilia*. Nor is she altogether unaware of both the shallowness and the cruelty of snobbery. The pain inflicted on the sensitive by the snobbish is finely depicted in Cecilia's confrontation with the aristocratic Delviles, and in Evelina's acute sufferings when she is pointedly ignored by the exclusive set which thinks she is a 'toad-eater'—a poor relation or acquaintance who acts as companion to a rich lady. But for Fanny Burney, the Smiths and the Branghtons are a different species. They so obviously cannot make the grade; and nobody is to blame but themselves, if, when they try to enter the charmed circle, they are mercilessly pushed out.

However much the satire directed against Mr. Smith and the Branghtons may be justified by their complacency, selfishness and ill-nature (and it must be said to their creator's credit that she contrives to endow each one of them with such a disposition that the satire seems fully justified), the impression remains that they are instinctively regarded as representatives of the mercantile community and the lower-class aspirants who try to launch out as gentlemen; they do symbolise the residents of Snow Hill and Holborn. However, what seems class-conscious snobbery is sometimes more a fastidious squeamishness about manners, which drives her into giving a disproportionate importance to the elegancies.[2] This squeamishness about manners made Hazlitt very impatient with her: 'The author appears to have no other idea of refinement than that it is the reverse of vulgarity; but the reverse of vulgarity is fastidiousness and affectation'.[3]

Fanny's beloved sister, Susan, while the two were still in their teens, noticed a 'prudery' in her character. Their niece records the comment in her introduction to the *Diary and Letters* (I, p.xi) :

> The characteristics of Hetty [another sister] seem to be wit, generosity, and openness of heart :—Fanny's—sense, sensibility, and bashfulness, and even a degree of prudery.

On one occasion a polite gentleman courteously paid her a compliment when a somewhat doubtful French novel was being discussed :

> '... It is not, indeed, a work that recommends very strict morality; but you, we all know, may look into any work without being hurt by it.'
> I felt hurt then, however, and very gravely answered,
> 'I cannot give myself that praise, as I never look into any books that could hurt me.'
> He bowed, and smiled, and said that was 'very right', and added,
> 'This book was written by an officer; and he says, there are no characters nor situations in it that he has not himself seen.'
> 'That, then,' cried I, 'will with me always be a reason to as little desire seeing the officer as his book.' (*Diary*, II, 234-5)

Queen Victoria could hardly have bettered that. Fanny Burney curbed her gift for writing plays for fear she would have to invent speeches for indelicate characters. Yet the modern reader is shocked by the brutal horseplay invented by this squeamish girl for the supposedly comic scenes of *Evelina*, where the gross Captain Mirvan, expert in practical jokes, 'smokes' old Madame Duval, who is a guest staying at the elegant country house of his mother-in-law, Lady Howard. For a 'frolic', he disguises himself as a highwayman, mauls her and bruises her, throws her into a ditch, and ties her up in it with a stout rope (II, ii).

However, Fanny Burney's squeamishness was not an affectation, and her prudishness had no taint of hypocrisy. Her shy, gentle, idealising temperament was genuinely distressed by the indelicate; moreover, she never made a ridiculous exhibition of such distress. Horace Walpole correctly testifies to her character :

> Dr. Burney and his daughter, Evelina-Cecilia, have passed a day and a half with me. He is lively and agreeable; she half-and-half sense and modesty, which possess her so entirely that not a cranny is left for affectation or pretension (to the Countess of Ossory, 17 Sept 1785; *Letters*, V, 426)

Though there was undoubtedly a touch of snobbishness in Fanny Burney's character, it was not the kind that pays deference to money; wealth, without culture and elegance, held no attractions for her. In her personal life she proved how willingly, how courageously, she could dispense with money. It was with complete sincerity that she spoke of her 'indifference to all things but good society' (*Diary*, I, 55), when Mr Thrale suggested a match between her, penniless as she was, and his rich nephew, Sir John Lade. The way she responded to the rich but 'inelegant' Mr. Barlow has already been seen. At long last, an elegant man did appear. At forty she fell in love with the aristocratic, but utterly penniless, Monsieur d'Arblay, a member of the colony of French aristocrat emigrés who had settled near her sister's house in Surrey. After the first few meetings she described d'Arblay to her father as 'one of the most delightful characters I have ever met, for openness, probity, intellectual knowledge, and unhackneyed manners' (*Diary*, V, 394). From the worldly point of view, it was a thoroughly imprudent match. Her father wrote begging her to desist and predicting utter disaster :

> I . . . beg, warn and admonish you not to entangle yourself in a wild and romantic attachment, which offers nothing in prospect but poverty and distress, with future inconvenience and unhappiness. (*Diary*, v, 426)

But she knew that for her poverty would not be a deterrent to happiness :

> Happiness, is the great end of all our worldly views and

proceedings, and no one can judge for another in what will produce it. To me wealth and ambition would always be unavailing; I have lived in their most centrical possessions, and I have always seen that the happiness of the richest and the greatest has been the moment of retiring from riches and from power. Domestic comfort and social affection have invariably been the sole as well as the ultimate objects of my Choice . . . M. d'Arblay has a taste for literature and a passion for reading and writing as marked as my own; this is a sympathy to rob retirement of all superfluous leisure. (*Diary*, V, 431)

'And never, never was union more blessed and felicitous', affirms the memorandum added in her diary more than thirty years after the marriage, long after d'Arblay's death (*Diary*, V, 429).

If Fanny Burney found a cultured taste and elegance of manners indispensable, like her heroine, Mrs. Delvile, 'she required to obtain her favour, the union of virtue and abilities with elegance' (VI. i). Like Addison and Steele, she sought a harmonious union of all the virtues of the mind and the heart in a finished gentleman. Further, in her life as in her works, she showed a strong tendency to idealise a few people to whom she attributed all the virtues. In this respect, she was once again like Mrs. Delvile, who 'magnified their virtues (of those she admired) till she thought them of a higher race of beings' (VI, i). Therefore, like Richardson, she often portrays idealized heroes and heroines, offering them as models for imitation. Evelina thinks of Orville as 'one who seemed formed as a pattern for his fellow-creatures, as a model of perfection' (II, xxvii). Like Sir Charles Grandison, Fanny Burney's commended man or woman 'is everything' (*Grandison*, VI, xxv). The hero Delvile is hailed as an 'exemplary young man' (VIII, iii). Cecilia finds after close observation that he lacks no single quality (III, ix). When he first read *Evelina*, Dr. Burney noted with approval: 'there is a *boldness* in a it (Lord Orville's character) that struck mightily, for he is a man not *ashamed* of being better than the rest of mankind' (*Diary*, I, 17).

The Burney-Richardson heroes, Orville-Grandison, stand almost *in loco parentis* to the young heroines; they are their mentors and protectors; Orville repeatedly offers to be a true brother to Evelina. Passion and sex never break in on the fraternal-paternal role. A touch of jealousy is all that is permitted to Orville or Delvile to establish their role of lovers. 'Esteem', not passion, attaches the hero to the heroine. 'I see, and I adore the purity of your mind,' says Orville to Evelina (III, xvi). When Evelina quivers with emotion it is because she is seized with gratitude for his brotherly solicitude.

In other respects also the Burney novels show affinity with *Sir Charles Grandison*. The analysis of moral predicaments, especially in *Cecilia*, bears a close resemblance to Richardson's, though it is carried out with somewhat less solemnity. Like Richardson, the stand which Fanny Burney takes on matters of virtue and integrity is uncompromising, though she is less overtly, and much less voluminously, didactic. If Richardson's favourite word is 'punctilio', hers is 'propriety'. In the novels of both writers, the emotional life of a young heroine is the focus of interest, and it is through her idealizing eyes that the ideal gentleman is visualized. Richardson's propensity to judge a man from the woman's point of view and to create the ideal gentleman in the image of the ideal husband has been pointed out in the chapter on Richardson. It has also been shown that much of the reader's impatience with Sir Charles's intolerable perfection is due to the fact that Richardson tries to combine in him the highest degree of virtue with the highest degree of elegance—just such a combination as a young woman's romantic adulation will find in her knightly hero.

If Fanny Burney's portrayal of the perfections of Orville, the ideal gentleman, is more acceptable than Richardson's portrayal of Grandison, it is because she is able to maintain more realistically, and with more charm, the point of view of an angelically innocent seventeen-year-old girl. Since the sensitive Evelina feels very keenly the deprivation of a father's love, her idealization of Orville appears to be a psychological touch. Moreover, Lord Orville is not made so overpoweringly perfect as Sir Charles Grandison; the other hero, Delvile, Cecilia's ideal, though he also shows Grandisonian tendencies, is even allowed to have a few human limitations.

If Fanny Burney's technique is not altogether like Richardson's, the virtues and disciplines she recommends through the creation of the hero and heroine are very similar to those insisted upon by Richardson. A keen sensibility, control of this sensibility by means of reason and self-denial, integrity of mind and uprightness of conduct are the princihal constituents of the ethic they both advocate.

By the time Fanny Burney began to write her novels, sensibility had of course become an indispensable constituent in the make-up of any worthwhile character in fiction. Fortunately her works are free of the ridiculous aberrations of the sensibility cult. But the admired or good among the Burney characters are all manifestly people of sensibility. Lord Orville is 'a man of sense and of feeling' (I, xxiv); the imperturbable suavity recommended in some quarters is not practised by him; 'a deep sigh' (III, xi) escapes him, 'his countenance [is] so much altered' (III, v) when he apprehends danger to Evelina or fears that she does not love him. Delvile's sensibility is constantly demonstrated in the generosity, gentleness and 'delicacy' of his actions, and in his acute sufferings, leading to a serious physical breakdown, when he is torn apart by the conflict within himself between love and duty. Cecilia's sensitive mind, like Richardson's Clementina's, is temporarily unhinged by her sufferings so that the author gets repeated opportunities to write in the sensibility trend.

If evidence of the reactions of the first readers had not survived, a modern reader would find it difficult to believe that hundreds of fashionable ladies and gentlemen, not to speak of stern blue-stockings, hardened politicians and grave moralists, found the pathos and emotional suspense of these novels almost too keen to endure. Only the exceptional moral power of the writer, and her signal triumph in plunging the depths of the human heart, made such agony bearable for them. Months after she first read *Cecilia*, Mrs. Chapone, one of the sage leaders of the contemporary moral reform movement, still had a tremor in her voice when she described the first impact of the novel on her to a distinguished circle of ladies, with the author sitting blushing in the corner (*Diary*, II, 256). The famous politician Wyndham, even when studying his brief for the impeachment of Warren Hastings, could not turn his mind away from the sufferings of Evelina. During the trial he walked up to Miss Burney who, in her position as Keeper of the Robes, sat in the Royal Box in the Great Hall, to declare that he could not tear himself away from the hero and heroine, so much had she 'twined, twisted, twirled them round our very heart-strings' (*Diary*, IV, 138).

Though her novels extol sensibility and exploit its reigning cult, like Richardson, the first great advocate of sensibility in the English novel, Fanny Burney spends much energy emphasizing the necessity of keeping it well under the control of reason, and of gauging its quality by the test of the principles of morality. Cecilia is given what her creator considers the highest compliment, when she is lauded as 'so rational ! so just ! so feeling, yet so wise !' (VII, ix). Vain indulgence in grief, so beloved of the heroine of sensibility, is repeatedly condemned in *Cecilia*. A lady, as much as a gentleman, is expected to show fearless courage, just as a gentleman, and not only a lady, is required to give proof of his sensibility and to guard his chastity. The Burney novels do not dwell upon sexual chastity in the male as laboriously as Richardson's; nevertheless, the standard expected of the Burney hero is just as strict. 'The right line of conduct is the same for both sexes,' as Mr. Villars makes it clear to Evelina (II, xviii).

Fanny Burney, like Richardson, lays particular stress on the necessity of curbing sensibility in the relationship between man and woman. 'Partiality' must be immediately subdued by reason and self-denial, if any 'impropriety' is suspected in the choice. The Rev. Mr. Villars writes his sternest letter to Evelina showing her that she has fallen in love with Lord Orville not, as she ought to have done, with the aid of reason, but only with the aid of imagination. A model lady, on the contrary, will allow herself to give her 'esteem' to a man only when her reason, after carrying out a dispassionate study of the man, permits her to grant it. It is interesting to note the functions attributed to reason, imagination and intuition in these final decades of the Age of Reason:

'... *Imagination* took the reins, and *reason*, slow-paced, though sure-footed, was unequal to race with so eccentric and flighty a companion. How rapid was then my Evelina's progress through those regions of fancy and passion whither her new guide conducted her' ... Lord Orville ... seems to have deserved the idea you formed of his character; but it was not time, it was not the knowledge of his worth, obtained your regard; your new comrade had not patience to wait any trial; her glowing pencil, dipt in the vivid colours of her creative ideas, painted to you, at the moment of your first acquaintance, all the excellencies ... (III, vi)

In curbing the turbulence of fancy and passion, more important than the role even of reason, is that of the 'inward monitor, who is never to be neglected with impunity' (*Cecilia*, VII, iii). If neglected, it burdens the soul with guilt, which 'is alone the basis of lasting unhappiness' (*Cecilia*, VIII, v). On the other hand, the sense of having acted rightly, brings with it 'the sweets of a self-approving mind' (*Cecilia*, VIII, ii). Cecilia finds it gives her comfort even in the cruellest grief and most miserable deprivation.

All the characters who are treated with any approval in the Burney novels consider moral obligations of primary importance. Even as she confesses to her guardian, 'my feelings are all at war with my duties', Evelina affirms :

Yet so strong is the desire you have implanted in me to act with uprightness and propriety, that, however the weakness of my heart may distress and afflict me, it will never, I humbly trust, render me wilfully culpable. The wish of doing well governs every other. . . (III, xi)

An individual who is governed by such a wish will put his talents to the best use. In doing so, he will consider his highest obligation to be the duty of helping his fellow-men. On the rich, in particular, is imposed the duty of charity. To dissipate her magnificent fortune only in luxuries for herself Cecilia considers an offence against virtue and propriety. 'Her affluence . . . .she considered as a debt contracted to the poor' (I, vii).

When she is disappointed in love, her only relief from grief is in charity, and making plans for charity:

> In her sleep she bestowed riches, and poured plenty upon the land; she humbled the oppressor, she exalted the oppressed; slaves were raised to dignities, captives were restored to liberty, beggars saw smiling abundance. . . . From a cloud in which she was supported by angels, Cecilia beheld these wonders. . . (VIII, vi)

Fanny Burney does not often become as fatuous as this, but obviously the 'benevolism' cult was too powerful to allow her to remain altogether uninfected by it. However, at times, she herself feels that Cecilia becomes somewhat excessive in scattering her largesse during the period when she is disappointed in love. When she has to renounce her magnificent fortune in order to marry Delvile, she is made to realize the 'error of profusion' even in charity, and to learn to circumscribe her donations 'by prudence' (X, x).

Prudence, in fact, is necessary not only to rise above passion and vice, but to order, regulate and refine the virtues themselves, and to bring them together into a harmonious union. Only when such a union has been effected will an individual be able to act at all times with 'propriety', a quality for which Fanny Burney reserves her highest approval. In a fervent passage Evelina speaks of 'the strong desire implanted' in her 'to act with propriety' (III, xi); Cecilia is praised by Delvile for 'the chaste propriety of your character' (X, ii). Another name for propriety is 'delicacy'. The total impression given by Lord Orville, who manifests all the virtues, in all their just proportions, is of a 'high-bred delicacy' (II, x).

This propriety or delicacy, which requires so fine a balance of so many different virtues, can be manifested only by a person endowed with 'good sense'. Cecilia shows 'such *propriety of mind* as can only result from the union of good sense with virtue' (V, vii). Like her successor Jane Austen, Fanny Burney values 'a strong understanding' in both men and women. Sensibility, integrity and discipline are of no avail without a fine intelligence and a sound judgment.

The function of good sense is to prevent excess in any

direction. Those who possess it, like Cecilia, 'try, at least, to approach that golden mean, which like the philosopher's stone, always eludes our grasp, yet always invites our wishes' (II, iv). Good sense teaches a man to be virtuous with good-breeding; to behave, 'much like a Gentleman, and [go] to Heaven with a very good Mien', as Steele remarked, appreciating the urbane tolerance with which Swift discussed religion (*The Tatler*, no. 5). The high-minded Orville's ideal is never to behave in public with 'unseasonable gravity', and to deftly 'adopt the conversation to the company' (III, iii), even though the frivolity of the company is disagreeable to him. He can always manage the pert and irresponsible with suavity. Similarly Cecilia, though she disapproves of the flightiness of the rich families in the neighbourhood is 'peculiarly careful not to offend them by singularity of manners' (IX, iv). Gone are the days when the Puritan enthusiast was praised for asserting his righteousness in the face of all the world.

This ideal of a way of life in which urbanity, elegance and intelligence lend grace to upright and humane conduct, was the ideal placed before the English gentleman and lady by many writers throughout the eighteenth century. Fanny Burney is its most vivacious advocate. She is not a writer of the highest stature; she had nothing either very original or very profound to contribute to the novel. But so well did she give voice to the ethos of her times, and so considerable were her powers of observation and her creative talent, that contemporaries of the stature of Edmund Burke could declare in all sincerity that their experience of human nature had been enriched by a reading of her works :

> There are few—I believe I may say fairly there are none at all that will not find themselves better informed concerning human nature, and their stock of observation enriched, by reading your *Cecilia*. They certainly will, let their experience in life and manners be what it may. The arrogance of age must submit to be taught by youth.[4]

There was certainly something in 'little Burney' on account of which, as Johnson saw, 'Richardson would have been really afraid of her. . . Harry Fielding, too, would have been afraid of her'.[5]

9 Who Was then the Gentleman?

> That was not an age of Faith,—an age of heroes. —Carlyle.[1]
> And all that rais'd the Hero, sunk the Man. —Pope.[2]

Who and what was then this gentleman of the novelists? Does an analysis of the ideals that are recommended and the vices that are execrated in the novels of the century reveal distinct and characteristic features which give him a recognizable identity? Moreover, since the concept of the gentleman is essentially a class concept, are the views that the different novelists express coloured by their own class background?

Observed from certain angles these novelists and their gentlemen seem strangely different from one another. Fielding's literary personality is so radically different from Richardson's that one does not expect the ideal gentlemen of these two novelists to display similar features. Nor will it be easily supposed that Fielding, generally described as 'robust' and 'manly', will recommend for imitation the same sort of man as Sterne, who is so often regarded as a morbid sentimentalist. Similarly, Fielding the clear-eyed realist, with his full and varied experience of life, will ordinarily not be expected to look for the same perfect gentleman as Fanny Burney, the young lady of seventeen who is anxious to make her 'entrance into the world' with decorum and propriety. And can the hero of this young lady—the fashionable lord moving in high society drawing-rooms where he is the observed of all observers—be associated with the heroes of Goldsmith, who idealizes a simple, credulous, suffering pastor, and makes his model gentleman wander about the countryside as a tramp, singing old ballads and mysteriously helping the helpless? Can there be any similarities between these two idealized figures portrayed by Goldsmith, and Smollett's wild young gentlemen or his eccentric, valetudinarian misanthrope ? Nor at first sight will any striking family resemblances be discernible between Smollett's angry heroes and Mackenzie's ideal gentleman, his timid tearful man of feeling, 'a child in the drama of the world'. And the extraordinary fantasy of Henry Brooke's portrayal of the ideal gentleman would seem to be woven by a mind which has not much in common with either Smollett's or Mackenzie's.

If the artistic personalities of these novelists reveal sharp differences, and their ideal characters seem to be apparently very different from one another, their education, social background and family antecedents also are by no means similar. Fielding, Smollett, Sterne, Brooke and Mackenzie were descended from gentry families, though the fathers of the first three were in straitened circumstances. Goldsmith's father was a poor Irish clergyman, a gentleman at least by concession. Only Richardson and Fanny Burney had no claims to gentility. Once again, only excepting these last two, they all received the traditional classical education given to gentlemen, though most of them could not afford the kind given to the sons of the very wealthy.

Furthermore, the social circles in which these writers moved and their occupational backgrounds show a variety which leads us to expect that a variety of ideals and aspirations will be expressed in their novels. Brooke moved in fashionable court circles in his early life, Mackenzie in fairly wealthy Scottish society, in the company of writers and philosophers of some standing. Through her father, Fanny Burney had access to a large circle of bohemians, as well as to fashionable and cultured society even before she published *Evelina*; between the publication of her first and second novel she spent much of her time at Mrs. Thrale's house in the company of Dr. Johnson, and was eagerly sought after by society gentlemen and ladies, as well as by bluestockings, writers and politicians.

Sterne went up to Jesus College, Cambridge, as a sizar. He was then ordained priest, and he is the only clergyman among our novelists. After the first volumes of *Tristram Shandy* were published, London society began to lionize Sterne; he became a great social success, and tremendously enjoyed being one.

Unlike Sterne, Goldsmith felt humiliated by his sizar's status at Trinity College, Dublin. Later he studied medicine at Edinburgh and Leyden, and then wandered over Europe, piping and singing, or participating in philosophical disputations at the universities, to earn his living. Returning to England, he lived on the brink of starvation in a London garret, served as usher in a poor school, 'wrote like an angel' on all sorts of subjects, and spent the evenings talking 'like poor Poll' in the company of Johnson and the brilliant members of the Literary Club.

Fielding, in spite of his origin which he traced to the Hapsburgs, had little access to the world of the wealthy and fashionable, except in his boyhood at his grandmother, Lady Gould's, and at Eton; he spent his early adult life in London as an impecunious dramatist and theatre-manager, and then as a law student at the Middle Temple. Soon after, he plunged into the unsavoury controversies of political journalism. His second wife was his first wife's maid. The last years of his life were spent as Justice of the Peace for Westminster, cleaning up the legal malpractices and the widespread corruption, crime and violence in the London of his days.

During his chequered career Dr. Smollett was apprentice to a medical practitioner, an unsuccessful and embittered dramatist, and a surgeon's mate in the Royal Navy, which took him to the West Indies. Returning to London with a wife from Jamaica, he soon gave up the practice of medicine for literary work. As a writer he proved hard-working and resourceful; his substantial income enabled him to entertain a number of guests, but he was perpetually involved in feuds with his fellow-writers, and spent a term in prison for libel.

Richardson served a seven-year apprenticeship to a printer and proved uncommonly scrupulous and diligent; he then married his master's daughter—and printing press. When his first wife died, his choice judiciously fell on the sister of an eminent book-seller. He spent his life in his printing press supervising his workmen through a peep-hole, writing novels about baronets, countesses and waiting-maids, and carrying on a vast correspondence with literary women and wealthy ladies about his all-absorbing characters.

One would normally expect such differences of family

background, education, environment, experience and temperament to be reflected in the works of these novelists, and would therefore expect from them different types of novels, projecting a variety of different types of ideals. From the preceding chapters it is clear that each of these novelists indeed has an individual personality, and that the novels written by some of them are even sharply antagonistic in tone and attitude to those written by some of the others. Their heroes and idealized characters are in many ways very different from one another. But our analysis of the novels has also revealed that all these novelists debate the same questions about life and feel the pull of the same forces. This is perhaps not surprising, since they belong to the same age. What is, however, astonishing is that their meditations on the problems of life and on the values that will bring happiness and fulfilment to the individual and to society result in their all building up essentially the same type of ideal figure, as regards both social position and basic attributes of character. The hero is always a landed country gentleman, or at least settles down as one when the novel draws to a conclusion. The idealized figure is paternal, benevolent, considerate, conscious of his duties and social obligations. His graciousness, courtesy and good-breeding are usually emphasized, though the kind and degree of these vary according to the tastes of the individual writer. The novelist may seem to toy with the idea of presenting a good servant lad or a brilliant beggar boy as a hero, but such characters are ultimately metamorphosed into philanthropic country gentlemen. The social origin, environment, education and temperament of the novelists seem to have no relevance when it comes to showing allegiance to this ideal of the benevolent country gentleman.

When in actualizing the figure of this ideal gentleman, one novelist is pulled more in one direction and another more in another, it seems to be a matter of individual temperament and personal preferences, rather than of education, or social origin and environment. For some the ideal gentleman is less wealthy than for others; the degree of homeliness or sophistication which he is given varies from novelist to novelist. Brooke and Richardson, who moved in very different social circles expect the same impeccable good breeding from their paragons. If Richardson is solemn and didactic, and expects his hero to be conventionally virtuous and unremittingly chaste, and, on the other hand, Fielding is ironical and gay, and allows his characteristic heroes to sow their wild oats, it would be facile to account for the difference by pointing to the supposedly upper class background of the one and the middle class, tradesman background of the other. Similarly in the case of Sterne and Smollett, one a clergyman, the other a medical man and journalist, the differences in professional status have little bearing on the shades of difference in the ideals projected by them.

The ideal which is thus so persistently celebrated in this literature is perhaps more pedestrian, and less exciting, than that recommended in any other. For many modern readers there is a dissatisfying lack of complexity and tension in these novels. Their chief concerns and preoccupations seem extraordinarily tame to our times. It seems curious that the intellect, and the ethical fervour, and the literary talents of these writers should have been content to confine themselves to meditating on the duty, benevolence and goodness of the country gentleman, to discuss the role that 'the passions' must play in his life, to gauge the degree of prudence and sensibility that he must develop, and to decide how he must strike the right balance in matters of good breeding and courtesy. The more complex issues of life seem to have left these novelists quite untouched. They seem unaware of the non-rational urges in man's nature, of the sinister and destructive aspects of his psychology. They are apparently untroubled not only by the tensions and conflicts which have assumed terrifying proportions in our age, but, curiously, even by questions which ages earlier than theirs found profoundly disturbing. The urge to explore all the glorious and all the terrifying potentialities of man's nature inspired the writers of the Renaissance and Jacobean periods to come to grips with life in a quite different way, and to project heroes whom the modern reader finds far more interesting and moving than the heroes of these novelists.

The reason for such a circumscribed vision is that the aspirations and fears of the eighteenth century for man and society converged on the figure of the gentleman *qua* gentleman. This becomes understandable when we remember that these were the decades in English history when the land-owning gentleman class had risen to the height of its political, social and economic power. The position and influence of the aristocracy and gentry had been growing stronger ever since the Glorious Revolution of 1689, and the half-century before the Fr nch Revolution marks the most flourishing period of their supremacy. The power of patronage they enjoyed covered every worth-while office in the administration. They claimed as legitimate sinecures for themselves and their dependents obsolete offices which nobody dared abolish. The House of Commons no less than the House of Lords was regarded as the property of the land-owning class; the aristocracy still put whole families into the lower house; local government was likewise in the hands of the landowners, for the justices of the peace were almost always appointed from among this class.

When the land-owner, the law-maker and the law-giver originate from the same class, it is to be expected that government will function for the benefit of that class. It is customary for historians to compare the English governing class of the decades preceding the French Revolution very favourably with its European counterpart. The sense of responsibility with which it managed affairs is frequently praised; its sense of justice and its enlightened policies in agriculture and land-development are emphasized. Unlike most of the European aristocracies, the members of the English governing class claimed for themselves 'no special privileges of any great consequence', and even 'eschewed the fiscal privileges which continental nobilities demanded as their birth-right'.[3] While the European nobility exacted crippling taxes, the landed gentlemen of England imposed upon themselves a land tax as high as four shillings in the pound. The hidebound rigidity and arrogant exclusiveness of the European aristocracy compare very unfavourably with the fluidity of the English class-structure and its more liberally constituted upper class consisting of 'aristocracy' and 'gentry'. The genial camaraderie which the English landed gentleman established with his tenantry, the ease with which he and his younger sons ventured into trade, the readiness he showed to enrich and strengthen the family by even entering into marriage alliances with the wealthy merchant, ensured an essentially more healthy life to the English governing class.

By tradition and temperament a much greater proportion of the English ruling class was imbued with a sense of social purpose; many more members of the class were actuated by a sense of responsibility to the state and to the people over whom they felt they had been placed as guardians. A paternal attitude to the tenantry, and a relationship of *bonhomie* with farmers and merchants in the countryside, established often on the hunting and sporting field, were a traditional part of the English landlord's way of life.

If, for establishing this way of life, credit must be given to the liberality and benevolence of the English upper class, due weight must also be given to its shrewd far-sightedness and its enlightened sense of self-interest. As J.L. and B. Hammond, who drew up a fiercely eloquent indictment of the upper classes in *The Village Labourer*, point out, 'selection and assimilation... and not exclusion are the true means of preserving a class monopoly of power... the English aristocracy understood the advantages of a scientific social frontier'.[4] Similarly, the careful attention which was given to many estates, and the patriarchal role which the landlord often adopted towards his 'people' paid substantial dividends; more prosperous farmers gave higher rents, and more contented and loyal tenants gave valuable support at election times.

There can be no doubt that the ruling classes on the whole ruled primarily in their own interest, and that they were not above weighting the law heavily in their own favour. Writers like the radical Hammonds look upon the parliamentary legislation sanctioning enclosures as bare-faced robbery which destroyed the peasantry as a class; they make an excellent case for regarding all the penal and poor law legislation of the period as selfish and ruthless measures devised to safeguard and enrich those who were empowered to enact the laws. Recent research has shown that the blame put by such writers on the enclosing landlords for the impoverishment of the peasantry is exaggerated. Nevertheless, even recent historians, except those who are definitely inclined to be partial towards the propertied classes, do not hesitate to affirm: 'Those that owned the land, owned the institutions of government and ran them in their own interests. More and more crimes against property became capital offences'.[5]

Writing shortly after the end of this period, William

Cobbett turned away from the heartless system of exploitation with bitter revulsion :

> There is in the men calling themselves English country gentlemen something superlatively base. They are, I sincerely believe, the most cruel, the most unfeeling, the most brutally insolent.[6]

Even if one concedes that Cobbett was likely to be carried away by his radical zeal, it is certain that as the century advanced the law became increasingly ferocious in protecting property and game against the starving masses, and that the 'labouring poor', as the greater part of Englishmen had come to be classed, found themselves much nearer the starvation line than at the beginning of the century. The savage system under which the poor were driven from parish to parish is the peculiar product of this period. The seemingly humane laws which made it incumbent upon every parish to take care of its destitute, in practice resulted in the most inhuman persecution of the infirm and dying. Old, ailing men and women were hounded out beyond the parish boundary to avoid the cost of their illness and funeral; pregnant women, even in the pains of labour, were cast out, so that the parish might not become liable for the maintenance of the mother and child.

As the poor were deprived of even their paltry rights to the common fields, and evicted out of their hovels to provide more and more land for the landlord, the gulf between the lord and the labourer became wider. The gentlemen of England lived in the most abundant profusion, making a public and ostentatious display of wealth.

Conspicuous consumption became an obligatory part of a great gentleman's way of life. The virtue analysed by Aristotle under the name of 'magnificence' had seldom found more conscientious followers than the upper classes of this period. Many of them had read Aristotle's description of this exclusively patrician virtue :

> ... this also seems to be a virtue concerned with wealth... it is a fitting expenditure involving largeness of scale ... the magnificent man will spend such sums for honour's

sake; for this is common to the virtues. And further he will do so gladly and lavishly; for nice calculation is a niggardly thing ... and a work has an excellence—viz. magnificence —which involves magnitude ... Hence a poor man cannot be magnificent, since he has not the means with which to spend large sums fittingly ... A magnificent man will also furnish his house suitably to his wealth (for even a house is a sort of public ornament).[7]

Some innate instinct in the eighteenth century English gentleman prompted him to embrace this Aristotelian virtue, especially in its manifestation of turning houses into 'a sort of public ornament'. Every substantial gentleman, and often even the not so substantial one, felt it incumbent upon himself to pour forth enormous sums in order to build, expand, decorate and furnish his country 'seat', and to enlarge and beautify the extensive gardens and parks surrounding the estate. Many spent prodigious amounts building artificial lakes and waterfalls and changing the courses of rivers so that they might 'serpentize' prettily through the estate; acres of parkland were planted with trees to merge artistically into the distant wooded hills, in the new style of romantic landscape architecture popularized by Capability Brown. The nouveaux-riches tried to make good their pretences by spending hundreds of pounds to put up 'ruins' of towers and temples which, covered with 'ancient' ivy, would look as if they were about to crumble in their venerable old age.

The novelists do not seem to be enthusiastic about this new interest in architecture and landscape gardening that was changing the face of the countryside. Smollett pictures the architectural activity of his contemporaries in an angry scene in *Humphry Clinker*. He shows the upstart daughter of a city merchant marrying into an old gentry family and frittering away a considerable fortune on repeated renovations to the 'venerable' old Gothic mansion, till it presents a ridiculous mixture of styles (11 Oct, by Matt). Fielding devotes a long and unusually elaborate descriptive passage to show us Squire Allworthy's country seat. Laughing self-consciously about the obviously picturesque quality of the description, he gives the chapter (I, iv) the title, *The Reader's Neck Brought into Danger by a*

Description. The reader who knows that Ralph Allen, the original of Squire Allworthy, lived in one of the most beautiful of the Palladian houses built during this period, will note with some surprise that Allworthy's seat is in 'the Gothic stile of building'. Richardson of course was out of his depth when it came to describing gentlemen's estates, and the description he attempts of Grandison's country house (VII, v) has not escaped the ridicule of critics

But the interests and tastes of the novelist and the landed gentleman were not infrequently quite different. Wanton and inconsiderate as much of the expenditure on the new architectural craze was, it must be said to the credit of the English gentleman that this prodigal expenditure was usually lavished with good taste and imagination. During these decades the science of architecture became the popular study of the man of fashion, and the countryside was transformed into a thing of aesthetic beauty, an actually realized Gainsborough painting presenting itself every few miles to the traveller's eyes. Dukes, baronets and even prime-ministers personally supervised every detail of the building, furnishing and decoration of their houses, and proved themselves men of superb taste. The Continent was ransacked for pictures and *objets d'art*; at home a new impetus was given to the art of furniture, culminating in the elegance of Chippendale and Sheraton. The eighteenth century is perhaps the greatest period of English domestic architecture; the most magnificent of the 'stately homes of England' were built or rebuilt and enlarged during this century. The wealthy gentry usually lived in enormous manor houses consisting of twenty-five to forty large rooms, not counting the cellars, larders, butteries, brew-houses, bake-houses and dairies.

The magnificence of the gentlemen's estates presented an appalling contrast to the mud hovels of the starving poor. But in spite of the glaring contrasts of opulence and destitution, and the built-in opportunities for exploitation and oppression in the hierarchical system, even those writers who seem to be outraged by the corruption and cruelty of the system, even those who draw scathing pictures of its iniquity, are not willing to question the validity of the stratified class structure. It is only at the end of the century that a few radical voices are raised, and even then only to be immediately stifled. Tom

Paine trying to awaken society to 'the rights of man', dared to propose a death duty of ten per cent, out of which the landless population would be compensated for the loss of their 'natural inheritance'; he was soon hounded out of the country. A Newcastle school-teacher, Thomas Spence, ventured to advocate public ownership of all land; he was arrested on a charge of sedition and effectively silenced.[8]

On the other hand, the system found ardent champions among the most enlightened men of the century. Samuel Johnson, a man whose name has become a byword for 'sturdy independence', unfailingly generous to the unfortunate, broodingly conscious of that truth which he enunciated so clearly, 'slow rises worth by poverty oppressed', was a staunch supporter of the principle of subordination as has already been shown in the second chapter. Edmund Burke, a man of high principles if ever there was one, a statesman who spoke out fervently for the liberty of the American colonies, who rose magnificently in defence of a distant and alien Indian people against the autocrats of his own nation, was conscious of no irony when he drew up a licence endorsing the right of the man of property to preserve and perpetuate a system which, especially in pre-Revolutionary France, permitted him to grab as much as he wished from the starving millions:

> ... The people, without being servile, must be tractable and obedient ... The body of the people must not find the principles of natural subordination by art rooted out of their minds. They must respect that property of which they cannot partake. They must labour to obtain what by labour can be obtained; and when they find, as they commonly do, the success disproportioned to the endeavour, they must be taught their consolation in the final proportions of eternal justice.[9]

Both Johnson and Burke were even willing to underrate their own worth when measuring it against the importance of the gentlemen with imposing ancestral lines and ancestral mansions. In 1772 Burke wrote to the Duke of Richmond:

You people of great families and hereditary trusts and fortunes, are not like such as I am, who, whatever we may be by the rapidity of our growth and even by the fruit we bear, flatter ourselves that, while we creep on the ground, we belly into melons that are exquisite for size and flavour, yet still we are but annual plants that perish with our season, and leave no sort of traces behind us. You, if you are what you ought to be, are in my eye the great oaks that shade a country, and perpetuate your benefits from generation to generation.[10]

To enable these great oaks to perpetuate from generation to generation those benefits which they had appropriated to themselves, in addition to the strength and laws of the state, there was a powerful instrument—the Anglican Church. As the Hammonds cryptically comment, 'the English Church was the very thing to keep religion in its place'; and, we may add, to keep the common folk in theirs. A substantial proportion of the upper class looked upon the Church not as a spiritual force, but as a stabilizing agent, a useful arm of the law. Moreover, the Church provided younger sons and other dependents with a comfortable livelihood. Even Burke defended religion primarily on the ground that it 'is the basis of civil society'.[11]

The hierarchical gradation in the Established Church was no different from that in the established secular society. The Archbishop of Canterbury enjoyed £25,000 a year and two palaces; the Bishop of London received £ 0,000. At the other end, at least twenty per cent of the ten thousand and odd benefices in the country were worth less than £75 per year; like the parson of Goldsmith's *Deserted Village* at least three per cent of the clergy had to consider themselves 'passing rich with forty pounds a year'. Like Parson Adams many a curate was only too grateful to share the remains of a joint sitting with the servants in the kitchen of the gentleman's house.

Faith and fervour had long since gone out of religion; however, to abide by its formalities had come to be recognized as a part not only of expediency, but of good breeding and the gracious life. 'A wise *Epicure* would be *Religious* for the sake of *Pleasure*; Good Sense is the Foundation of both;' the Marquess of Halifax said, instructing his daughter.[12]

However, even those most tepid in their attitude towards Christianity were scandalized if the Church was attacked, just as even the most fervent critics of the Establishment were outraged if the sacred principle of subordination was questioned. Gibbon, who thought that 'an age of light and liberty would receive, without scandal, an inquiry into the human *causes* of the progress and establishment of Christianity' (*Autobiography*, pp. 144-5), was surprised to find that he had stirred up a hornet's nest, and thought it wisest to return to the peace of his Alpine retreat.

As previous chapters have shown, there is a similar disturbing contradiction in the presentation of social and economic questions in many of the novels of this period. The clear-sighted awareness which the novelists show of the degenerate and tyrannical conduct of the gentry is nullified by the tacit supposition that gentility is the supreme blessing. The passionate exposure of the iniquity and ruthlessness of the system fails to have any artistic logic when the most glorious reward which the novelist reserves for the hero is to be absorbed into the class that operates the system. The contradiction ultimately weakens both the moral and artistic effect of the novels. Industry, virtue and moral struggle have little meaning when the gentleman hero is debarred from all profitable activity if he does not have an ancestral estate to manage.

Having confined himself within the rigid framework imposed by the class structure, the novelist can do little else except exhort the gentleman to perform his duty, to live the life of reason, prudence and good-breeding, and to be just and benevolent to the creatures placed under him. Riches, privilege and power are granted to him without question; if he is not restrained by moral conventions and enlightened by reason, he will become dissolute and tyrannical.

Power to do great good or great evil was invested in the almighty squire. Richardson's Mr. B. can intimidate not only all his servants but the whole countryside and carry out his nefarious designs on the 'low-born' Pamela with complete impunity. Fielding's Lady Booby can send the village belle to Brideswell if she fancies the girl's lover. Most of the squires in *Joseph Andrews* harass the neighbouring farmers, shoot their dogs and seduce their daughters. At Wakefield, the squire abducts both the daughters of the Vicar. On the other hand, the Allworthys and Grandisons and Sir Launcelots and Mr. Fentons can restore plenty to a smiling land, and bring hope and cheer into the cottages of scores of impoverished families. Plots which turn on events of this kind seem melodramatic and puerile to the modern reader; but the social conditions provided plenty of opportunities for such ruthlessness and such benevolence. The tyrannical rake and the paternal landlord were both common existing types.

In such a society, benevolence and a sense of social responsibility will necessarily be regarded as the most commendable virtues. Benevolence is not a virtue that needs to be insistently recommended in a socialistic state; it is essentially the virtue of a society organized around the gentleman, just as a ruthless tyranny is its most dreaded vice. Embarking on his project of presenting the most noble human being, Richardson could think of only two qualities which such a man 'can properly rise to'—'philanthropy and humanity' (*Letters*, 24 March 1751). The same two qualities are the essential components of that virtue of 'good-nature' which Fielding selected as the most commendable attribute of man. Sterne selected for advocacy 'the one virtue of compassion', and spoke of 'philanthropy, and those kindred virtues to it, upon which hang all the law and the prophets' (*Sermons*, I, p. 50, xlviii). Goldsmith, projecting his vision of the ideal man, invented the fanciful figure of Sir William Thornhill, *alias* Burchell, who goes about the countryside in a romantic disguise dispensing charity to the needy, and sweet ginger-bread to their children. Mackenzie presented the ideal man as a country gentleman with the significant name of Benevolus (*Lounger*, no. 96). Smollett, the scathing satirist, ended his career by conjuring up the quixotic 'benevolist' Sir Launcelot, and the misanthropic 'benevolist' Squire Matthew Bramble. Henry Brooke dreamed of a retired merchant-prince, rich beyond the dreams of ambition and benevolent beyond the dreams of the poor. Even John Wesley, preacher to massive congregations of labourers and coal-miners, could not think of presenting a more inspiring ideal than Brooke's and, 'retrenching' some unorthodox passages, published a revised edition of *The Fool of Quality* for the benefit of the public.

Inseparable from the persistent advocacy of benevolence is

the emphasis given to the ideal of social responsibility. When to an individual has been granted the privilege of being 'blessed', as Gibbon said of himself, with 'the double fortune of. . . birth in a free and enlightened country, in an honourable and wealthy family. . . . the lucky chance of an unit against millions' (*Autobiography*, p. 180), a correspondingly heavy burden of responsibility is placed upon him. The behaviour of many a light-hearted squire and nobleman made the familiar proverb 'What's a gentleman but his pleasure ?' ring only too true, but the expressed ideal of the gentleman's hand-book had remained much the same since Sir Thomas Elyot defined it in 1531 in *The Gouernour* (II, i) :

> They shall nat thynke howe moche honour they receiue, but howe moche care and burdene. . . Let them thynke the greatter dominion they haue, that therby they sustayne the more care and studie. And that therefore they muste haue the lasse solace and passetyme, and to sensual pleasures lasse opportunitie.

Besides, at the same time as they endeavoured to fulfil their obligations, the gentlemen would be laying the foundation of their own happiness—for happiness, as they were often told, is the reward of the life of virtue. This is the 'Truth', which it is 'enough for man to know, Virtue alone is happiness below' (*Essay on Man*, iv, 309-10). The truth was evident to anyone who cared to reason it out :

> Let me see then wherein consist the most lasting pleasures of this life : and that so far as I can observe is in these things : First, Health, without which no sensual pleasure can have any relish. Secondly, Good Reputation, for that I find everybody is pleased with, and the want of it a torment. Thirdly, Knowledge, for the little knowledge that I have, I find I would not sell at any rate, nor part with for any pleasure. Fourthly, Doing Good. I find the well-cooked meat I ate today does now no more delight me; nay, I am diseased after a full meal. The perfumes I smelt yesterday now no more affect me with any pleasure. But the good turn I did yesterday, a year, seven years hence,

continues still to please me as often as I reflect upon it. Fifthly, the expectation of eternal and incomprehensible happiness in another world also carries a constant pleasure with it.[13]

In such an atmosphere it was natural for poets to ask, without any suspicion that there could be another answer, 'What is Virtue but superior Sense ?' (Edward Young, *Epistle to Mr. Pope*). To Locke, to Addison, to Fanny Burney, to Richardson even, Virtue is but an aspect of common sense and clear logic; it manifests itself in an elegant good breeding, in politeness and propriety of manners. They see 'the reasonableness of Christianity'[14] and the good sense and profitableness of Christian ethics. To the popular mind the *Spectator* essays first made virtue, duty, religion, good sense and good breeding all seem to be one. Good form became as much the gentleman's duty as the obligation to act the paternal, magisterial role on his country estate, and the patriotic and independent role in parliament.

Good breeding indeed becomes a primary duty at a time when the members of the leisured classes are constantly thrown upon one another for entertainment and diversion. When the gentleman is debarred from all monetarily profitable activity and when at the same time there are no developed media of entertainment, people have constantly to look to one another for their amusement. In such a situation, the art of living in society, of elegant and considerate behaviour and polite conversation, becomes a matter of the first importance. Even John Wesley sat down to copy in several issues of the *Arminian Magazine* extracts from *The Refined Courtier*, an old treatise on etiquette, compiled out of the well known Italian courtesy book, *Galateo* by Della Casa.[15]

If the wealthy élite has no routine and serious employment, leisure can quickly turn into ennui, and ennui into the dissipation of gambling and sexual excesses. As Voltaire's Candide was told by the Turc, '*le travail éloigne de nous trois grands maux, l'ennui, le vice, et le besoin*'.[16] The rake who has an obsession for women and the gambler who has an obsession for cards and preposterous bets on which he stakes fabulous sums, are two common phenomena of the fashionable circles of this period. Both types are found not only among the triflers, but even among the extremely talented, highly accomplished public men of the period, men who rose high in the service of the state and eloquently championed liberal causes.

However, the propensity to such excesses can be taken care of by good sense, a feeling for propriety, a consciousness of social responsibility and an inclination for philanthropy. The tediously multiplied sketches of frivolous and criminally foolish gentlemen of leisure in the novels, essays and even the poetry of the period are presented as salutary warnings against such folly, extravagance and dissipation.

So it is the message of good sense and moderation, good breeding and philanthropy, that is reiterated all through the century. No really vexing or insoluble problems troubled the élite of those days. Society seemed to have attained stability. The European governing classes lived in an atmosphere of elegant culture and cosmopolitan fraternization. In England there was a calm and long interregnum after the political and religious upheavals of the seventeenth century. The hounds of liberty, equality and industrialism were soon to be unleashed on the gentleman's traces, and 'the peace of the Augustans' was to be shattered by the fury of revolution and romanticism. But, as yet, there was no problem about preserving the *status quo*; all that it was necessary to do was to improve matters slightly within the fixed framework.

Human nature itself had come to be regarded as a not very complex problem; it was thought that it could be easily kept under control by the discipline of reason. The faith in reason, especially in the early part of the century, made human problems seem easy of solution. Men like Pope felt that it was easier to understand and improve mankind than to probe the mysteries of the universe. Our times have proved it otherwise, and our literature is a reflection of our bewilderment. In those days the calm confidence expressed by the 'judicious Locke' was shared by most of the educated : 'The faculty of reasoning seldom or never deceives those who trust to it.'[17] Reason was able to govern desires, and make the passions obedient. It was to be used to arrive at the golden middle path which was indubitably the path of virtue, steering clear of the excesses on either side to which the human propensities lead when unchecked by reason.

This road to virtue and the right modes of living had been explored and described by the 'ancients' in their literature and philosophy. In Aristotle, in Cicero, and in Horace, the paths of virtue and wisdom had been clearly mapped out; since then they had been tried and tested by the experience of centuries. Now 'to follow Nature' and reason, was 'to follow them'.

In the later years of the century, the curb placed by reason on the emotions was eroded by waves of sensibility, and by subversive voices which had begun to preach that passion could perceive more truths than reason. The restrained, decorous sensitiveness preached by Addison as an aspect of good breeding turned into a morbid exhibition of feeling. A similarly morbid psychological reaction turning with exaggeration upon the doctrine of well-bred propriety and civilized elegance, was the hankering after the primitive, the uneasy flirtation which some writers and thinkers carried on for a time with the idea of the noble savage.

In the minor writers of the period, and not infrequently in the major, the pull in contrary directions of these opposing forces, rationalism and sensibility, elegance and primitivism, produces some very confused writing. Even writers of the stature of Goldsmith are not certain of their values and produce works which have such divided aims that they tempt critics to give a variety of contradictory interpretations.

A period like this is not a time which gives rise to dazzling heroes, magnificent warriors, noble saints, or tortured martyrs; nor is it a time when the writer longs to create such heroic characters. Desiring to create a noble and exalted character, all that they can rise to is to think, 'philanthropy and humanity is all that he can rise to' (Richardson to Lady Bradsaigh 24 March 1751). It is not a time for Hamlet or Faustus, Antony or Tamburlaine, Satan or Prometheus, for poems about heaven and hell. It professes attitudes which can easily stultify literature and limit the vision. These characteristics of the period infuriated Carlyle who spoke of it with his most vitriolic scorn, branding it as an age of 'spiritual paralysis', 'soul extinct, stomach well alive'. 'Perhaps in few centuries that one could specify since the world began was a life of Heroism more difficult for a man,' was his verdict as he saw Johnson and Burns valiantly struggling to rise to heroism in such an age. He felt nothing but disgust for its talk about philanthropy and humanity: 'Consider them, with their tumid, sentimental vapouring about virtue, benevolence—the wretched Quack-Squadron . . .'[18]

But if fixed standards, belief in a stable hierarchical society, confidence in reason and in tried, traditional values can sometimes stultify life and art, they can also give a solid, firm basis for some forms of literature. The time is right for a realistic and critical exposition of day to day life, observed with humour and humanity, and with moral conviction. A diversified social scene, which offers sharp contrasts of luxury and misery, and affords countless opportunities for displaying cruelty and selfishness, or humanity and generosity, when observed by a writer with a strong belief in a few tried moral values, provides rich descriptive and emotional material for a novel.

Moreover, if the English Augustans enjoyed peace, stability, comfort and elegance, the sorrow and suffering that is a part of the human condition had not been banished from life:

> Infelicity is involved in corporeal nature, and interwoven with our being . . . the armies of pain send their arrows against us on every side . . . and the strongest armour which reason can supply, will only blunt their points, but cannot repel them. (*Rambler*, no. 32)

Take a look at the armies of pain, only on the physical plane. Illness, disease and surgical operations had to be endured in those days of primitive medicine without analgesics and anaesthetics, antiseptics and antibiotics. Experiments were continually being made with painful, revolting cures; jaundice, it was believed, would be cured if nine live lice were swallowed every morning.[19] For women, there was the annual martyrdom of child bearing; twelve to sixteen children were common. This was the lot of the gentleman as well as of the citizen and the labourer. So was a kind of squalor in the midst of the elegance. Sitting amidst the magnificent beauty of his Cannons, the Duke of Chandos wrote frantically to a friend in Jamaica, for bitterwood to line his baby daughter's cradle which was infested with bugs.[20] Fashionable ladies were accustomed to carrying long pointed 'scratchers' to reach down their backs to the lice.

And always in the background there was 'the black fear of death which saddens all'. Small-pox came and emptied whole nurseries within a few days. At such times only reason, and the philosophy which taught 'the threats of pain and ruin to despise', could come to the rescue. Not much imagination is required to see that the eighteenth century was not altogether denied opportunities for proving its strength and moral resources, nor quite deprived of the raw material for creating significant works of art.

But it was tired of the enthusiasm about heroism and greatness and saintliness, and suspicious of 'the poet's eye in fine frenzy rolling'. Running as a thread through this whole literature is an antagonism to the 'great' man; writers of varied temperaments repeatedly insist that the good, simple man must be placed higher than him.

The concept of nobility, the idea of the gentleman, seems to have changed significantly from the earlier concept of the ideal gentleman as the perfect 'courtier'; a resplendent public figure and an undaunted adventurer, seeking glory, defying death,

> Still climbing after knowledge infinite,
> And always moving as the restless spheres.
>
> (*Tamburlaine*, II, vii)

The restless ambition and dazzling versatility had now spent themselves and given place to more placid values. The ideal of the 'courtier' had turned into the ideal of the country gentleman; that magniloquent word 'honour' had been replaced by the candid word 'honest'. Pride, the typical heroic virtue, had gradually come to be seen as no fit virtue for the Christian gentleman. The traditionally praised attributes of courage and prudence still remained virtues; but courage was now advocated in its nobler aspect of bearing misfortune with fortitude and equanimity, not in its aspect of arrogant assertion of victory and dominion over others. Prudence was still inculcated, but it was sought to be purified of all the Machiavellian cunning and suave dissimulation associated with it in earlier periods, and was asked to clasp hands with its opposites, sincerity and open-heartedness.

The traditional heroic virtues are essentially self-regarding, aiming at the highest development of the individual personality. The new scale of values is essentially more humanitarian, noticeably more aware of those standing in the outer cold. It stresses at least two qualities that seem to be now newly perceived as virtues—pity and tolerance. Now the gentleman is no longer to live with the hauteur and exclusiveness of the aristocrat, but is continuously to give proof of 'the expanded heart' (*Grandison*, VII, vii).

The 'false scale of happiness' that put the dazzling qualities of 'the rich, the honour'd, fam'd and great' above the simple, domestic pieties is exposed, and 'all that rais'd the Hero' is shown to have 'sunk the Man' (*Essay of Man*, iv, 287-94). Even as late as Dryden, 'desire for greatness is a god-like sin' (*Absalom and Achitophel*, i, 372); but now Pope proclaims, 'the honest man's the noblest work of God', and in many writers of the century greatness comes to be equated with all that is destructive and despicable. In literature even the unsuccessful, ineffective, awkward, credulous man comes to be regarded as a more praiseworthy person than the clever, sophisticated, successful man of the world.

Men like Chesterfield, who still favour 'the shining character of a complete gentleman, *un galant homme, un homme de cour*' (*Letters*, 27 May 1753), who has mastered all the politic gifts that bring worldly success, now represent a small, select section of society that still clings to an earlier tradition, and looks often towards France for culture and enlightenment. The popularity of Chesterfield's *Letters* as a book of advice shows that the worldly and fashionable still feel the pull of this way of life, but most of the literature of the period that attempts to inculcate values is fast embracing the more homely, 'honest' virtues. It is not at all surprising that even Chesterfield's public voice is consistently raised on the side of the manly, English virtues. In the numerous witty essays he wrote for public consumption in *The World* and *Common Sense*, Chesterfield frequently ridicules the craze for French sophistication.

The widely-shared faith in these new values leads to a move awya from the town and the courts of princes which come more and more to be associated with corruption, duplicity, cringing flattery and every sort of soul-destroying vice. On the other hand, in the country, on the family estate, there is scope for the exercise of all the cherished virtues—for paternalism and benevolence; for a few steadfast, loyal friendships; for useful employment of one's talents in administering justice; for healthy entertainment obtainable from books and the wholesome sports of the countryside. Quite unlike the Restoration dramatists who present the country gentleman as a ridiculous boor, from Addison to Jane Austen no position is seen as more enviable than that of the gentleman with, as Jane Austen's Anne Elliott calls it, 'the duties and dignity of a resident land-holder' (*Persuasion*, ch. xv).

This ideal came to be preached with an added enthusiasm and force, because it had a literary sanction in classical literature, especially in the poetry of Virgil and Horace. As Rachel Trickett demonstrates vividly, 'the country gentleman . . . saw himself through the glass of Horace.'[21]

The enthusiasm for this ideal became all the more keen because in England public life and the court had come to be linked with the long, corrupt regime of Walpole (in whose image Fielding created the 'great' gangster, Jonathan Wild) and with the dowdy Hanoverian court. George II, who reigned during the first half of this period, was more German than English, and kept stout unfashionable German mistresses; George III, who reigned during the second half, was well-meaning but homely, moralizing, and 'very stupid, really stupid. Had he been born in different circumstances it is unlikely he could have earned a living except as an unskilled manual labourer'.[22]

If the court was dowdy, the cultivated class itself had come to have a broader base; it had expanded to absorb within itself a new aristocracy of wealth, and with it the tastes and attitudes of the bourgeois turning into the *gentilhomme*. At such a time old ideas of culture and glory are bound to be modified to suit the talents, tastes and aspirations of men with a different outlook. Addison, who moved in the company of aristocrats, and himself occupied several prominent posts in public life, allows his new hero, Sir Andrew Freeport, to make his pile in trade by his own industry and acumen, and then to retire into the countryside with the honourable status of a country gentleman, determined to provide work for the poor and charity for the disabled, planning to drain marshes, plant woods and to so contrive 'that not a shower of rain, or a glimpse of sunshine, shall fall upon my estate, without bettering some part of it' (*The Spectator*, no. 549). Swift, who moved with the most distinguished politicians and noblemen of his day, and was perhaps the finest intellect in the whole literature of the century, considers that the man who makes 'two ears of corn grow where one grew before' is worth 'the whole race of politicians put together'.[23]

The militant patriotism of an earlier time that found its incentive in a thirst for glory, adventure and danger, and in the lure of the unknown, had now given place to a different patriotism, that received its incentive from an urge for prosperity, stability and peace. It was ready to settle down and make an England that had put its religious and political revolutions behind it into a rich, prosperous land, leader of the world in agriculture, commerce and industry. The ideal gentleman now stands in country boots, dreaming not of glory and heroic honours on the battlefield, but of multiplying his acres and his cattle; of better breeds on better pastures, better wool, better cloth, better roads; more wood, more coal, more canals :

But all our praises why should Lords engross ?
Rise, honest Muse ! and sing the MAN of ROSS :
. . . .
Who hung with woods yon mountain's sultry brow ?
From the dry rock who bade the waters flow ?
. . . .
'Till Kings call forth th' Ideas of your mind,
(Proud to accomplish what such hands designed,)
Bid Harbours open, public Ways extend,
Bid Temples, worthier of the God, ascend;
Bid the broad Arch the dang'rous Flood contain,
The Mole projected break the roaring Main;
Back to his bounds their subject Sea command,
And roll obedient Rivers thro' the Land :
These Honours Peace to happy Britain brings,
These are Imperial Works and Worthy Kings.

(Pope, *Moral Essays*, iii, 249-54)

This new ideal was being translated into reality all over England during the course of the eighteenth century, by country gentlemen, by peers, and by 'Farmer George' himself, king and 'first gentleman' of Great Britain. Their leaders and models were Lord Townshend, whose agricultural enterprise brought him the nickname 'Turnip Townshend'; the Duke of Bridgewater, whose canals established a new system of river navigation all over England, Thomas Coke of Holkham afterwards Earl of Leicester, whose fat sheep and cattle made English pastures and English cattle-breeding famous all over Europe; leaders 'who plant [ed] like BATHURST, or who built like BOYLE' (*Moral Essays*, iv, 177).

The new ideal was also being expressed all through the century in good, as well as in extremely bad poetry; in every periodical magazine, and, as we have seen, in the novel by the foremost novelists, Richardson, Fielding, Smollett and Goldsmith.

The ideal, though not so much in its urge to build, improve and prosper, as in its glorification of the calm, leisured, reasonable life of the country gentleman, found its quintessential expression, right at the beginning of the century, in a poem entitled *The Choice*. To the modern reader it seems a thoroughly pedestrian poem which makes this much acclaimed way of life appear unbearably uninspiring and tame. However, throughout the century this poem enjoyed an immense and quite incredible success, proving the appeal of this ideal of the tranquil, prosperous country life that found 'substantial bliss' in everyday things; all its 'joys refin'd, sincere, and great'; all tried 'by solid reason, and let that decide'.[24]

Except in a poet of the stature of Pope, the celebration of this new ideal proves unsuited to poetry and often produces quite ridiculous examples of bathos. But in the novel, a form designed to portray life realistically and to express social concern, a form which could legitimately describe the art of day-to-day living in the most direct terms, the new ideal found a natural, and at its best a vividly human, expression, just as the old chivalric ideal had found its natural expression in the rapture and fine frenzy of lyric poetry and drama, and the grandeur of heroic epic and romance.

The deficiencies of the gentleman, and the iniquity of the

system of which he was the pivot, have only too often been sharply exposed in the preceding pages. The novelists also have only too often been severely criticised for not having the courage and the imagination to question the validity of the gentleman-oriented social organization, though they were clearly aware of its injustice and cruelty. Yet, if we are tempted to dismiss the novelists of the eighteenth century as timid, because they did not venture to suggest that the gentleman should be hurled down from his pedestal, we must recollect that even a thinker as radical as Harold Laski, wrote with melancholy and fear about 'the passing of the gentleman' as late as 1932 :

> No one, I believe, will see the passing of the gentleman without a brief annotation of regret. In the period of his apogee he was a better ruler than any of his possible rivals. I, at least, would rather have been governed by Lord Shaftesbury than Mr. Cobden, by the gentlemen of England than by the Gradgrinds and Bounderbys of Coketown. . . Nor is it certain that we shall replace him by a more admirable type.[25]

Nor is it certain that the ideals pictured in the eighteenth century novel are uninspiring and unoriginal. No mature reader can fail to perceive the vitality, the honesty and the depth of the moral vision of these writers as it concentrates on the domestic sphere, and on the problems and conflicts of every day life. The sharp critical sense, the keenly observant eye, the delightful humour and the common sense wisdom with which these novelists confront life should be obvious to every perceptive reader, and are qualities commonly pointed out in discussing their contribution to literature. But in the judgment of many modern readers, to emphasize such qualities is merely to imply that these novelists deserve only that faint praise which damns a writer to oblivion.

It is all the more necessary therefore to stress that the humanity and passion with which these novelists confronted social wrongs were a new and important challenge offered to man's sense of values, and his idea of his moral personality. The intellectual excitement and the emotional complexity of Renaissance and Jacobean literature must not blind us to the fact that it shows scarcely any awareness of the sufferings, or even of the humanity, of the large majority of mankind, that it is almost totally unconcerned about the wants and the aspirations of this majority, and about the degradation to which it is compelled to submit. A few memorable passages like the one in which King Lear, driven out of his palace by his daughters, becomes conscious of the plight of the 'poor naked wretches', do not change the fact that concern for the downtrodden majority is not an integral part of this literature. The literature of the eighteenth century is the first to become conscious that the mass of mankind is not material only for comedy, that the challenge it offers to literature, and to man's moral character, is noble and heroic, and not without potentialities for the expression of passion and disillusionment. It is the first to realize that the exploitation and degradation of the ordinary man by social, political and legal institutions, and by the agents of money and power, are themes with which literature must concern itself.

Notes

CHAPTER 1

1. John Locke, *Some Thoughts Concerning Education*, ed. R.H. Quick, Cambridge, 1913, p. lxiii.
2. To John Wilkes, 16 March 1759; James Boswell, *The Life of Samuel Johnson*, ed. George Birkbeck Hill, rev. L.F. Powell, 6 vols., Oxford, 1934, I, 348.
3. Rev. Thomas Wilson to Richardson, 29 July 1752, cit. A.D. McKillop, *Samuel Richardson, Printer and Novelist*, Chapel Hill, 1936, p. 206.
4. Sterne's comment on Smollett, *A Sentimental Journey*, ed. Ian Jack, 1968, 'In the Street— Calais', p. 99.
5. *The English Comic Writers*, *The Compleat Works of William Hazlitt*, ed. P.P. Howe, 21 vols., 1930-4, VI, 121.
6. Charles Kingsley's description of Brooke in the preface to *The Fool of Quality*, ed. E.A. Baker (with biographical preface by Charles Kingsley), 1906, p. xxxvii.
7. Sermon delivered 24 Aug. 1744, St. Mary's Church, Oxford; cit. Samuel Shellabarger, *Lord Chesterfield*, 1935, p. 206.

CHAPTER 2

1. *Biographia Literaria*, 1905 (George Bell); 'Satyrane's Letters', letter 2, p. 250.
2. William Harrison, *Description of England*, 1577, cit. G.M. Trevelyan, *English Social History*, 1962, pp. 164-6.
3. Walter Bagehot, 'Sterne and Thackeray' in *Literary Studies*, ed. R.H. Hutton, 1910, II, 321.
4. Diana Spearman, *The Novel and Society*, 1966, p. 211.
5. See E.A. Baker, *The History of the English Novel*, vol. IV (1933), p. 89, and Irvin Ehrenpreis, 'Fielding's Use of Fiction: The Autonomy of Joseph Andrews' in *Twelve Original Essays on Great English Novels*, ed. Charles Shapiro, Detroit, 1960, pp. 31, 35.
6. Ian Watt, *The Rise of the Novel*, California, 1962, pp. 269-70.
7. As by W.M. Sale, 'From Pamela to Clarissa', in *Age of Johnson, Essays Presented to C.B. Tinker*, New Haven, 1949, pp. 131-2; to some extent by Ian Watt, *op. cit.*, pp. 220-2; but see Diana Spearman's remarks on the subject, *op. cit.*, pp. 178-82.

8. *The Citizen Turn'd Gentleman*, title of a comedy written 1762 by Edward Ravenscroft.
9. H.W. Thompson, *A Scottish Man of Feeling*, Oxford, 1931, p. 125.
10. Daniel Defoe, *The Compleat English Gentleman*, ed. Karl D. Bülbring, 1890, pp. 256-7.
11. The Earl of Egmont's Diary, 4 Feb. 1745, cit. A.D. McKillop, *Samuel Richardson, Printer and Novelist*, North Carolina, 1936, p. 29.
12. David Hume, *Essays Moral, Political and Literary*, cit. James Sutherland, *A Preface to Eighteenth Century Poetry*, Oxford, 1948, p. 99.
13. See A.S. Turberville, *The House of Lords in the Eighteenth Century*, Oxford, 1927, pp. 5-8.
14. Edmund Burke, *Thoughts on the Causes of the Present Discontents*, ed. F.G. Selby, 1912, p. 3.
15. It must however be said that the English governing class had not seized the fiscal and other legal privileges which the European aristocracies claimed for themselves.
16. See Turberville, *op. cit.*, pp. 29-31, p. 437; Sarah Tytler, *The Countess of Huntingdon and Her Circle*, 1907, pp. 30-1.

CHAPTER 3

1. James Boswell, *The Life of Samuel Johnson*, ed. George Birkbeck Hill, rev. L.F. Powell, 6 vols., Oxford, 1934, III, 54.
2. This has been pointed out by W.E. Alderman in 'Shaftesbury and the Doctrine of Moral Sense in the Eighteenth Century', *PMLA*, xlvi (19'1), pp. 1087-94.
3. See F.T. Blanchard, *Fielding the Novelist—A Study in Historical Criticism*, Yale University Press, 1926, pp. 193-4.
4. David Fordyce, *The Elements of Moral Philosophy*, 1754, pp. 263-4; cit. R.S. Crane, 'Suggestions Toward a Genealogy of the "Man of Feeling" ', *ELH*, Dec. 1934, pp. 205-30; p. 205.
5. Voltaire, *Oeuvres*, XLIX, 56-7, cit. Samuel Shellabarger, *Lord Chesterfield*, 1935, p. 388.
6. W.A.C. Steward and W.P. McCann, *The Educational Innovators*, New York, 1967, p. 23.
7. A.A. Evans, 'The Impact of Rousseau on English Education', *Researches and Studies, University of Leeds Institute of Education*, XI (Jan. 1955), pp. 15-25; p. 24.
8. Machiavelli, *The Prince*, tr. W.K. Marriott, n.d., pp. 122, 14-3.
9. See G.E. Mingay, *English Landed Society in the Eighteenth Century*, 1963, p. 145; Dorothy Marshall, *English People in the Eighteenth Century*, 1956, p. 240; J.H. Plumb, 'Nobility and Gentry in the Early Eighteenth Century', *History Today*, V (Dec. 1955), pp. 816-7.
10. The two satirical treatises, *An Essay on Polite Conversation*, and *A Complete Collection of Genteel and Ingenious Conversation*, and the

NOTES 283

following essays—'On Modern Education', 'Of the Education of Ladies', 'Hints towards an Essay on Conversation', 'A Treatise on Good Manners and Good Breeding' and 'Hints on Good Manners'.
11. Nicholas Hans in *New Trends in Education in the Eighteenth Century*, 1951, makes a statistical study of 713 cases of sons of gentlemen who received their secondary or higher education during the eighteenth century and became famous enough to figure in *The Dictionary of National Biography*. The study shows that approximately 33% were educated at home, 44% at one among the nine well-known public schools, 14% at grammar schools, 8% at private schools, and 1.5% at dissenting academies.
12. Ruth Kelso, *The Doctrine of the English Gentleman in the Sixteenth Century*, University of Illinois Studies in Language and Literature, XIV (1929), pp. 111-9.
13. Wallace Notestein, *English Folk*, 1938, p. 88.
14. See Nicholas Hans, *op. cit.*, D.A. Winstanley, *Unreformed Cambridge*, Cambridge, 1935; Christopher Wordsworth, *Scholae Academicae, Some Account of the Studies at English Universities in the Eighteenth Century*, Cambridge, 1910.
15. D.A. Winstanley, *op. cit.*, pp. 213-4.
16. *The Collected Works of Oliver Goldsmith*, ed. Arthur Friedman, 5 vols., Oxford, 1966, I, 336. Isaac Newton, Richard Bentley and quite a few others who rose high, went up as Sizars. The position of Sizars improved a little towards the end of the century, but as late as 1840, at some colleges they dined after the other undergraduates had finished. —see Winstanley, *op. cit.*, p. 202.
17. Lord Charlemont to Lord Bruce, 17 July 1774; See *The Letters of Philip Dormer Stanhope, Earl of Chesterfield*, ed. John Bradshaw, I.P. xxvii.
18. Cit. J.H. Plumb, *Men and Places*, 1966, p. 72.
19. See Joseph Burke, 'The Grand Tour and the Rule of Taste', in *Studies in the Eighteenth Century*, ed. R.F. Brissenden, Canberra, 1968, pp. 231-50.

CHAPTER 4

1. To the Countess of Bute, 20 Oct. NS 1752; Lady Mary Wortley Montagu, *Letters and Works*, ed. Lord Wharncliffe, 3 vols., 1837, III, 39. In an earlier letter, after passing several strictures on *Clarissa*, she declared : 'I look upon this and *Pamela* to be two books that will do more general mischief than the works of Lord Rochester.'—1 March NS 1752; III, 23.
2. Samuel Coleridge, *Anima Poetae*, cit. Frank Bradbrook, 'Samuel Richardson', *Pelican Guide to English Literature*, ed. Boris Ford, 1963, IV, 293.
3. Mrs. Chapone; cit. B.W. Downs, *Richardson*, 1928, p. 119.

4. From the earlier descriptive title for *Clarissa*, in the Forster Collection, printed in *Selected Letters of Samuel Richardson*, ed. John Carroll, Oxford, 1964, p. 77, note 64.
5. David Daiches, *A Critical History of English Literature*, 2 vols., 1961, II, 709.
6. See R.F. Brissenden, *Samuel Richardson*, 1965; Frank Kermode, 'Richardson and Fielding', Cambridge Journal, IV (1950), pp. 106-14, p. 110.
7. Samuel Johnson, *Life of Rowe*; cit. H.G. Ward, *Richardson's Character of Lovelace*, MLR, VII (Oct. 1912), pp. 494-8.
8. 'But how have I suffered from the Cavils of some, from the Prayers of others . . . Mr. Lyttleton . . . Mr. Cibber, and Mr. Fielding, have been among these.'—Richardson to Aaron Hill, 7 Nov. 1748, *Letters*, p. 99.
9. '. . . The supposed Tragical (tho' I think it Triumphant) Catastrophe, which cannot recommend it as to Sale, as a prosperous and *rewarded Virtue* could.'— to Aaron Hill, 26 Jan. 1746/7, *Letters*, p. 83.
10. Brigid Brophy, 'The Rococo Seducer', London Magazine, May 1962, vol. II, no. 2, pp. 54-71.
11. *Advice to a Daughter*, *The Complete Works of George Savile, First Marquess of Halifax*, ed. Walter Raleigh. 1912, pp. 10-17.
12. Diana Spearman, *The Novel and Society*, 1966, p. 193.
13. J.E. Austen-Leigh, *Memoir of Jane Austen*, ed. R.W. Chapman, Oxford, 1926; cit. A.D. McKillop, *Samuel Richardson, Printer and Novelist*, North Carolina, 1936, p. 248.

CHAPTER 5

1. Henry Fielding, *Journey from this World to the Next*, I, vii.
2. Leslie Stephen, *A History of English Thought in the Eighteenth Century*, 1927, II, pp. 377-80.
3. See esp. James A. Work, 'Henry Fielding, Christian Censor', in *The Age of Johnson*, Essays Presented to C.B. Tinker, New Haven, 1949; Sheldon Sacks, *Fiction and The Shape of Belief*, California, 1964; Michael Irwin, *Henry Fielding, The Tentative Realist*, Oxford, 1967.
4. See F.T. Blanchard, *Fielding the Novelist— A Study in Historical Criticism*, Yale University Press, 1926, pp. 49-50.
5. *Ibid.*, p. 193.
6. *Ibid.*, pp. 193-4.
7. Sheldon Sacks, *op. cit.*, p. 117, agrees with this view, but many other Fielding scholars do not accept it.
8. See Diana Spearman, *The Novel and Society*, 1966, pp. 208-9.
9. John Brown's famous *Estimate of the Manners and Principles of the Times* (1757) expressed a similar pessimism and dismay.

10. This is disputed by some critics; e.g. William Empson, 'Tom Jones' in *Henry Fielding, A Collection of Critical Essays*, ed. Ronald Paulson, Englewood, Cliffs, N.J. 1962, and by A.E. Dyson, *The Crazy Fabric*, 1965, pp. 28-30.
11. William Empson, *op. cit.*, pp. 130-5.
12. A.E. Dyson, *op. cit.*, pp. 28-30.
13. See F. Homes Dudden, *Henry Fielding— His Life, Works and Times*, 2 vols., Oxford, 1952, II, 794.
14. William Empson, *op. cit.*, pp. 128-9.
15. John Middleton Murry, *Unprofessional Essays*, 1956, p. 51.
16. See Muriel Jaeger, *Before Victoria*, 1967, pp. 59-80.
17. James Boswell, *Private Papers*, IX, 16; 19 March 1772, cit. R.A. Leigh, 'Boswell and Rousseau', *MLR*, XLVII (July 1952), p. 304.
18. Ford Madox Ford, *The March of Literature*, 1939, pp. 572, 588-90.
19. William Empson, *op. cit.*, p. 126.
20. However, Fielding had a very high opinion of Chesterfield; in *Joseph Andrews* (III, i) he singled him out as a splended exception among 'high people'.
21. See Middleton Murry, *op. cit.*, pp. 24-5.
22. See A.E. Dyson, *op. cit.*, pp. 25-6, H.N. Fairchild, *The Noble Savage, A Study in Romantic Naturalism*, New York, 1961, p. 88.
23. Leslie Stephen, *Hours in a Library*, 1879, p. 178.
24. See *inter alia, Jonathan Wild*, III, iii; *Amelia*, IV, iv, VIII, iii, VIII, xiii.
25. Wilbur Cross, *The History of Henry Fielding*, 3 vols., New Haven, 1918, III, 77.

CHAPTER 6

1. The three quotations are from *Roderick Random*, II, xx, *Humphry Clinker*, letter of 2 June, by Matt, and *Roderick Random*, I, xvi.
2. See William Bowman Piper, *The Large Diffused Picture of Life in Smollett's Early Novels, SP*, vol. LX (Jan. 1963), pp. 45-56; Ronald Paulson, *Satire in the Early Novels of Smollett, JEGP*, July 1960, pp. 381-402; M.A. Goldberg, *Smollett and the Scottish School*, Albuquerque, 1959, Robert Giddings, *The Tradition of Smollett*, 1967. Mr. Piper and Mr. Paulson think that the fact that Roderick and Peregrine turn out to be such unpleasant heroes is a technical consequence of Smollett's as yet not very successful experiments in seeking to adapt the then fashionable form of the novel to the purposes of satire. Mr. Piper describes the protagonists of the first three novels as 'blank characters' who are not meant to make any 'personal demand on our sympathies' nor are they to be judged as realistically depicted people. On the other hand, Mr. Paulson admits that the brutal nature of the protagonists of the first two novels seriously disturbs the

reader. This happens because Smollett is attempting to incorporate the *persona* of the Juvenalian verse satirist in the novel; however, the novel, a realistic form concentrating attention on a hero in whose personal history the reader gets interested, and whom he judges as a human being, was not readily amenable to such an adaptation; hence, Smollett's first two novels are 'unsatisfactory performances'. Mr. Goldberg and Mr. Giddings attempt even more emphatically to vindicate the sensitiveness of Smollett's moral perception and his philosophical seriousness. According to them the unpleasant characteristics of the heroes are part of a systematically worked out moral purpose, the author's aim being to correct and reform his heroes, and to give them a reward only when they are cured of their vices. Mr. Goldberg sees Smollett's heroes each as a study in a conflict between a pair of opposing forces in human nature; Mr. Giddings sees Perry's imprisonment in a debtor's prison as a cataclysmic experience 'which it would perhaps not be pretentious to compare with the heath scenes in King Lear'!

3. H.W. Meikle, 'New Smollett Letters', *TLS*, 21 July 1943, p. 360.
4. The first edition contained several coarse passages and venomously personal attacks which Smollett cut out in the second edition printed seven years later. Modern editors have always preferred to print the text of the second edition, some eighty pages shorter, and several degrees less coarse; the 'Oxford English Novels' edition, ed. J.L. Clifford, 1964, now makes the original text available. The expurgated passages will be found restored on pp. 65-6, 242, 244, 263-4, 273-4, 325-31, 424-6, 655-60, *inter alia*, of this edition.
5. R. Paulson, *op. cit.*, p. 396.
6. See Alexandre Beljame, *Men of Letters and the English Public in the Eighteenth Century*, 1897, pp. 1-8; J.H. Plumb, *Men and Places, Essays on the Eighteenth Century Scene*, 1966, pp. 100, 107-8.
7. See James R. Foster, 'Peregrine Pickle and The Memoirs of Count Grammont', *MLN*, Nov. 1951, no. 66, pp. 469-71, and Vivian de Sola Pinto, *Enthusiast in Wit, A Portrait of John Wilmot, Earl of Rochester*, 1962.
8. See Thomas R. Preston, 'Smollett and the Benevolent Misanthrope Type', *PMLA*, March 1964; vol. 79, pp. 51-7.
9. See George Saintsbury, *The English Novel*, 1931, p. 121; A.D. McKillop, *The Early Masters of English Fiction*, 1962, p. 169; R. Giddings, *op. cit.*, p. 139; two recent writers on the eighteenth century novel have seen that this work is unjustly underrated; see R.D. Mayo, *The English Novel in the Magazines, 1740-1815*, 1962, pp. 277-86; and A.R. Humphreys in *Pelican Guide to English Literature*, 1962, IV, 329.
10. See Oswald Doughty, 'The English Malady of the Eighteenth Century', *RES*, Jan. 1926, vol. 2, no. 5, pp. 257-69.
11. This resemblance has been pointed out by T.R. Preston, *op. cit.*, pp. 54-6, and by A.D. McKillop, *op. cit.*, pp. 176-7.

12. L.M. Knapp, 'Smollett's Self-Portrait in The Expedition of Humphry Clinker', in *The Age of Johnson— Essays Presented to Chauncey Brewster Tinker*, New Haven, 1949, p. 154.
13. L.M. Knapp, *Smollett*, p. 184.

CHAPTER 7

1. *The Deserted Village*, 11. 385, 253-4. However in *The Citizen of the World* (letter xi) Goldsmith praised 'luxury', because it 'increases our capacity for happiness'.
2. See Macdonald Emslie, *Goldsmith's 'The Vicar of Wakefield'*, 1963, pp. 12-4.
3. E.A. Baker, *The History of the English Novel*, 1934, V, 81-2.
4. Robert H. Hopkins, *The True Genius of Oliver Goldsmith*, Baltimore, 1969; for the statements see pp. 188, 207, 212, 226.
5. See however, R.H. Hopkins, *op. cit.*, pp. 128-35, who calls it 'one of the cleverest and most misunderstood essays of the entire eighteenth century'.
6. William Makepeace Thackeray, *The English Humorists*, ed. J.C. Castleman, New York, 1916, p. 249.
7. E.A. Baker, *op. cit.*, V, 82.
8. *Diary and Letters of Madame d'Arblay*, ed. by Her Niece, 7 vols., 1842-6, I, 59.
9. Richardson's remark about Sir Charles Grandison, 'who, imitating the divinity, regards the heart rather than the head...' (VI, liv, 897).
10. See particularly *The Mirror*, nos. 35, 39, 40.
11. Fielding frequently condemned the glorification of the military conqueror, but the problem of colonialism is not considered by him. Mackenzie's distaste for the newly returned Nabobs and 'Nabobinas', who 'turned our barn-door fowls...by garlic and pepper...into the form of *Curries* and *Peelaws*' is evident in *The Lounger*, nos. 17 and 56.
12. Cit. E.A. Baker, *op. cit.*, V, 126.
13. Robert Burns to John Murdoch, 15 Jan. 1783, cit. H.W. Thompson, *A Scottish Man of Feeling*, Oxford, 1931, p. 218.
14. Lady Louisa Stuart to Scott, 4 Sept. 1826; collected by Sir Wilfred Parlington in *The Private Letter Books of Sir Walter Scott*, p. 272, cit., Q.D. Leavis, *Fiction and the Reading Public*, 1932, pp. 154-5.
15. Cf. Fielding's description of Sophia Western's eyes : 'Her black eyes had a lustre in them, which all her softness could not extinguish.' *Tom Jones*, IV, ii.
16. For examples of this pertinent whistling see *Tristram Shandy*, I, xxi; II, ii; III, xlii; IV, viii; IV, xxix.
17. See for example E.A. Baker, *op. cit.*, V, 103-4.
18. Keats to Benjamin Bailey, 22 Nov. 1817; *The Letters of John Keats*, ed. M.B. Forman, 1952, p. 67.

19. W.L. Cross, *The Life and Times of Laurence Sterne*, New Haven, 1929, p. 549.
20. Margaret R.B. Shaw, *Laurence Sterne, The Making of a Humorist*, 1957, p. 60.
21. Of course some critics do not find Sterne so delightful. Their views may be represented by the following passages : ' ... that amoral person Sterne... He fondled his sensibility, he never tired of playing with it; he was a debauched sentimentalist aware of his vices, and voluptuously enjoying all its sweetness.'—E.A. Baker, *op. cit.*, V, 95-6. 'He showed...a corrupt heart and a prurient imagination. He is a literary prostitute. He cultivates his fineness of feeling with a direct view to the market.'—Leslie Stephen, *History of English Thought in the Eighteenth Century*, 2 vols., 1927, II, 441.
22. Ignatius Sancho to Sterne, 21 July 1766, *The Letters of Laurence Sterne*, ed. L.P. Curtis, Oxford, 1935, pp. 282-3. W.L. Cross thinks that Sancho's letter, copied in Sterne's own hand in his Letter Book, was 'elaborated' by Sterne; see *The Letters of Laurence Sterne*, York ed; New York, 1904, p. 119.
23. W.L. Cross, *Life*, p. 553.
24. Sterne is referring to Smollett.
25. Dr. Warburton to Sterne, 15 June 1760, *Letters of Laurence Sterne*, ed. L.P. Curtis, pp. 112-4.
26. Walter Bagehot, *Literary Studies*, vol. II, 1910, pp. 287-8.
27. William Hazlitt, *The Complete Works*, ed. P.P. Howe, 21 vols., VI, 121.

CHAPTER 8

1. *Diary and Letters of Madame d'Arblay*, ed. by Her Niece, 7 vols., 1842-6, I, 103.
2. Johnson's gloss in the *Dictionary* is interesting :
   Elegance 1. Beauty rather soothing than striking; beauty without grandeur; the beauty of propriety rather than greatness.
   Elegancy 2. Anything that pleases by its nicety. In this sense it has a plural.
3. William Hazlitt, *The Complete Works*, ed. P.P. Howe, 21 vols., 1930-4; VI, 124-5.
4. The Rt. Hon. Edmund Burke to Miss Fanny Burney, 29 July 1782; *Diary and Letters of Madame d'Arblay*, II, 148-9.
5. *Ibid*, I, 71.

CHAPTER 9

1. *On Heroes and Hero-Worship*, Lecture V, World's Classics, ed., 1935, p. 224.

NOTES

2. *Essay on Man*, iv, 294.
3. G.E. Mingay, *English Landed Society in the Eighteenth Century*, 1963, pp. 14, 284.
4. J.L. and Barbara Hammond, *The Village Labourer, 1760-1832*, 1919, p. 14.
5. J.H. Plumb, *Men and Places*, 1966, p. 33.
6. William Cobbett, cit. Harold Nicolson, *Good Behaviour*, 1955, pp. 195-6.
7. Aristotle, *Ethics*, IV, ii; tr. Sir David Ross, Everyman ed., 1954, pp. 85-8.
8. See Mingay, *op. cit.*, p. 267.
9. Edmund Burke, *Reflections on the Revolution in France*, ed. Thomas H.D. Mahoney, New York, 1955, p. 287.
10. Cit, Hammond, *op. cit.*, pp. 24-5.
11. Burke, *op. cit.*, p. 102.
12. George Savile, First Marquess of Halifax, *The Complete Works*, ed. Sir Walter Raleigh, pp. 2-7.
13. The passage occurs in one of the notebooks of John Locke; cit. Maurice Cranston, *Locke*, 1961, p. 28.
14. Title of an essay by Locke, 1695.
15. Y.M.M. Wahba, 'The Literature of Polite Education in England, 1755-1800', unpub. dissertation 1957, Bodleian Library, Oxford, p. 108.
16. Voltaire, *Romans et Contes*, ed. H. Benae (Garnier), Paris, n.d., p. 220.
17. John Locke, *The Conduct of the Understanding*, ed. Thomas Fowler, Oxford, 1892, sec. iii, p. 7.
18. Carlyle, *op. cit.*, lecture V, pp. 224-30.
19. Elizabeth Burton, *The Georgians at Home*, 1967, p. 247.
20. Plumb, *op. cit.*, p. 92.
21. Rachel Trickett, *The Honest Muse*, Oxford, 1967.
22. Plumb, *op. cit.*, p. 46.
23. Jonathan Swift, *Gulliver's Travels*, 'A Voyage to Brobdingnag'; *Prose Works*, ed. Temple Scott, 12 vols., 1897-1908, VIII, 140.
24. John Pomfret, *The Choice*, 11. 97, 75, 88-9; *Supplement to the British Poets*, ed. Thomas Park, 1899, vol. I.
25. Harold Laski, *The Danger of Being a Gentleman and Other Essays*, 1939, pp. 29-31.

KEY TO THE NOTES

Works to which frequent reference is made are abbreviated in the notes as follows :
Characteristicks : Shaftesbury, *Characteristicks of Men, Manners, Opinions, Times.*

HC	: Smollett, *Humphry Clinker.*
JA	: Fielding, *Joseph Andrews.*
Life	: Boswell, *The Life of Samuel Johnson.*
PP	: Smollett, *Peregrine Pickle.*
RR	: Smollett, *Roderick Random.*
SJ	: Sterne, *A Sentimental Journey.*
Thoughts	: Locke, *Some Thoughts Concerning Education.*
TJ	: Fielding, *Tom Jones.*
TS	: Sterne, *Tristram Shandy.*

Select Bibliography

The editions mentioned are those to which reference is made in the notes. Unless otherwise stated, the place of publication is London.

Addison, Joseph : *The Guardian, The British Essayists*, ed. A. Chalmers, Vols. XIII-XV, 1802.
——: *The Spectator*, ed. G.G. Smith, 8 vols., 1897-8.
——: *The Tatler*, ed. G.A. Aitken, 4 vols. 1898-9.
Austen, Jane : *The Collected Novels of Jane Austen*, ed. J.C. Squire, 1928.
Boswell, James : *The Life of Samuel Johnson*, ed. George Birbeck Hill, rev. L.F. Powell, 6 vols., Oxford, 1934.
Brooke, Henry : *The Fool of Quality or The Adventures of Henry, Earl of Moreland*, ed. E.A. Baker (with biographical preface by Charles Kingsley), 1906.
Burney, Fanny (Madame d'Arblay) : *Evelina or The History of A Young Lady's Entrance Into The World*, ed. Edward A. Bloom, (Oxford English Novels), 1968.
——: *Cecilia or Memoirs of An Heiress*, ed. A.R. Ellis, 2 vols., 1882.
——: *Diary and Letters of Madame d'Arblay*, ed. by Her Niece, 7 vols., 1842-6.
——: *Early Diary, 1768-78*, ed. A.R. Ellis, 2 vols., 1889.
Chesterfield, Philip Dormer Stanhope, Earl of : *The Letters of Lord Chesterfield To His Son*, ed. Charles Stokes Carey, 2 vols., 1872.
——: *The Letters . . . With The Characters*, ed. John Bradshaw, 3 vols., 1926.
——: *Miscellaneous Works*, with *A Memoir of His Life* by M. Maty, 4 vols., 1779.

Castiglione, Count Baldassare : *The Boke of the Courtier*, done into English by Sir Thomas Hoby, ed. Walter Raleigh, 1900.

Day, Thomas : *The History of Sandford and Merton*, revised Cecil Hartley, n.d.

Defoe, Daniel : *The Compleat English Gentleman*, ed. Karl D. Bülbring, 1890.

Elyot, Sir Thomas : *The Boke Named The Governour*, intr. by Foster Watson, (Everyman), n.d.

Fielding, Henry : *Joseph Andrews*, ed. P.N. Furbank, 1954.

——: *Tom Jones*, ed. R.P.C. Mutter, 1966.

——: *Amelia*, ed. A.R. Humphreys, 2 vols., (Everyman), 1966.

——: *Jonathan Wild The Great*, ed. A.R Humphreys, (Everyman), 1964.

——: *The Journal of a Voyage To Lisbon*, ed. A.R. Humphreys, (Everyman), 1964.

——: *The Covent-Garden Journal*, ed. G.E. Jenson, 2 vols., 1915.

——: *The Complete Works of Henry Fielding*, ed. W.E. Henley, 16 vols., 1903.

Gibbon, Edward : *Autobiography*, ed. O. Smeaton, (Everyman), 1932.

Goldsmith, Oliver : *The Collected Works of Oliver Goldsmith*, ed. Arthur Friedman, 5 vols., Oxford, 1966.

Hobbes, Thomas : *Leviathan*, intr. W.G. Pogson Smith, Oxford, 1952.

Johnson, Samuel : *Works of Samuel Johnson*, 9 vols., (Oxford English Classics), 1825.

Locke, John : *The Conduct of the Understanding*, ed. Thomas Fowler, Oxford, 1892.

——: *An Essay Concerning Human Understanding*, ed. A.C. Fraser, 2 vols., Oxford, 1894.

——: *Some Thoughts Concerning Education*, ed. R.H. Quick, Cambridge, 1913.

Mackenzie, Henry : *The Man of Feeling*, ed. Brian Vickers, 967.

——: *The Man of the World*, New Universal Library, n.d.

——: *Julia de Roubigné*, 2 vols., 1787.

——: *The Mirror*, vols., XXXV-XXXVII of *The British Essayists*, ed. Alexander Chalmers, 1802.

SELECT BIBLIOGRAPHY

———: *The Lounger*, vols., XXXVIII-XL of *The British Essayists* ed. Alexander Chalmers, 1802.
Mandeville, Bernard: *The Fable of the Bees, or Private Vices, Public Benefits*, ed. F.B. Kaye, 2 vols., Oxford, 1924.
Montagu, Lady Mary Wortley : *Letters and Works*, ed. Lord Wharncliffe, 3 vols., 1837.
Peacham, Henry : *The Compleat Gentleman*, ed. G.S. Gordon, Oxford, 1906.
Richardson, Samuel : *Pamela*, ed. M. Kinkead-Weekes, 2 vols., (Everyman), 1967.
———: *Clarissa*, ed. John Butt, 4 vols., (Everyman), 1967.
———: *Sir Charles Grandison*, 2 vols., 1783.
———: *Familiar Letters*, etc., ed. B.W. Downs, 1929.
———: *Selected Letters of Samuel Richardson*, ed. John Carroll, Oxford, 1964.
Pope, Alexander : *The Poetical Works*, ed. A.W. Ward, 1956.
Rousseau, Jean Jacques : *Emile*, tr. Barbara Foxley, 1963.
———: *La Nouvelle Héloise*, Libraire de Paris, n.d.
Savile, George, First Marquess of Halifax : *The Complete Works*, ed. Sir Walter Raleigh, Oxford, 1912.
Saussure, César de : *The Letters of Monsieur César de Saussure, A Foreign View of England in the Reign of George I and George II*, ed. Madame Van Muyden, 1902.
Shaftesbury, Anthony Ashley Cooper, Third Earl of : *Characteristicks of Men, Manners, Opinions, Times*, 3 vols., 1727.
Smith, Adam : *An Inquiry into the Nature and Causes of the Wealth of Nations*, ed. James E. Thorold Rogers, 2 vols., Oxford, 1880.
Smollett, Tobias : *Roderick Random*, (World's Classics), 1959.
———: *Peregrine Pickle*, ed. Walter Allen, 2 vols., (Everyman), 1967.
———: *Peregrine Pickle*, ed. James L. Clifford, (Oxford English Novels), 1964. (This prints the text of the first ed., and is occasionally referred to in the notes).
———: *Ferdinand Count Fathom*, (Ballantyne Press), Edinburgh, n.d.
———: *Sir Launcelot Greaves*, (Ballantyne Press), Edinburgh, n.d.
———: *Humphry Clinker*, ed. Charles Lee, intr. Howard Mumford Jones, (Everyman), 1966.

---: *The Adventures of An Atom*, (Ballantyne Press), Edinburgh, n.d.

---: *Travels through France and Italy*, vol. XI of *The Works of Tobias Smollett*, ed. W.E. Henley, 1900.

---: *The Letters of Tobias Smollett*, ed. Edward S. Noyes, Harvard, 1926.

Steele, Sir Richard : *The Complete Plays*, ed. G.A. Aitken, (Mermaid Series), n.d.

---: *The Guardian, The British Essayists*, ed. A. Chalmers, vols. XIII-XV, 1802.

---: *The Spectator*, ed. G.G. Smith, 8 vols., 1897-8.

---: *The Tatler*, ed. G.A. Aitken, 4 vols., 1898-9.

Sterne, Laurence : *The Life and Opinions of Tristram Shandy, Gent.*, (World's Classics), 1947.

---: *A Sentimental Journey*, ed. Ian Jack, 1968.

---: *The Journal to Eliza*, ed. Ian Jack, 1968.

---: *Second Journal to Eliza*, ed. Margaret R.B. Shaw, 1929 (authorship doubtful).

---: *The Sermons of Laurence Sterne*, The Sutton Issue of *The Life and Works of Laurence Sterne*, New York, 1904.

---: *The Letters of Laurence Sterne*, ed. Lewis Perry Curtis, Oxford, 1935.

Swift, Jonathan : *Prose Works*, ed. Temple Scott, 12 vols., 1897-1908.

Walpole, Horace : *The Letters of Horace Walpole*, ed. Peter Cunningham, 9 vols., Edinburgh, 1906.

Index

Addison, Joseph 15, 37-9, 45, 69, 85, 90, 97, 117, 236, 247, 269, 271, 275, 276
  The Guardian 117
  The Spectator, 15, 38-9, 50, 68, 73, 81, 85, 90, 100, 114, 236, 269, 276
  Adviser, The 98
Akenside, Mark 165
Allen, Ralph 126, 263
Arblay, General d' 246
Architecture 89, 188, 262-4
Aristotle 262, 271
Armstrong, Dr. John 165
Ascham, Roger 67
Austen, Jane 37, 43-4, 98, 121, 252, 275
  Emma 44, 48
  Persuasion 43, 275
  Pride and Prejudice 43
  Sense and Sensibility 15

Bacon, Sir Francis 67, 70
Bagehot, Walter 20, 232
Barlow, Mr. 237-8, 246
Barrie, Sir James
  The Admirable Crichton 34
Barrow, Isaac 212
Bathurst, Allen Bathurst, first Earl of 277
Berkeley, George, Bishop of Cloyne 63
Boswell, James 19, 27, 49, 115, 147
  Life of Johnson 19, 27, 64, 115
Boyle, Richard, Earl of Burlington 217

Bradsaigh, Lady Dorothy ('Mrs. Belfour') 41, 105-6, 109, 114
Brathwaite, Richard 67
  The English Gentleman 22
  The English Gentlewoman 22
Bridgewater, Francis Egerton, third Duke of 277
Brooke, Henry 23, 36-7, 39, 56-7, 72, 77-81, 88, 255, 257, 267
  The Fool of Quality 23-4, 77-81, 267
Brown, Lancelot ('Capability') 262
Buckingham, George Villiers, Duke of 83
Burke, Edmund 52, 71, 253, 264-5
  Reflections on the Revolution in France 71
Burney, Dr. Charles 240, 246-7
Burney, Frances, Madame d'Arblay 14, 37, 43-7, 68-9, 94, 237-40
  Cecilia 14-15, 46-7, 236, 239-40 242, 244, 248-51, 251-3
  Diary and Letters 69, 239-40, 243, 245-6, 250
  Early Diary 238
  Evelina 15, 43-5, 237-49, 250-3, 255
Burney, Susan 245
Burns, Robert 213, 272
Butler, Joseph, Bishop 63
Byron, Lord George Gordon 115, 223

Campbell, Mungo 115
Carlyle, Thomas 254, 271
Castiglione, Count Baldassare 67, 69, 83-4

Il Cortegiano 67, 83-4
Cervantes 126, 234
   Don Quixote 42, 180, 182
Chandos, James Brydges, Duke of 272
Chapone, Hester (née Mulso) 109, 249
Charles II 67, 83, 97, 100
Chaucer, Geoffrey
   Legend of Good Women 118
   Roman de la Rose 21
   Wife of Bath's Tale 21
Chesterfield, Philip Dormer Stanhope, fourth Earl of 16, 47, 49, 63-7, 70, 74, 81, 83-6, 90, 93-5, 152, 165, 206
   Common Sense 274
   Letters 16, 63-7, 74, 83-4, 90, 93-5, 152, 155, 206, 274
   The World 47, 90, 274
Cheyne, Dr. George 29
Chudleigh, Elizabeth, Duchess of Kingston 52
Cicero 271
Cibber, Colley 109
Class System 17-54, 258-62, 262-8
   Merchant class 37-46, 239, 241-2
   'Subordination' 18, 28, 264-5
Cobbett, William 261
Coleridge, Samuel Taylor 17, 97, 124
Collier, Jeremy 100
Coke, Thomas, Earl of Leicester 86, 277
Crisp, Samuel 240
Cromwell, Oliver 18

Day, Thomas 34-6, 77, 80
   Sandford and Merton 34-5, 77, 80
   The Dying Negro 35
Defoe, Daniel 42, 70, 119
   The Compleat English Gentleman 19, 41-2
   Tour thro' the Whole Island of Great Britain 119
Dorset, Charles Sackville, Earl of 83
Dryden, John 50, 274

Absalom and Achitophel 274
Duelling 114-6

Education 55-8, 63-5, 73-95
   Dissenting Academies 81, 87
   Grand Tour 86, 89-95
   Schools 73-7
   Universities 43, 85-9, 92
Eglintune, Alexander Montgomerie, ninth Earl of 115
Elizabethan (Renaissance) Age and Literature 10, 21-2, 38, 67, 70, 83, 118, 258, 273, 276, 277-8
Elyot, Sir Tomas 67, 82, 83, 268
   The Governour 82, 268

Fielding, Henry 9, 12, 16, 23-6, 37, 47, 56-7, 60, 69-70, 74, 76, 82, 88, 98, 104, 108, 120-1, 123-60, 165, 167, 175, 193-4, 212, 234, 243, 254-6, 258, 262, 266, 275, 277
   Amelia 10, 26-7, 82, 126, 128-36, 144-6, 148, 150-5, 158-60, 212-3
   The Champion 131, 157
   The Covent-Garden Journal 47, 128, 130, 135-6, 145-6, 151-4, 212
   Essay on Conversation 152
   Of Good-Nature 127
   The Fathers 90
   Inquiry into the Causes of the Late Increase of Robbers 140
   The Jacobite's Journal 108
   Jonathan Wild 150-1, 159-60, 275
   Joseph Andrews 17, 24, 74, 85, 85-6, 90, 126, 135, 141, 150-1, 154-7, 204, 212, 218-9, 265, 266
   Journey From This World to the Next 141, 143, 157
   Knowledge of the Characters of Men 137
   Miscellanies 150-1
   Tom Jones 24-6, 52, 53-4, 56, 60, 69, 74, 120-1, 123-32, 134-50, 155, 157-9, 175, 212
   Tom Thumb 150

INDEX

Voyage to Lisbon 157
France, attitude to 85-6, 89-95, 274

Gainsborough, Thomas 263
Garrick, David 165
George II 147, 275
George III 68, 275, 277
George IV (as Prince of Wales) 178
Gibbon, Edward 86, 266, 268
   Autobiography 86, 266, 268
Gisborne, Thomas 96
   Enquiry into the Duties of Men 97
Goldsmith, Oliver 12-4, 52, 70-2, 73, 89, 151, 179, 186, 192-204, 217, 255-6, 265, 267, 271, 277
   Citizen of the World 186, 198-201
   The Deserted Village 71, 193, 203, 265
   The Good-Natured Man 51, 198-9, 203-4
   Life of Richard Nash 71, 200
   Polite Learning 89
   The Vicar Wakefield 13, 50, 71, 193-204, 218-9
Gower, John
   Confessio Amantis 21
Grammont, Count de 100
Guevara, Antonio de
   Dial of Princes 72

Halifax, George Savile, Marquess of 106, 265
Hamilton, James Douglas, Duke of 115
Harrison, William 20
   Description of England 20
Hastings, Warren 208, 250
Hazlitt, William 13, 124, 235, 244
Hawkins, Sir John 125
Highmore, Susanna 105
Hobbes, Thomas 58, 60, 61
   Leviathan 61
Hoby, Sir Thomas 67
Hogarth, William 37, 154
Horace 271, 275

Humanitarianism/benevolence 208, 266-8, 278-9
Hume, David 50
Huntingdon, Selina, Countess of 16, 48
Hutcheson, Francis 58-9, 63, 64

Illegitimate Children 49-50, 147
Inchbald, Elizabeth 104
India 208-9, 264
Institution of a Gentleman 20

Jonson, Ben
   Every Man Out of His Humour 21
Johnson, Samuel 9, 15, 18-9, 27-8, 55, 64, 70, 88, 94, 102, 115, 125, 159, 191, 204, 239, 243, 253, 255, 264, 272
   Dictionary 18-9
   Life of Milton 159
   Rambler 9, 70-1, 272
   Vanity of Human Wishes 191

Keats, John 60, 222
Kingston, Evelyn Pierrepont, Marquis of Dorchester, and Duke of 93

Lade, Sir John 246
Lamb, Charles 223
Laski, Harold 278
Laud, William 63
Law, William
   A Serious Call 22
Legge, William, second Earl of Dartmouth 16
Le Sage, Allian-Rané 162
Literary Theory and Criticism 50-2
Locke, John 9, 33, 55-8, 68, 72-3, 76-7, 81-5, 92, 268-70, 270-1
   Conduct of the Understanding 56
   Essay Concerning Human Understanding 56
   Thoughts Concerning Education 11-2, 55-8, 73, 76, 81-4, 92
Louis XIV 68
Lyttleton, Lord George 165

Machiavelli 67, 70
Mackenzie, Henry 14, 40, 51, 56-7, 60, 77-81, 88, 104, 113, 193, 204-17, 220, 234, 236, 255, 267
  Julia de Roubigné 209-10
  The Lounger 206-7, 209, 214-5
  The Man of Feeling 14, 51, 204-10, 213, 215
  The Man of the World 14, 40, 77-80, 205, 207, 209-11, 215-17, 218
  The Mirror 206-7, 209, 211
Mandeville, Bernard 60, 61-3, 66
  The Fable of the Bees 50-1, 61-3
Manners 15, 67-71, 151-4
Marlowe, Christopher
  Tamburlaine 273
Milton, John 101
  Of Education 83
Mohocks 178
Mohun, of Okehampton, Charles, fifth Baron 115
Montagu, Lady Mary Wortley 97, 106, 112, 120, 123-4, 160
Montaigne 72
Mulso, Hester (see Chapone)
Murphy, Arthur 123

Newton, Sir Isaac 191
Noble Savage 154, 193, 207-8, 271
Nottingham, Daniel Finch, second Earl of 93

Paine, Thomas 46, 264
Peacham, Henry 49, 83
  The Compleat Gentleman 21
Pitt, Sir William 230
Plato 166
Pomfret, John
  The Choice 277
Pope, Alexander 69, 90, 149, 190-1, 254, 270, 274, 276, 277
  The Dunciad 90, 243
  Epilogue to the Satires 190
  Epistle to Dr. Arbuthnot 190
  Epitaph for Newton's Tomb 191
  Essay on Man 28, 59, 192, 268, 274
  Moral Essays 276-7
Prévost, Abbé 212

Religion 15-6, 60, 113-4, 144, 149, 265-6, 269
  Latitudinarianism 57, 60-1, 127-8, 212
  Methodism 16
  Puritanism 253
Restoration Society, Manners, etc. 38, 68, 70, 100, 178, 215, 275
Richardson, Samuel 9, 11-2, 27-30, 37, 40-1, 56-7, 70, 72, 76, 82, 83, 91, 94, 96-127, 176, 247-50, 253-7, 263, 267, 269, 277
  Clarissa 11, 30-2, 41, 98-108, 113-4, 117-8 174, 176
  Letters 41, 99-101, 103, 105-9, 120, 123-4, 127, 267
  Pamela 11, 12, 15, 27-30, 32, 56-7, 72, 76, 85, 98, 104, 105, 113, 266
  Sir Charles Grandison 11, 27, 33, 40, 57, 72, 82-3, 98, 102, 105, 107-21, 126, 247-9, 274
Rochefoucauld, duc de la 67
Rochester, John Wilmot, Earl of 83, 100, 178
Rousseau, Jean-Jacques 35-6, 56, 58, 64-7, 70, 72, 77-82, 212
  Emile 14, 36, 56, 64-7, 70, 72, 77-80, 206-7, 210, 215
  La Nouvelle Héloise 67, 78, 212

Saussure, César de 18
  A Foreign View of England 18
Scott, Sir Walter 213
Sedley, Sir Charles 83, 100
Sensibility and Sentiment 14, 15, 60-1, 64, 78, 100, 112-3, 151, 167, 180-1, 184-6, 193-235, 249-50, 252, 271
Shaftesbury, Anthony Ashley Cooper, first Earl of 58

INDEX

Shaftesbury, Anthony Asnley Cooper, third Earl of 58-61, 63, 64, 112, 127-8, 166, 193, 209, 212
  Characteristicks 58-60
Shelley, Percy Bysshe 223
Shirley, Laurence, fourth Earl of Ferrers 52
Shakespeare William
  All's Well That Ends Well 96
  King Lear 279
  Sonnet lxvi 220
Sheridan, Richard Brinsley 214
  The School for Scandal 214
Smith, Adam 86-7, 91
  The Wealth of Nations 87
Smollett, Tobias George 9, 12-3, 16, 47, 51, 58, 72, 74-6, 87, 92-3, 94, 120, 133, 161-91, 193, 212, 226, 255-6, 258, 262, 277
  Adventures of an Atom 165
  Ferdinand Count Fathom 162, 163-4, 166-7, 180
  History of England 180
  Humphry Clinker 12, 15, 47, 120, 164, 166-70, 179-81, 184-91, 262
  Letters 164-5
  Peregrine Pickle 12, 58, 72-3, 75-6, 87, 92-3, 94 161-9, 171-9, 181, 189-90
  Roderick Random 12, 42-3, 53, 74, 161-72, 181, 189-91
  The Regicide 165
  Sir Launcelot Greaves 12, 53, 179, 181-4, 267
  Travels Through Italy 164
Spence, Thomas 264
Steele, Sir Richard 15, 18, 37-9, 71, 90, 91, 97, 117, 179, 236, 247, 253
  The Conscious Lovers 39
  The Guardian 91, 108, 118,
  The Spectator 15, 38-9, 50, 68, 73, 81, 85, 90 100, 114, 236
  The Tatler 18, 39, 253
Stephen, Sir Leslie 124, 156

Sterne, Laurence 13, 56, 76, 91-2, 179, 186, 193-4, 216-35, 254-6, 258, 267
  Journal to Eliza 223
  Letters 222, 224, 228-33
  Sentimental Journey 91, 217, 220, 222-6, 230
  Sermons 91, 224, 227-8, 229-32, 233-4, 267
  Tristram Shandy 13, 57, 76-7, 90, 91, 186, 217-35, 255
Stuart, Lady Louisa 213
Swift, Jonathan 69-70, 73, 88, 149, 253, 276

Thackeray, William Makepeace 109, 124
Thrale, Mrs. Hester Lynch 27, 236, 240, 255
Thrale, Henry 246
Townshend, Charles, Viscount (Turnip Townshend) 277

Vanbrugh, Sir John
  The Provoked Husband 52
Virgil 275
Veblen, Thorstein
  The Theory of the Leisure Class 82
Voltaire 64, 190, 269

Walpole, Horace, Earl of Orford 41, 47, 48-9, 86, 127, 246
Walpole, Sir Robert 147, 275
Warburton, William, Bishop 230
Wesley, John 14, 16, 63, 267, 269
Wharton, Philip, Duke of 100
Wilkes, John 191
Wordsworth, William 209
  Elegiac Stanzas 211
Wyndham, William 250

Young Edward 192
  Epistle to Mr. Pope 269
  Night-Thoughts 192